MW01526306

OAHU RESTAURANT GUIDE 2005

WITH HONOLULU AND WAIKIKI

Robert & Cindy Carpenter
www.hawaiirestaurantguide.com

OAHU RESTAURANT GUIDE 2005
WITH HONOLULU AND WAIKIKI

1st Edition

ISBN 1-931752-36-2
Library of Congress Control Number: 2005924850

Printed in the United States of America.

Holiday Publishing Inc.

Post Office Box 211
Havana, IL 62644

Post Office Box 11120
Lahaina, HI 96761

holidaypublishing@yahoo.com

www.hawaiirestaurantguide.com

OAHU RESTAURANT GUIDE 2005
WITH HONOLULU AND WAIKIKI

TABLE OF CONTENTS

Hawaiian Islands

INTRODUCTION

It's been said that there are those who eat to live and those that live to eat. Since you're reading this you probably already have a leaning toward the latter group. Well, join the club! Food has taken on an importance never seen before. That's not to say that Mom's cooking wasn't good. What better place can you think of to develop your own sense for comfort food than at the kitchen table? However, with restaurants popping up on every corner and 24 hours of food shows airing daily, culinary pursuits have definitely come of age.

Hawaii is a perfect place to explore this newfound enthusiasm. Here in the islands you'll find people from around the world blending and sharing the best of their cultures. Naturally the local dining scene reflects this international view where noodle shops and Continental dining venues make perfectly compatible neighbors. Then to make things that much more interesting, Hawaii people like to throw in some fusion cuisine and a little contemporary sushi to complete the neighborhood mix. You won't find that back in Ohio!

This book was written in an attempt to define this wonderful disarray. Knowing full well that this was a nigh on impossible task we took off happily into the fog and aren't quite sure if we've emerged yet! Let's just say that five years, six islands, and 1500 assorted restaurants, dining spots, and take-out windows later, you now have in your hands a copy of the 2005 Oahu edition of the Hawaii Restaurant Guide series.

Along the path of creation we've found ourselves doing a bit of experimenting. Before putting pen to paper there first had to be research, which of course was our favorite part of the undertaking. Being self-confessed culinary vagabonds, what better way to combine our vices than an extended dining tour across the Hawaiian Islands? As the adventure continued, it started taking on a bit of a Keseyian spin. When the term fusion confusion became part of our vocabulary, we knew it was time to state a criterion. Here is what we determined.

Experience has shown us that our readers want to be empowered. They don't care for travel experiences that include being shoved on a bus and handed a meal voucher. Nor do they like being led around to all the standard guidebook hot spots. No, they want to go it alone and make their own decisions, so we resolved to arm them with as much information as possible.

To start with, people need to have accurate information concerning the physical location, website address, phone number, hours of operation, dress code, style of cuisine, credit cards, and price range of each establishment. Then they like to see actual menu items with prices to determine budgeting. What might be medium priced to one person could be something entirely different to another.

Our restaurant selection process follows suit. We decided early on not to waste time writing about places we wouldn't bother revisiting and skipped right to creating an A list. Why waste time beating up on also-rans when there are so many wonderful places to talk about? The results have been assembled in a collection that covers all tastes and styles from five stars to hole-in-the-walls.

Of course no restaurant guide would be complete without impressions. People have repeatedly told us that they want to know what to expect before they arrive. This can run the gamut from dealing with parking to personal preferences like waterfront dining. In our comment sections we try to deal with real world issues and leave the chamber of commerce spin to the paid inclusion publishers.

Finally, all of this was done at our own expense. Too much of what readers encounter is slanted by compensation. In the world of travel, that comes in many forms. It could be through free rooms, complimentary meals, or outright cash payment. Regardless, the resulting work becomes an advertorial instead of an unbiased review. It's hard to be objective when they roll out the red carpet!

So plan to visit Hawaii! Explore the renowned pleasures of sights and sounds to be found in the islands. But while you're there, be sure to discover some of the culturally diverse culinary experiences unique to America's Pacific Paradise!

Robert & Cindy Carpenter
Authors

ISLAND CUISINES

HAWAIIAN CUISINE

It has been said that everybody in Hawaii came from someplace else which also holds true for many of the food sources we think of as native to the island chain. The Hawaiian Islands are geologically very young. They are also among the most remote places on earth with nearly three thousand miles of open ocean separating the islands from any major land mass. Hawaii's youth and isolation led to the evolution of a unique but nutritionally sparse flora and fauna.

The first arrivals in Hawaii are thought to have been a small dark people whose origins hail back to Southeast Asia. Archaeologists believe that these people lived off what they found which didn't go much beyond fish, birds, and a few native plants. Many like to think of those earliest inhabitants as the legendary Menehune, but they, like their history, disappeared into the annals of time. It wasn't until the Polynesians voyaged to Hawaii with their domestic animals and "canoe" plants that the island food resources achieved any variety.

These ancestors of the modern Hawaiians were great mariners. A thousand years ago they began sailing their double-hulled voyaging canoes up from Tahiti bringing with them dogs, pigs, and fowl as well as coconuts, sweet potatoes, breadfruit, bananas, taro, yams, arrowroot, and sugarcane. They also brought the Polynesian style of cooking which includes broiling over hot coals, boiling with hot stones, and baking in an underground oven. It is this latter method, cooking in an imu, that holds center stage at Hawaiian luaus today.

Ancient Hawaiians lived in ahupua'a which were land divisions reaching from the top of the mountains down adjoining ridges to the ocean. These triangular watersheds theoretically contained all the elements required to sustain the community. Trees for building canoes grew up on the mountain. The uplands supported dry land crops like sweet potatoes and yams. Down along the stream beds taro was grown in paddies called loi. Then, beyond the coconut and breadfruit trees, lay the ocean with its wealth of fish, mollusks, and seaweeds.

The Hawaiian diet was simple but healthful. Fish provided the bulk of the common people's protein with domestic animals and fowl reserved primarily for the chiefs and special occasions. The staple starch was poi made from the steamed and pounded corms of the taro plant. When conditions wouldn't allow for taro cultivation sweet potatoes or breadfruit were used as substitutes. Taro greens and seaweed filled the need for leafy vegetables by supplying vitamins and minerals. Finally, bananas and coconuts were important for good health.

Today these traditions continue. Modern Hawaiians usually cook much like everyone else, but they make a point to hold luaus to celebrate milestones in life. Island favorites like kalua pig, lomi lomi salmon, chicken long rice, laulau, haupia, and of course poi are staples at these events. If you get the chance, try to attend a luau and experience the original Hawaiian cuisine.

CHINESE CUISINE

The Chinese have influenced the socio-economic and culinary scenes of the islands to the point that it would be hard to imagine Hawaii without them. Beginning in the mid 1800's they were the first immigrant group recruited to work in the sugar cane fields. From those humble beginnings the Chinese went on to become the merchant class and landlords of Honolulu.

The Chinese experience in Hawaii is more than a list of menu items and real estate investments. It's a meaningful part of Hawaiian history. The early Chinese immigrants came from southern China, so naturally they brought that style of cooking with them. After they arrived it didn't take long for them to figure out that there wasn't much of a future working on the plantations, so as soon as their contracts expired they moved on.

These free but unemployed farmers looked around and saw opportunity. Where the Hawaiians had once raised taro and fish the Chinese saw rice paddies and duck ponds. Intermarriage provided access to idle land that soon became truck gardens and small farms. Since trading is a way of life for the Chinese, the port of Honolulu quickly had its own Chinatown full of shops and small eateries.

Today you see the effects of this history throughout the islands. The dominant Chinese cuisine in Hawaii is Cantonese. This is what most North Americans picture when they think about eating Chinese, so the methods and menu items are quite well known. Preparations like dim sum and stir-fries are popular in that region and are standards on menus in Hawaii.

True Chinese cooking is a healthful cuisine. Chefs in China instinctively strive for balance and harmony in meal preparation. This can be accomplished by using a variety of cooking methods and ingredients. No Chinese cook would ever serve an entire deep-fried meal; rather he or she would always include vegetable dishes and serve steamed rice on the side.

To fully enjoy a Chinese meal make sure you choose a variety of dishes, levels of spiciness, and cooking methods. This is dining banquet style, but it can still be done at a fairly reasonable cost. Some restaurants have made things easier by selecting an assortment of dishes and offering them as a package, but those set menus can be a bit on the middle-of-the-road side. Make your meal an adventure and select the items yourself—just watch out for the chicken feet!

No trip to Honolulu is complete without a visit to Chinatown. Take a walk and look for the shops with the barbequed pork and smoked ducks hanging in the windows. Down off King Street you'll find markets packed with people selling vegetables you've never seen and fish so fresh they're still swimming. Finally, stop for lunch at a place where you're the only ones speaking English and there isn't a fork in sight. That's when you'll know why they call it Chinatown.

JAPANESE CUISINE

Like so many others the Japanese experience in Hawaii is tied to sugar. The first immigrants began arriving from Japan soon after the end of the American Civil War. At first it was a trickle, but after the Reciprocity Act Of 1876 removed tariffs on Hawaiian sugar, the trickle turned into a torrent. That was the age of industrialized sugar, and enormous amounts of manpower were required. Today Americans of Japanese ancestry play a major role in Hawaiian society. This is reflected through Hawaii's wide variety of Japanese dining venues.

It has been said that the Japanese eat with the eyes as well as the mouth. This becomes apparent after visiting one of their restaurants. Instead of having a single main entrée dominating the table, Japanese diners prefer a variety of smaller servings. The dishes are served separately on various plates and bowls artistically arranged around the table.

The ultimate fine dining experience is the kaiseki. This is also known as royal dining or dining in courses and involves considerable ceremony as well as an elegant dinner presentation. An elaborate array of special courses is served that might include items such as an exquisite appetizer, assorted sashimi and sushi, miso soup, a tempura course, a seafood dish, a small steak, pickled vegetables, steamed rice, cold noodles, and dessert.

A more common choice is the teishoku or complete meal. This Japanese equivalent of the prix fixe dinner consists of an appetizer, soup, pickled vegetables, one or two entrees, rice, and perhaps dessert. Anyone interested in exploring Japanese cuisine would do well to start with a teishoku as the variety allows the diner to do some sampling and not be overwhelmed by the menu.

Within the various meal presentations you will find a variety of preparation styles. Thanks to the spread of international dining, visitors to Hawaii often think of sushi and sashimi as typical Japanese food. While those are popular items in Japan, their cuisine goes far deeper than that. Beyond the temptations of the sushi bar you will find several major styles of cooking.

First comes yakimono, which are grilled or broiled dishes. Teriyaki and yakitori are classic examples of yakimono. That knife-wielding chef in a teppanyaki house is also doing a form of yakimono cooking. Then there's agemono where meats or vegetables are fried in oil. Tempura with its light puffy coating is probably the most recognizable form of agemono. Finally you have nabemono where thinly sliced pieces of meat and vegetables are gently simmered in a fragrant broth using a chaffing dish placed on the tabletop. Shabu shabu and sukiyaki are traditional nabemono dishes.

So walk into a Japanese restaurant with confidence, and after a half-bow to the hostess get ready for a truly unique and exceptional dining experience.

PORTUGUESE CUISINE

Portuguese culinary tradition is the odd man out among ethnic cuisines in Hawaii. Where all the rest are Asian in origin Portuguese is European. When the Asians serve a starch it is nearly always rice. For the Portuguese starch means bread or beans. Asians love stir-fries. The Portuguese prefer stews. In spite of all these differences, Portuguese cooking has become a valued part of the Hawaiian melting pot.

The Portuguese have always been a seafaring people. During the fourteenth and fifteenth centuries Portuguese ships embarked on a great wave of global exploration. Those adventurers brought back spices and foods that were unheard of in Europe. The resulting trade routes reached around the world exposing the Portuguese to exotic places and exotic places to the Portuguese.

The first Portuguese plantation laborers arrived in Hawaii during the 1870's and were actually from the Azores and Madeira. This was a rather natural development as sugarcane had been part of the Madeira agricultural scene for hundreds of years. These European immigrants differed from their Asian counterparts as they intended to stay in Hawaii permanently. Their families brought hearth and home along with the entire range of Portuguese cuisine.

Hearty soups, stews, and casseroles were a rather new concept in the islands but old favorites among the Portuguese. Usually these were enhanced with the wide variety of spices and flavors that had come into their possession through global exploration. Portuguese sausage or linguica with its garlicky zest has gone on to become a mainstay breakfast item across the islands. In Hawaii you'll find eggs and Portuguese sausage right next to Egg McMuffins and breakfast burritos on fast food restaurant menus.

Another island favorite is Portuguese Bean Soup. If Hawaii people had to name the recipes that make their top ten list, Portuguese Bean Soup would be there every time. Somehow it doesn't seem to matter what a restaurant normally serves or where its price range falls, this local comfort food combining beans and vegetables with ham hocks and Portuguese sausage manages to make its way into the rotation as soup of the day.

Finally, there is the Portuguese tradition of baking bread. Everywhere you go in Hawaii you'll find menus offering French toast made with Portuguese sweet bread. Also known as pao doce, this local favorite has taken on another identity as Molokai Sweet Bread. Visitors to that island will see local people boarding the plane carrying loaves for those at home. Another Portuguese specialty is the sugary doughnut without a hole known as the malasada. Traditionally served as a special treat the day before Ash Wednesday, malasadas were prepared using the family's remaining butter and eggs before starting the lean times of Lent.

KOREAN CUISINE

Immigrants from Korea began arriving in Hawaii during the early 1900's. Like their fellows, the early arrivals came to work on the plantations. Although that era is all but over, the migration continues today as Koreans seeking economic opportunity leave their homeland for Hawaii and other parts of North America.

Koreans strive for balance and harmony in all aspects of their lives. This is never more obvious than at the table, where they look to food as a cure for physical and mental ailments as well as for sustenance. Their cuisine is low in fat and very healthful with an emphasis on grilled or broiled meats, soups, and fresh vegetables. Some of the cooking methods favored by Koreans involve tableside preparation using a grill or by simmering meats and vegetables in broth, while others require pan or deep-frying.

One item that has almost come to mean Korean is kim chee. Interestingly enough both of this pickled relish's principal ingredients came from other places. The Dutch introduced cabbage to the Koreans and the chili peppers that give kim chee its fire were brought from Portugal. This zesty condiment is nearly always seen on Korean tables and adds zip to offset the mildness of rice.

Contrary to general impressions not all Korean food is highly seasoned. In fact many of their favorite menu items could pass as comfort food. If you like teriyaki then you'll enjoy the marinated grilled meats. Koreans are more of a beef-eating nation than other Asian countries. It is thought that invading Mongols introduced cattle to Korea hundreds of years ago. Other protein sources common to the Korean diet include poultry and fish as well as soybean products.

For those who really like to know the details, some of the ingredients used as flavoring in Korean cuisine include chrysanthemum leaves, daikon, ginger root, garlic, enokitake, shimeji and shiitake mushrooms, hot green and red peppers, green onions, mirin, miso, nori, sesame oil and seeds, pine nuts, soybean sprouts, soy sauce, tofu, and wakame.

Combination meals are usually offered giving the diner a chance to experience a variety of items. These dinners begin with several small dishes of salads and pickled vegetables. Turnips, potatoes, kim chee, seaweed, bean sprouts, and garlic bulb pickles among others will be offered. Soup made of oxtails, fish, chicken or vegetables, many times with the addition of a beaten egg or dumplings, are important courses in a Korean meal. Popular entrées commonly seen include bulgoki, kal bi ribs, and chun. As in other Asian cultures desserts are limited to fruits and special occasion items.

Most island Korean restaurants tend to be less formal establishments where one can enjoy a healthful dinner of wonderfully prepared foods at a reasonable cost.

FILIPINO CUISINE

Filipinos constituted the last major group of immigrants recruited to work on Hawaii's sugar cane and pineapple plantations. Their arrival during the early to mid-1900's was a reaction to legal restrictions placed by the US Congress on importing foreign workers. The Hawaiian planters needed cheap field labor, and as the Philippines were a US Territory, it became the logical alternative.

Although at first glance one might assume that Philippine culture would be Southeast Asian in nature that is not at all the case. Early visits from the east followed by three hundred years of Spanish occupation and fifty years as a US Territory heavily influenced Filipino daily life. The result is a cuisine that is truly global in nature.

Early traders from China and Malaysia are thought to have been the first outsiders to seriously impact the culinary traditions of the Filipino people. The use of egg roll wrappers in lumpia, rice, curry, coconut, coconut milk, patis, soy sauce, and noodles all had their origins in eastern cuisines.

Then came the Spanish who truly made an impression on the daily diet in the Philippines. Tomatoes, onion, garlic, beans, pimientos, and olive oil have become everyday components in Filipino dishes. During the late 1890's America was at war with Spain and the islands came under US military rule. Although Filipino people enjoy American dishes as well as their own, little of what we consider true Filipino food could be attributed to that period of history.

Today the Filipino influence on the culinary arts in Hawaii might not be as noticeable as that of some other Asian cuisines as there are not many restaurants serving an exclusively Filipino menu. However, that doesn't mean that visitors won't be exposed to Filipino food. Many island restaurants incorporate Filipino styles and dishes in their menus. You just have to know what to look for.

Filipino cooks like to mix all of a dish's ingredients together rather than preparing and serving them separately. A classic example of this is adobo, which is a stew made from pork and/or chicken that has been marinated in garlic and vinegar. Another is chicken relleno, which is a roasted and boned chicken that is stuffed with a pork, onion, raisin, pimiento, and hard-cooked egg stuffing.

Then come the veggies! Filipino culinary tradition calls for the use of an extremely wide variety of vegetables. Most Western visitors won't easily identify many of them, but a walk through a Filipino grocery or Chinatown will give you the idea. Of course, no meal would be complete without rice or pancit noodles to round things out.

Finally, the Filipinos are fond of sweets. Look for leche flan, fruit lumpia, or cascaron and you'll know you've found the dessert section of the menu.

THAI CUISINE

People from Thailand were among the first modern immigrants who did not come to Hawaii seeking work on the plantations. Their arrival over the last thirty years was part of a general movement out of Southeast Asia by those looking for more promising forms of economic opportunity. As many before them had already discovered, a quick way to create an income in a new land is to open a restaurant and introduce the neighborhood to your native cuisine. Hawaii with its large Asian ethnic population was a natural for these new entrepreneurs. Thai cuisine has quickly become a local favorite.

Thai cuisine reflects an interesting history of interaction between people throughout Indochina. Thanks to its central location Thailand became a crossroad for foreign travelers and exotic ideas. Immediately to the north lies China with its ancient traditions of stir-frying and the use of noodles. Among that group were Buddhists preparing vegetarian dishes. From the west came people from India making curries and Arabs cooking skewer-broiled meats. And of course don't forget the ever-present Portuguese and their tiny red hot peppers!

Chefs from Thailand have a whole arsenal of flavors at their disposal. Some of the ingredients commonly used include Thai chilies, Kaffir lime leaves, lemon grass, ginger, mint, basil, curry, peppers, and the ever-present fish sauce known as nam pla. Thai food may be ordered spiced mild, medium, or hot. However, since mild dishes can miss the point and hot is best reserved for the Thai's we suggest that people consider ordering medium. Then in order to moderate the spicy flavors, be sure to include at least one dish that is made with coconut milk and have it all served along side a steamer basket of sticky rice.

A meal in a Thai restaurant is generally served all at once and then shared between the diners, rather than in courses. Usually a number of dishes are presented giving everyone an opportunity to sample a variety of items. Great effort is made to balance out the contrasting tastes and textures in order to promote harmony in the meal. Unlike many Asian countries a fork and spoon are used in dining. The fork is used for cutting and pushing food onto the spoon, and the spoon gives the diner the ability to fully appreciate the flavorful sauces.

A good rule to follow in making dinner selections is to always ask, "What do the locals order?" Here there are favorites like anywhere else. Starting with the appetizer section consider the Thai Crispy Noodles or Satay Chicken. Then follow up with a Green Papaya Salad and a bowl of Tom Yum Soup. Next comes the main event where dishes like Evil Prince Shrimp, Pork Pad Pet, Chicken Panang Curry, and Beef with Thai Basil Sauce appear high on the list. Finally, make sure to include a dish of Pad Thai Noodles and dinner is served.

Try to visit a Thai restaurant while in you're in Hawaii. You'll discover an exciting new cuisine that truly broadens the horizons of culinary adventure.

VIETNAMESE CUISINE

The end of the Vietnam War signaled the beginning of a major migration of Vietnamese people to Hawaii and North America. What started out as a political exodus has turned into a classic movement of people seeking a better way of life. Hawaii has been an attractive location for resettlement because of its mild, temperate climate and the presence of other Asian cultures. Today their presence has become so visible that there are those who refer to the central part of the Honolulu Chinatown historic district as Little Saigon.

While you are walking around Chinatown notice the small Vietnamese eateries that seem to be popping up on every street corner. At one time, Chinese immigrants operated these shops. Now those people have moved on to other endeavors and the latest wave of arrivals have taken their place. Many of these places are pho shops. Pho is pronounced "fuh" and is an aromatic rice noodle soup made with a clear, rich beef stock. A plate of fresh herbs such as Thai basil and cilantro along with bean sprouts and jalapeños is served on a separate plate. You flavor this popular breakfast or lunch dish to your own specifications.

Vietnamese cuisine is the result of many years of cultural blending. Like the other countries in Southeast Asia, the ebb and flow of history brought in successive waves of new people and customs. The original inhabitants of Vietnam are thought to have moved down the coastline from southern China. Then others from the east and west arrived looking for trade. There were occupations, first by the Chinese and then by the French. Throughout that time the people of Vietnam were learning new culinary methods and techniques.

As you peruse a Vietnamese menu you will witness those influences through the use of everything from lemongrass and curry paste to croissants and baguettes. Naturally, the Asian staple starch appears as a major item. Not only do you see rice served steamed as a side dish but it also appears in noodles and as rice paper for wrapping. Vietnamese foods have a delicate fresh taste and are never heavy in texture or flavor. Herbs are used as greens as well as for flavor. Dishes made with curry may be ordered spiced according to personal preference.

A Vietnamese meal is served family style where everyone samples each dish. Preparation is not a detailed or complicated endeavor but rather is a gathering of fresh healthful ingredients handled and cooked as little as possible. A favorite example is the banh hoi. This popular dish is made by taking grilled marinated meat slices and placing them onto a rice paper wrapper piled with pickled daikon and carrots, bean sprouts, romaine, rice vermicelli, and fresh mint leaves. This is then rolled up like a burrito and dipped into a light, flavorful sauce.

Vietnamese cuisine is the new kid on Hawaii's culinary block. Although some of the surroundings may be a little basic, go in and try this wonderful taste experience just once and you will find yourself wanting to go back for more!

LOCAL FOOD

Local food is the Hawaiian Everyman's version of homegrown comfort food. Its roots go back to the plantation days when people were recruited from around the world to work the sugar cane and pineapple fields. Although they lived in separate camps the workers gathered in small groups for lunch and that is where the blending of cultures began.

The field workers' diet was pretty simple. Just about everyone had a tin of rice and some kind of meat and vegetable. A Japanese worker might bring some teriyaki beef and his Portuguese comrade might have a can of sardines. The Koreans would certainly bring along some kim chee and the Filipinos their adobo and lumpia. Then in a kind of Hawaiian potluck the workers would share what they brought bringing variety to an otherwise ordinary lunch in the field.

That was the beginning of local food, but what does it look like today? When you think local food think of something simple a plantation family would keep in their pantry. First comes the staple starch, which is nearly always rice. Then you have canned meat of which Spam, Vienna Sausages, sardines, corned beef, and beef stew predominate. To add a little interest there would be a jar of mayonnaise and a bag of macaroni with which to make a simple mac salad. Then the upcountry farmers would bring down their cabbage and dinner would be served.

Most visitors to Hawaii experience local food at one of the diners that can be found just about everywhere in the islands. The standard offering is what is commonly called a plate lunch. For six or seven dollars you get a choice of meat such as teri chicken, katsu pork, or mahi mahi, "two scoop" rice, and a scoop of mac salad. The whole affair comes appropriately served in a Styrofoam carryout container complete with plastic table service. Bon Appetit!

Now if a big bowl of noodle soup is more your style, local food can accommodate you as well. The staple item here is known as saimin. The history of this dish is interesting. The Chinese say it has a Japanese origin and the Japanese say it came from China, so they both must be right! To make saimin, first you must have a stock. In the Japanese tradition this would be a dashi which is a broth made from nori flavored with bonito shavings. Since this is a little lean for many tastes the choices take off from there. Some places use a chicken stock and others a beef broth. Determining your preference and figuring out who is using what is part of the adventure of exploring the local food establishments.

Then come the noodles that by tradition are made from wheat flour, eggs, and water. This "long rice" is complemented with a little meat and perhaps an egg as well as some Chinese cabbage to top the whole thing off. Local diners will buy a teri beef stick or two to add flavor to their bowl or to eat along side with some hot mustard. Make sure you try adding a dash of hot sauce for added zest.

PACIFIC RIM CUISINE

In a geographical sense Pacific Rim refers to all of the nations that border the Pacific Ocean. This area not only includes Japan, Korea, China, and Southeast Asia but it also takes in Australia, New Zealand, and all of Polynesia as well as South, Central, and North America. However, no matter how large that seems physically, in a cultural sense the Pacific Rim involves even that much more.

People from diverse cultures have shared their culinary traditions since the beginning of time. This interaction has greatly accelerated as global commercial activity, improved communications, and personal travel experiences impacted the general public. During the 20th century our new awareness of different culinary tastes and practices began to change people's expectations regardless of where they stood on the economic ladder. Witness the evolving trends of American dietary culture as we went from Italian and Chinese to Mexican and Thai. Once we began to sample exciting new flavors we didn't want to stop.

This brings us to a better understanding of the dynamics behind the Pacific Rim movement. Watching the explosion of mass-produced ethnic convenience foods, what enterprising young chef wouldn't try to capitalize on a new trend? Taking advantage of opportunity, professional chefs began using their classic training to blend ingredients from one group of countries and cooking methods from another to produce results that are on a higher level than the sum of the parts.

For instance, grilled beef tenderloin with shiitake mushrooms in a Marsala demi glace served with mashed Hawaiian taro and Okinawan sweet potatoes is a far cry from a grilled steak and baked potato. The combination uses Chinese, French, Italian, Hawaiian, Okinawan, Continental European and American foods and methods to elevate the diner's experience. The chef's education and experience in blending flavors led to the resulting balanced and pleasing entree.

In the Hawaiian Islands visitors sometimes wonder if they are experiencing Pacific Rim or Hawaii Regional Cuisine. Hawaii Regional Cuisine showcases locally produced fish, meats, fruits, and vegetables combined with local ethnic styles and classic cooking techniques to produce an upscale contemporary version of Hawaiian "local food". Pacific Rim Cuisine draws upon a much broader geographic area when sourcing its ingredients and cooking methods and ends up as an innovative fusion of cuisines from all around the Pacific Rim.

A visit to a Pacific Rim restaurant is like a visit to a foodie theme park. As you read the menu, try and picture the ingredients and tastes the chef is combining before you make your selection. Not all the world's tastes and textures are to everyone's liking. By thinking about what you really enjoy and then following your own lead you will be much better prepared to select those dishes more likely to please and experience a truly enjoyable dining experience.

HAWAII REGIONAL CUISINE

There was a time when dining in Hawaii was less than a stellar experience. Much of what appeared on restaurant menus had to be shipped in over long distances. Things that could be arrived frozen and those that couldn't arrived tired. Then, in an attempt to please the visitors, the local chefs tried to prepare classic cuisine under less than ideal circumstances. As you can imagine, cooking Continental out of a can didn't work very well.

Along came the late '80's and a group of young chefs decided that something had to be done to change the situation. They began to talk with local farmers, fishermen, and ranchers about the types of products needed to raise the level of their culinary offerings. Then, in order to create new and exciting dishes, these chefs began merging local cultural influences with their newfound sources of supply and Hawaii Regional Cuisine was on its way to being born

In the original group there were twelve chefs who banded together and formally created the Hawaii Regional Cuisine movement. Those twelve are: Sam Choy, Roger Dikon, Mark Ellman, Bev Gannon, Jean Marie Josselin, George Mavrothalassitis (Mavro), Peter Merriman, Amy Ferguson Ota, Philippe Padovani, Gary Strehl, Alan Wong, and Roy Yamaguchi. Their goal was to combine fresh island products with local ethnic cooking styles and classic techniques in a contemporary upscale regional cuisine unique to Hawaii.

Hawaii Regional Cuisine is a fusion of elements from both eastern and western cultures. Much of the inspiration comes from the meager beginnings of the plantation camps and what islanders call "local food". Add that to an innovative group of classically trained chefs and the freshest of local products and you get truly unique preparations unlike anything you've ever experienced.

There are an amazing variety of offerings on a Hawaii Regional Cuisine menu. Naturally, fresh island fish like opakapaka and mahi-mahi appear regularly, but so do local aquaculture products like Kahuku prawns and Keahole lobster. Look for the Asian preparations and Polynesian sauces that take these specialties one-step beyond. Then to complement the seafood dishes, you might find innovative items like pineapple chicken or macadamia crusted lamb rounding things out.

While you are traveling in the islands keep an eye out for restaurants operated by any of the twelve original Hawaii Regional Cuisine chefs. They will surely provide you with a memorable evening of dining enjoyment. There is also a new group of young up and coming chefs who are doing wonderful work in Hawaii. These people call themselves the Hawaiian Island Chefs and include Steven Ariel, Chai Chaowasaree, Hiroshi Fukui, Teresa Gannon, George Gomes, Wayne Hirabayashi, D. K. Kodama, Lance Kosaka, Jacqueline Lau, Douglas Lum, James McDonald, Mark Okumura, Russell Siu, Goren Streng, and Corey Waite. Look for them. They are the new wave and they're here today.

Legend

Dress Code and Restaurant Price Symbols are based upon dinner. Lunch is usually a less expensive meal with more casual attire acceptable.

Restaurant Prices:

$	<$10
$$	$10-25
$$$	$25-$40
$$$$	$40+
Ent Card	Entertainment Card

The Entertainment Card travel discount card offers sizeable discounts and may be purchased for many geographic areas. You can view the benefits and order a directory and card at www.entertainment.com. At this writing the cost for the Hawaii package is $35.00. Fine, moderate, and casual dining choices are offered at many locations in Hawaii but are most common on Oahu. These books are released in limited quantities every November and do sell out. Either order early online or ask at your local bookstore. Make sure that you get the membership card with your copy. It should be attached inside the front cover.

Credit Cards Accepted:

AE	American Express
CB	Carte Blanche
DC	Diners Club
DIS	Discover
JCB	Japan Credit Bank
MC	Master Card
V	Visa

Days of Operation:

Su	Sunday
Mo	Monday
Tu	Tuesday
We	Wednesday
Th	Thursday
Fr	Friday
Sa	Saturday
X	Except

Example: XMo=Every Day Except Monday

Service Code:

Bru=Brunch **Buf**-Buffet

Cuisine Code:

Amer	American
Asian	Asian
Car	Caribbean
Chi	Chinese
Cof	Coffee
Cont	Continental
Ec	Eclectic
Euro	European
Fili	Filipino
Fre	French
Ger	German
Grk	Greek
Haw-Reg	Hawaiian Regional
Haw	Hawaiian
Ind	Indian
Indo	Indonesian
Isl	Island
Ital	Italian
Japan	Japan
Kor	Korean
Local	Local
LatAm	Latin American
Med	Mediterranean
Mex	Mexican
Org	Organic
Pac	Pacific
Pac-Rim	Pacific Rim
Port	Portuguese
Sea	Seafood
Spec	Specialty
Stk	Steak
Thai	Thailand
Trop	Tropical
Veg	Vegetarian
Viet	Vietnamese

Dress Code:

Casual	sandals, t shirts, shorts
Resort Casual	shirt with a collar, shorts with pockets, no flip-flops
Evening Aloha	long pants on gentlemen with closed-toed shoes
Formal	long sleeved dress shirt or jacket for gentlemen; inquire
Note:	Bathing suits and tank tops are suitable attire on the beach and by the pool. Cover-ups are an absolute must at even the most casual of dining spots.

Menu Items:

Nothing in the world of travel changes faster than restaurant menus. Everything from the seasonal availability of produce to which side of the bed the chef got up on impacts what you're offered when you sit down to dine. Nowhere is this more true than in Hawaii where the catch of the day really is caught that day. If the boats didn't bring opakapaka in, it just isn't available.

This guide attempts to help the reader come to his own conclusions. Menu items were chosen to give a well-rounded cross-section of the offerings and a sense of their depth and complexity. Signature dishes have been included whenever possible as they tend to be constants and best represent the expertise and direction of the chef. Finally, prices are always subject to change and should be viewed as guidelines of affordability.

Reservations:

It is always wise to call ahead. Even the most notable restaurants change their hours and days of operation. This is particularly true in travel destinations like Hawaii where business tends to be seasonal.

Spelling & Punctuation:

We have attempted to duplicate the spelling and punctuation as they appear on individual menus. If you think that some of them are unusual, you should have seen what they did to our spell check and grammar programs!

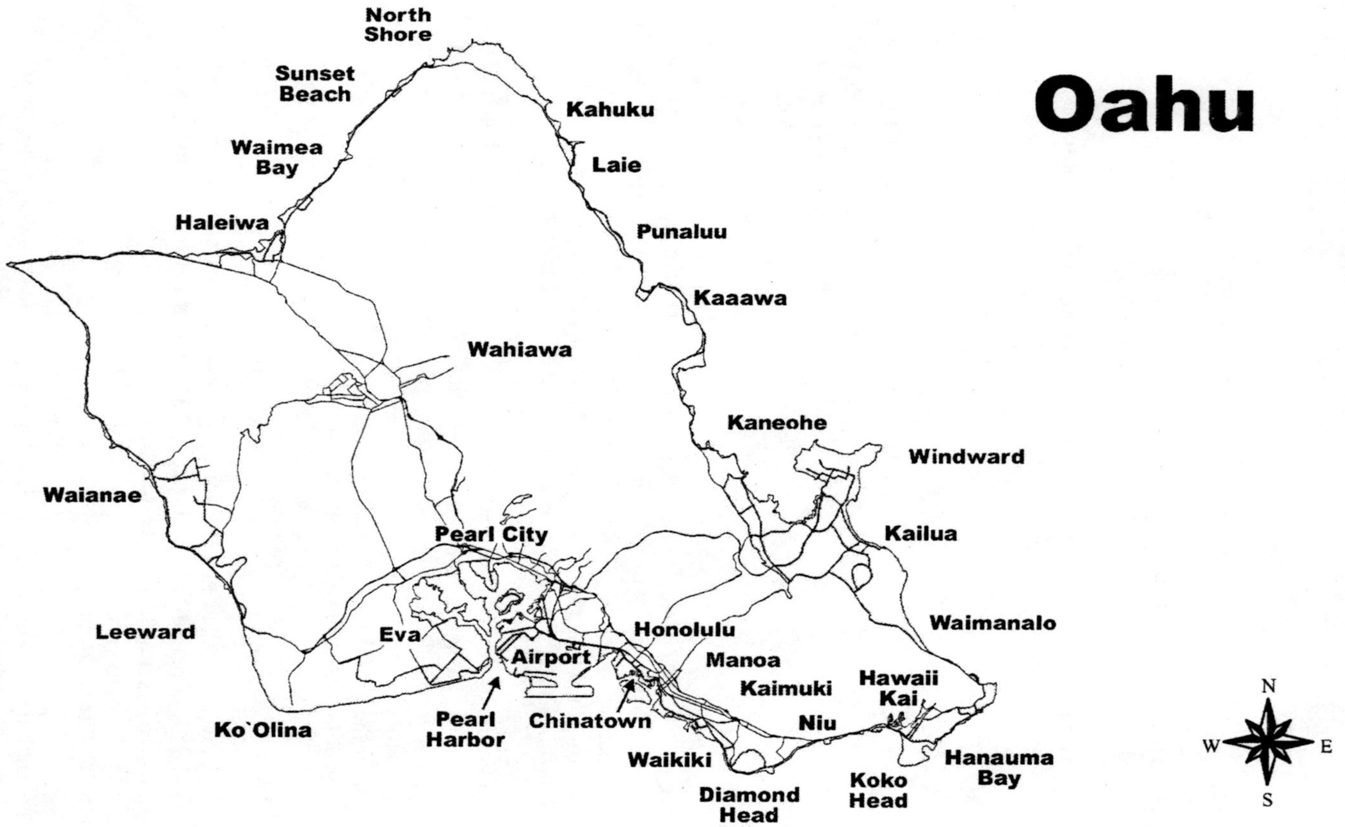

Oahu

North
Shore

Sunset
Beach

Waimea
Bay

Haleiwa

Kahuku

Laie

Punaluu

Kaaawa

Wahiawa

Kaneohe

Windward

Waianae

Pearl City

Kailua

Leeward

Eva

Honolulu

Waimanalo

Airport

Manoa

Kaimuki

Hawaii
Kai

Pearl
Harbor

Chinatown

Niu

Ko`Olina

Waikiki

Diamond
Head

Koko
Head

Hanauma
Bay

OAHU DINING

Kaimuki

12th Ave Grill

Authors' Favorite

1145C 12th Ave
Honolulu, HI 96816
808-732-9469
Web: None
Hours: L 11:30 AM-2:30 PM Mo-Fr
D 5:30 PM-9:00 PM Mo-Th
D 5:30 PM-10:00 PM FrSa
Cards: MC V
Dress: Resort Casual
Style: Amer $$

Menu Sampler:

Breakfast:
N/A
Lunch:
Salads & Small Plates: Smoked Ahi Salad Nicoise 9.95, Baked Macaroni & Cheese w/house smoked Parmesan 6.95, Garlic Bread 3.50
Sandwiches: Grilled Chicken Breast with lemon caper aioli 7.95, Smoked Ahi Sandwich-famous smoked ahi spread with tomatoes and sprouts 8.95
Large Plates: Kim Chee Steak grilled 14.95, Braised Short Ribs 16.95
Dinner:
Salads & Small Plates: Caesar w/croutons 7.95, Potato Pancakes w/fresh grated horseradish sauce 6.95, Fried Calamari w/tomato-lime tartar sauce 8.95
Large Plates: Hunter's Chicken with soft linguini 15.95, Smoked duck with sausage-cornbread stuffing, sautéed greens 24.95, Penne Pasta w/roasted butternut squash, alii mushrooms & goat cheese w/light cream sauce 15.95, Pan Seared Ribeye with Hearty Forrest Mushrooms sautéed in sherry 26.95
Desserts: Seasonal Fruit Crisp with Fresh Whipped Cream 5.95

Impressions:

Welcome to the newest hot spot on the Kaimuki dining scene. Word got out fast, and lines have been forming since the 12th Ave Grill opened. This neighborhood version of the trendy display-kitchen dining venues serves what management describes as contemporary American cooking. Best we can tell this is fusion cuisine with mainland roots and local spins. Simple dishes have been elevated by combining the best of many cultures. Things work amazingly well. Although the menu is unusual, the wait staff is knowledgeable and brings concepts across.

Kaimuki

3660 On The Rise Authors' Favorite

3660 Waialae Ave
Honolulu, HI 96816
808-737-1177
www.3660.com
Hours: D 5:30 PM-9:00 PM XMo
Cards: AE DC DIS JCB MC V
Dress: Evening Aloha
Style: Euro/Isl $$$

Menu Sampler:

Breakfast/Lunch:
N/A
Dinner:
First Flavors: Signature Dish of Ahi Katsu of ahi wrapped in nori and deep fried medium rare, wasabi-ginger sauce $10.95, 3660 Sampler Platter for Two-Oxtail and Foie Gras Tortellini, Sautéed Mushroom & Natural Jus; Ahi & Salmon Hash, Lomi Tomato with Ogo; Crispy Shrimp Won Tons, Spicy Soy Sauce; Shichimi Seared Ahi, Asian Slaw $15.95
Second Flavors: Clam & Corn Chowder with roasted red pepper crème fraiche $6.00, Asian Style Spinach and Wild Salmon Salad, spicy hoisin dressing $9.50
Entrées: Roast Rack of Macadamia Nut Crusted Lamb with cabernet mint sauce $28.00, New York Steak Alae pan seared with garlic, Hawaiian salt and butter, crisp onions $29.00, Chinese Steamed Fillet of Snapper in a Chinese black bean broth $25.00, Tempura Farm Raised Catfish with ponzu sauce $22.50
Taste of 3660: Four Courses-Pan Seared Scallop Salad, Crispy Calamari Spinach Salad, Medallions of Beef Tenderloin, Prawn, Dessert $36.60, wine $15
Sweet Endings: Harlequin Crème Brulee of vanilla bean custard and chocolate mousse glazed with a caramelized crust $7.00, White Chocolate Lemon napoleon with fluffy white chocolate, lemon mousse and fresh raspberries between layers of phyllo, lemon and raspberry sauces $7.00

Impressions:

3660 On The Rise has been a major part of the Honolulu dining buzz since it opened back in the early '90's. There behind Diamond Head, Chef Russell Siu creates award-winning fusion cuisine complemented by an excellent selection of wines from around the globe. Waialae Avenue might be a bit distant from the normal visitor haunts, but 3660 is quite easy to find. Park in the deck under the building, and take the elevator up to the lobby.

Oahu Dining

Honolulu

Aaron's **Authors' Favorite**

Ala Moana Hotel
410 Atkinson Drive
Honolulu, HI 94814
808-955-4466
www.tri-star-restaurants.com
Hours: D 5:30 PM-10:30 PM
Cards: AE DC DIS JCB MC V
Dress: Resort Casual
Style: Amer/Cont/Sea $$$$

Menu Sampler:

Breakfast/Lunch:
N/A
Dinner:
Appetizers: Black & Blue Ahi seared in Cajun spice $13.95, Escargot with sweet garlic & Parmesan Reggiano Gratinee $10.95, Foie Gras pan seared with a balsamic raspberry port wine reduction $18.00, Tiger Eye Sushi Tempura done tempura style with pear tomato salad and Chinese mustard sauce $13.95
Soups & Salads: Classic French Onion Soup $6.50, Blue Crab & Lobster Bisque $6, Grilled Asparagus w/goat cheese & walnut oil vinaigrette $7.50, Greek Maui Wowee Special w/chopped tomatoes, avocado, Maui onions, feta cheese, bay shrimp $8.95, Caesar Sarento's Style w/roasted garlic cloves $7.50
Entrées: Beef Filet ala 'Lexi" with Boursin cheese, olive oil mashed potatoes, & portobello mushroom $33.95, Steamed Island Onaga with baby Shanghai cabbage, soy-nori vinaigrette & sizzling hot peanut oil $29.95, Diver Sea Scallops with herb gnocchi, asparagus and shiitake mushrooms $27.95, Roasted Salmon with a smoked shrimp crust, mushroom orzo, red wine and honey thyme sauce $25.95, Abalone Medallions-Chicago Style or Almondine Butter $65.00, Grilled Rack of Lamb-herb crusted, sundried tomato jam, natural fennel jus $33.95, Veal Scallopine-porcini mushrooms & Madeira sauce $27.95

Impressions:

Those searching for a romantic dining experience would do well to consider an evening at Aaron's. Raised banquettes overlook the small window-side tables allowing everyone to enjoy the beautiful 36th floor view. The menu is upscale, the atmosphere clubby, and the service impeccable. Sophisticated patrons will appreciate the late night entertainment and extensive wine cellar. Valet parking is available at the hotel entrance street level on Atkinson Drive.

Honolulu

Akasaka Authors' Favorite

1646 B Kona Street
Honolulu, HI 96814
808-942-4466
Web: None
Hours: L 11:00 AM-2:30 PM Mo-Sa
D 5:00 PM-2:00 AM, 5:00 PM-12:00 AM Su
Cards: AE DC DIS JCB MC V
Dress: Resort Casual
Style: Japan $$

Menu Sampler:

Breakfast:
N/A
Lunch:
Sushi Combinations served with Kobachi, Miso Soup and Salad $12.95/$14.95 Teishoku-served with Miso Soup, Salad, Pickled Vegetables and Rice, Sashimi $12.95, Chicken Teriyaki $8.50, Butterfish Misoyaki $10.95, Combination Lunches include miso soup, salad, pickled vegetables and rice-choice of two entrees $12.95, choice of three entrees $16.95-choices include sashimi, tempura, beef or chicken teriyaki, chicken katsu, tonkatsu, udon or soba
Dinner:
A la Carte: Shrimp Tempura $9.95, Teishoku Dinner Combinations served with Vegetable Salad, Miso Soup, Pickled Vegetables & Rice, Scallop Butteryaki $12.95, Beef Teriyaki Teishoku 412.95, or choice of two entrees $18.95, choice of three entrees $24.95. NY Steak Dinner $15.50, King Crab Legs & NY Steak $23.95, Shrimp & Vegetable Tempura $8.95, Yakitori $6.75

Impressions:

If you are a sushi lover and are looking for the ultimate hideaway, you can't do better than Akasaka. This diminutive eatery is located behind the Ala Moana Shopping Center on a lane paralleling a parking lot off Kapiolani Boulevard. Inside you'll find a few tables, one tatami room, and a ten-seat sushi bar. The kitchen serves a surprisingly wide variety of Japanese specialties at prices that are quite reasonable by Honolulu standards. Akasaka serves until the wee hours making this a good choice for night owls.

Oahu Dining

Honolulu

Alan Wong's Restaurant Authors' Favorite

1857 S. King
Honolulu, HI 96826
808-949-2526
www.alanwongs.com
Hours: D 5:00 PM-10:00 PM
Cards: AE DC JCB MC V
Dress: Resort Casual
Style: Haw-Reg/Pac-Rim $$$$

Menu Sampler:

Breakfast/Lunch:
N/A
Dinner:
Appetizers: "Poki Pines" of crispy won ton ahi poke balls on avocado with wasabi sauce $12.50, Hot "California" Rolls…but with no rice-baked Kona lobster mousse wrapped in nori with crab avocado stuffing $14.00, Chinatown Roast Duck Nacho with homemade tapioca chips, avocado salsa $11.00
Salads: Ahi Cake-seared ahi and tomato terrine layered with grilled eggplant, Maui onions, basil, Big Island goat cheese lemongrass dressing $8.00, Whole Vine Ripened Tomato Salad with a li hing mui dressing $7.50, House Salad of greens with our Alan Wong's Special Oil Blend Vinaigrette $6.50
Entrées: Selections change nightly. Kiawe Wood Grilled Mahi Mahi with stir fried vegetables, wasabi sauce $27.00, Ginger Crusted Onaga, miso sesame vinaigrette, shiitake Enoki mushroom corn $33.00, Macadamia Nut-Coconut Crusted Lamb Chops with Asian ratatouille, roasted garlic smashed potatoes, red wine reduction $37.00, Pan Stew of Shrimp and Clams, Penne Pasta, chili garlic lemongrass black bean sauce $25.00, Braised Chinese Roast Duck Leg $28.00
Menu Tasting: Five Course without wines $65, with wines $90
Chef's Tasting: Seven Courses for $85/person (entire table must order)

Impressions:

Chef Alan Wong was a pioneer in the Hawaii Regional Cuisine movement. Back when many island chefs were still cooking from boxes Chef Alan was out developing local sources of supply. Today only the freshest ingredients are used in his fusion creations. These unique combinations are guaranteed to excite even the most jaded diner. Despite the world-class reputation, you'll find an informal, friendly atmosphere at this establishment. If you can find any way possible, try and include Alan Wong's in your visit to Honolulu. Reservations are a must!

Honolulu

Anna Miller's 24 Hour Restaurant
Pearlridge West
Kamehameha Highway
Aiea, HI 96701
808-487-2421
Web: None
Hours: BLD 24/7
Cards: AE MC V
Dress: Casual
Style: Amer/Isl $$

Menu Sampler:

Breakfast:
Two Eggs, Choice of Toast, Rice, Hash Browns or Cornbread-with Ham, Spam or Link Sausage $5.95, Bacon or Portuguese Sausage $6.25, Corned Beef Hash $6.95, Chicken Fried Steak $7.25. Banana Pancakes (3) $4.45
Lunch/Dinner:
1/3# Hamburger w/choice of cole slaw, macaroni salad, fries, or rice $6.45, Pastrami Reuben w/choice of cole slaw, macaroni salad, fries, or rice $7.25, French Dip w/au jus & choice of whipped potatoes, fries, rice, cole slaw, or mac salad $7.95, Mahi Mahi Sandwich w/cole slaw, mac salad, fries or rice $7.25
Entrees: Served with choice of rice, fries, or whipped potatoes and hot roll or cornbread- Chicken Katsu $8.75, Homestyle Meatloaf $8.95, Liver & Onions $8.65, Turkey & Stuffing $9.95, Fish & Chips $9.45, Deep Fried Scallops $9.75. Chicken Pot Pie with green salad and hot roll or cornbread $8.75, New York Steak $11.95 or T-Bone Steak $16.95 served with soup or salad, rice, fries, baked or whipped potato, hot roll or cornbread. Caesar Salad $6.95, with grilled chicken $7.95, with bay shrimp $7.75, Soup & Salad with roll $6.45
Desserts & Pies: Brownie Fudge Sundae $5.45, Malts & Shakes $3.95, Root Beer Float $2.95, Fresh Strawberry, Pecan, Cheesecake, or Macadamia Nut Pie $3.25, Fruit, Cream, Custard or Meringue Pie $2.95, Ala Mode $1.55

Impressions:

Honolulu people will drive from miles around to dine at Anna Miller's 24 Hour Restaurant. This crowd pleasing family dining spot serves their extensive menu all-day-every-day. If somebody wants dinner at six in the morning, they get it. How about a sunset breakfast? No problem! But the flexible service isn't all that brings in the patrons. The food is genuinely good and fairly priced. This would be a good choice for a traditional mainland meal in an eclectic social setting.

Oahu Dining

Hawaii Kai

Assaggio
Koko Head Marina Shopping Center
7192 Kalanianole Hwy.
Honolulu, HI 96825
808-396-0756
Web: None
Hours: L 11:30 AM-2:30 PM
D 5 PM-9:30 PM Su-Th
D 5 PM-10 PM FrSa
Cards: AE DC DIS JCB MC V
Dress: Resort Casual
Style: Ital $$

Menu Sampler:

Breakfast:
N/A
Lunch:
Appetizers, Soups, Salads: Fresh Clams Scampi Style $8.90, Minestrone or Tortellini in Brodo (broth) $2.90/$3.90, Tossed Green Salad $2.90
Entrées: Chicken Sorrentino with eggplant, cheese, and mushrooms in wine sauce $11.90, Fettuccini Alfredo with Broccoli $9.90, Lasagna $11.90, Meatball Sandwich $7.90, Eggplant Parmigiana Sandwich $7.90, Shrimp Scampi $13.90
Dinner:
Appetizers, Soups, Salads: Artichoke Pepperonata $7.90, Carpaccio with filet mignon $7.90, Vichyssoise or Pasta Fagioli $2.90/$3.90, Calamari Vinaigrette Salad $5.90, Caesar Salad (2 orders min.) $5.90 Sweet Broccoli Sauté $5.90
Entrées: Fettucine Alfredo w/broccoli $11.90/$14.90, Calamari Vegetable with squid strips and vegetables in garlic sauce with pasta $14.90/$16.90, Chicken Putanesca with garlic, anchovy, chili peppers and tomato sauce $14.90/$16.90
Desserts: Italian Spumoni $4.00, Homemade Cheesecake $4.50, Homemade Tiramisu $5.00, Zabaglione w/imported Marsala wine $4.50, Irish Coffee $5.00

Impressions:

As you head up the coast past Diamond Head you'll come to an area that would fit as well in Fort Lauderdale as it does in Hawaii. This is Hawaii Kai, home to Assaggio and the Koko Head Marina. Here at Assaggio's waterfront restaurant they take an upscale approach to décor and menu selections while maintaining reasonable prices. Tasty Italian food in generous portions makes Assaggio a great lunch choice while traveling around the island. Dress appropriately.

Honolulu

Auntie Pasto's
1099 S. Beretania
Honolulu, HI 96826
808-523-8855
Web: None
Hours: L/D 11 AM-10:30 PM
D Su 4 PM-10:30 PM
Cards: MC V
Dress: Casual
Style: Ital $$

Menu Sampler:

Breakfast:
N/A
Lunch/ Dinner:
Antipasti: Garlic Bread $3.50, Red Pepper Calamari $6.50, Garlicky Clams & Mussels $8.95, Garlic Bread $3.00, Mozzarella Marinara $5.95, Fire Roasted Artichokes $7.50, Soup-cup $2.95, bowl $3.95
Salads: Garden Salad $4.50/$7.95, Original Caesar $4.95/$7.95 with shrimp add $4.00, Caprese- Tomato Mozzarella Salad $5.95, Kitchen Sink Salad $8.95, It's Greek To Me $5.95, Romaine & Gorgonzola $4.95, Pimento & Anchovy $5.50
Pasta: Sausage & Peppers $8.25, Meatball or Meat Sauce $7.95, Spinach & Cream $8.95, Creamy Pesto $8.95, Carbonara $8.95, Seafood $8.95, Tuna with Tomato & Onion $7.95, Fried Eggplant $8.50, Fresh Mushrooms $8.50, Tomato or Butter & Garlic $7.25, Clams $9.25, Fresh Vegetables $7.95
Entrées: Veal Marsala $14.50, Chicken Piccata $11.95, Grilled Calamari $11.95, Eggplant Parmesan $8.95, Lasagna Roll $8.95, Manicotti $7.25, Calamari Steak $11.25, Cacciuco (seafood stew) $15.95, Homemade Gnocchi $8.25, Cheese Pizza $8.95, Sausage, Oregano, Ricotta, Peppers, Onions $10.50
Desserts: Tiramisu $4.95, Cheesecake $4.50, Crème Brulee $3.95, Sorbet $4.50

Impressions:

Auntie Pasto's is a warm, welcoming establishment with waiters in white aprons and tables laid with red checked linens. Besides the comfortable atmosphere this restaurant provides a tasty menu. The salads are crisp with zesty dressings, and the pasta dishes are well seasoned with full-flavored meats and sauces. Espresso, Cappuccino, and a complete bar are available as are wonderful desserts. The prices are reasonable, but you'll have to look for parking on the street. Visitors will find this to be a convenient stop after touring the museums and galleries.

Oahu Dining

Leeward

Azul
Ihilani Resort & Spa
92-1001 Olani
Kapolei, HI 96707
808-679-0079
www.ihilani.com
Hours: D 6:00 PM-9:00 PM Tu-Sa
Cards: AE DC DIS JCB MC V
Dress: Evening Aloha
Style: Med $$$$

Menu Sampler:

Breakfast/Lunch:
N/A
Dinner:
Appetizers: Mango Crab Cake crusted with capellini pasta, beurre blanc, chive oil 17.50, Sautéed Duckling Foie Gras, toasted scallion brioche, field greens, gastrique of balsamic and pomegranate 19.00, Azul Hukilau of today's catch of shellfish, white wine, chorizo and saffron with grilled focaccia 18.50
Soups & Salads: Consommé of Oxtail with an oxtail truffle crepe 9.50, Azul Salad with baby romaine, avocado relish, fresh island shellfish in a creamy citrus dressing 14.00, Prosciutto and Mozzarella Fresca, sun dried kunai pineapples, island watercress, aged balsamic vinaigrette 15.50
Entrées: Ahi Tournedos seared with a three pepper crust, duckling foie gras, truffle risotto and beurre rouge of port wine balsamic 38.00, Poached Maine lobster with a ragout of Kauai shrimp and saffron lobster sauce 45.00, Roast Rack of Lamb marinated in herbs and lightly crusted with pommery mustard, with dried fig feta cheese polenta 40.00, Sautéed Beef Tenderloin, wild mushroom crusted aged Angus beef with caramelized shallot confit and rosemary pinot noir jus 39.00, Weekly Menu Specials
Chef's Prix Fixe Menu 80.00

Impressions:

The Ihilani Resort & Spa is located in the wide-open spaces of southwestern Oahu, far from the hustle and bustle of Waikiki. This oasis of peace and serenity is the hub of the burgeoning Ko'Olina resort. Here you'll find Azul, the Ihilani's Four Diamond signature restaurant. The continentally influenced Mediterranean cuisine comes elegantly served and is complemented by a Wine Spectator award winning wine list. Patrons will find that the setting and service are impeccable. Reservations are required.

Waikiki

Bali By The Sea Authors' Favorite

Hilton Hawaiian Village Hotel
2005 Kalia Road
Honolulu, HI 96815
808-941-2254
www.hawaiianvillage.hilton.com
Hours: D 6-9:30 PM XSu
Cards: AE DIS JCB MC V
Dress: Evening Aloha
Style: Euro-Asian $$$$

Menu Sampler:

Breakfast/Lunch:
N/A
Dinner:
First Tastes: Seared Diver Scallops and Wild Mushrooms with sautéed celery root, truffle vinaigrette and watercress coulis $13.00, Escargot and Wild Mushroom En Croute with Raclette cheese $7.50, Bali By The Sea Sampler of crispy prawns, seared scallops, beet salad, and ahi avocado cake $18.00
Soups: Island Bouillabaisse-a savory seafood stew of shrimp and scallops and fresh island catch $9.75, Gingered Maui Onion Soup w/coconut milk $7.00
Entrées: Sautéed Island Opakapaka crusted with Macadamia nuts, chopped cilantro and sweet potato mousseline, asparagus, baby carrots and kaffir lime sauce $34.00, Roasted Duck Breast and Confit Leg with wild rice risotto croquette, French beans, squash and sauce cassis $30.00, Roast Rack of Sonoma Lamb with orange hoisin glaze, Molokai sweet potato mousseline, touille of fresh vegetables and spicy peanut demi glaze $39.50, Scallion Crusted Ahi Tempura with fern shoots and hearts of palm salad, sweet potato lemon grass trap and ponzu butter sauce $36.00, Poached Kona Lobster $44.00

Impressions:

For an outstanding evening's entertainment of romantic dining, take a stroll through the Hilton Hawaiian Village to Bali By The Sea. This award-winning Four Diamond restaurant combines a comfortable upscale atmosphere with a fine dining menu in one of the nicest oceanfront locations on Waikiki Beach. The chef combines French, Asian, and island influences to produce wonderful taste and texture combinations offered with an extensive wine list. Bali's pupus display the chef's talents and can become a complete meal with little prompting. When the sunset starts to fade and the lights come on along the shore, you'll know why you made the reservation.

Honolulu

Bali Indonesia
1901 Kapiolani Blvd.
Honolulu, HI 96826
808-949-2254
Web: None
Hours: L 11:30 AM-2:00 PM, Buffet or Menu
D 6:00 PM-9:00 PM, Buffet Mo-Th
Cards: AE MC V
Dress: Casual
Style: Indo $ Ent Card

Menu Sampler:

Breakfast:
N/A
Lunch:
Daily Buffet-$5.95/adult, $4.95/child-assortment of regular menu dishes
Dinner:
Dinner Buffet: Mo-Th $7.95/adult, $6.95/child-assortment from regular menu
Crackers: Shrimp Crackers w/Indonesian sauce $1.95, Belinjo crackers $1.95
Appetizers: BBQ Fish Cake wrapped in banana leaf with peanut sauce $6.95, Indonesian style egg roll stuffed with chicken, shrimp, carrots, bamboo shoots, and green onion, served with spicy peanut sauce $5.95, Deep Fried Tofu $5.95
Salads and Soups: Gado Gado-Mixed vegetables, tofu, eggs and shrimp crackers with peanut dressing $7.95, Beef Ball & vegetables in soup $8.95
Satays: Asst. Satay-marinated chicken, lamb & shrimp w/peanut sauce $12.95
Entrées: Javanese Style BBQ Chicken $8.95, Indonesian Style Curry Chicken, Egg, & Potatoes $8.95, Fried Spicy Beef w/chili sauce $9.95, Lamb cooked w/coconut milk sauce $9.95, Margarine Sautéed Prawns w/black sweet & sour sauce $9.95, Asst. Stir Fried Vegetables w/chicken, beef ball, and mushroom $8.95, Indonesian Style Fried Egg Noodle w/ meats & vegetables $8.95

Impressions:

Bali Indonesia's location is typical Hawaii. Instead of occupying a freestanding building, this dining spot can be found at the end of a strip mall. Inside, patrons will find a comfortably busy yet gentle atmosphere. The menu features fresh fruits and vegetables combined with ingredients like coconut milk, peanuts, and fresh herbs. Vegetarians would love this place, but those of us who like a little meat in our diet aren't left behind. Go online and check for coupons. A recent offering provided an eight-course banquet for $18.95 per person.

Honolulu

Big City Diner

Ward Entertainment Center
1060 Auahi Street
Honolulu, HI 96814
808-591-8891

Web:	None
Hours:	B 7:00 AM-10:30 AM Mo-Fr B 7:00 AM-11:00 AM SaSu L 11:00 AM-4:00 PM Mo-Fr L 11:30 AM-3:30 PM SaSu D 4:30 PM-Closing FrSaSu
Cards:	AE DIS MC V
Dress:	Casual
Style:	Amer/Isl $

Menu Sampler:

Breakfast:
Broiled NY Steak & Eggs with choice of starch $8.95, Loco Moco $5.95, Fried Rice & Eggs $5.75, Kimchee Fried Rice $5.75, Murphy's Famous Apple Pancakes with warm cinnamon sauce $6.50, Grilled Oatmeal Cakes $5.95
Lunch/Dinner:
Pupus: Wings Over Kaimuki with a guava bbq sauce $6.95, Calamari Tempura Strips $6.95, Roasted Garlic Fries $3.95, Chips & Homemade Salsa $3.95
Salads: Paniolo Chicken Salad with lime marinated chicken, roasted corn, tomato, cheeses, chips & cilantro over greens $7.95, Citrus Grilled Salmon Salad with ponzu vinaigrette $9.95, Oriental Chicken Salad $7.95
Big Burgers & Specialty Sandwiches: All served with fries. Burgers are ½ lb. patties cooked medium or otherwise. Magic Mushroom Burger-mushrooms sautéed in garlic, Marsala wine & butter $7.95, Grandma's Famous Kimchee Burger $7.95, The Big City Club adding avocado, jack and cheddar cheeses $8.95, Ultimate Grilled Eggplant Sandwich w/roasted red peppers, caramelized onion, melted jack cheese and roasted garlic mayo on sourdough roll $7.95
Entrees: Served w/choice of white or brown rice, soup or salad. Chinatown Chow Mein noodles stir-fried w/fresh veggies $7.95, Herb Roasted Tequila Chicken $9.95, Fresh Catch Pan Seared &Glazed $9.95, Baby Back Ribs $19.95

Impressions:

This bustling anytime diner has something to tempt any taste or appetite. Their varied menu has earned awards for "Best Family Restaurant". There is plenty of parking in the Ward Center lots making it easy to visit this fun place.

Hawaii Kai

BluWater Grill

Hawaii Kai Shopping Center
377 Keahole St
Honolulu, HI 96825
808-395-6224
www.bluwatergrillhawaii.com

Hours: LD 11:00 AM-11:00 PM Mo-Th
LD 11:00 AM-12:00AM FrSa
SuBru 10:00 AM-2:30 PM Su D 2:30 PM-11:00 PM
Cards: AE DC JCB MC V
Dress: Resort Casual
Style: Pac-Rim $$

Menu Sampler:

Breakfast:
N/A
Lunch/Dinner:
Pupus: Chicken Sate with spicy peanut dipping sauce and green mango slaw 5.95, Oven Roasted Seafood Dip with crisp tortilla chips 10.95, Shoyu-ogo Poke $Mkt, Kalua Pig Tostadas on crisp fried squid ink wontons with pureed sweet potato and mango-papaya salsa 6.95, Inside Out California Roll 12.95
Soups And Salads: Norwegian Salmon Chowder 7.95, BluWater Grill Caribbean Cobb Salad w/ginger grilled shrimp & candied mac nuts 12.95
Meats & Seafood: Mango and Guava Glazed Pork Ribs with Caribbean Slaw, Jamaican peas & rice 15.95, Scallops with soy-mustard-butter sauce 14.95, Hawaiian Barbecued Chicken over seared vegetable yaki soba noodles 11.95
Sandwiches: Crispy Kalua Pork Sandwich on a toasted taro roll with tropical fruit relish 7.95, Chicken Panini with basil mayo and dressed greens 8.95, Seafood Salad Melt of crab, shrimp, scallops, spinach, bacon, Gouda 10,95
Desserts: Warm Banana Blintzes with chocolate-caramel-rum sauce 4.95, French Kiss of Kahlua, Grand Marnier, hot chocolate, whipped cream 5.75

Impressions:

BluWater Grill is the handiwork of some long time Honolulu restaurant pros. These people recognized the potential of some available space overlooking the Hawaii Kai lagoon and created a fun waterfront-dining experience. First, they designed a menu around known customer preferences. Prices were then set at a reasonable level to encourage repeat visits. Finally, it all came together when the experienced chef began building flavors into his preps, and the crowds appeared.

Honolulu

Bravo Restaurant-Bar

Pearlridge Center
98-115 Kaonohi St
Aiea, HI 96701
808-487-5544

Web:	None
Hours:	LD 11:00 AM-10:00 PM Su-Th
	LD 11:00 AM-11:00 PM FrSa
Cards:	AE DC DIS JCB MC V
Dress:	Casual
Style:	Ital $$

Menu Sampler:

Lunch/Dinner:
Pizza: 8" & 12", Classic Cheese $7.25/$11.25, Veggie Gourmet $8.75/$14.75, Artichoke & Prosciutto $8.95/$14.95, Garlic Roma $8.75/$14.75
Sandwiches: choice of fries, pasta salad, rice or today's pasta, Homemade Meatball Sandwich $6.50, Chicken Parmigiana Sandwich $7.25
Salads & Soup: Spinach Salad $4.95/$8.95, Chopped Salad $6.95/$8.95, Chinese Chicken Salad with sesame dressing $8.95, Minestrone $2.95
Steak & Veal: choice of pasta, rice, or fries-Veal Parmigiana $13.95, T-Bone $16.95, Steak Sinatra with sautéed mushrooms, onions & peppers $18.95
Pasta: Seafood Harvest Linguine in a light tomato cream sauce $16.95, Sautéed Scallops with fresh mushrooms in a cream sauce on linguine $13.95, Baked Chicken Canneloni $10.95, Eggplant Parmigiana $9.75, Lasagna $12.95, Penne Pasta with Artichokes & Chicken $13.95, Homemade Ravioli $9.95, Baked Rigatoni $10.95, Fettucine Pasta w/Sliced Chicken & Mushrooms in a garlic cream sauce $13.95, Eggplant Siciliana $11.95, Combo Platters-2 items $12.95
Desserts: Fresh Fruit Italian Ices $3.25, Cappucino Ice Cream Sundae $3.95, Tiramisu $4.95, Death By Chocolate $4.75, Haupia Chocolate Pie $3.25

Impressions:

Visitors to the USS Arizona Memorial are close at hand to one of Honolulu's favorite Italian restaurants. Just up the hill from Pearl Harbor you'll find the Pearlridge shopping complex and Bravo Restaurant-Bar. This establishment serves an extensive menu of affordable Italian specialties. Don't be intimidated by the crowds or large size of the room. Service is efficient and accommodating. During peak meal times the parking lot around the restaurant fills up. However, if you're not afraid to walk a bit, you'll find plenty of room behind the stores.

Windward

Brent's Restaurant & Delicatessen

Kailua Business Plaza
629-A Kailua Road
Kailua Business Plaza
Kailua, HI 96734
808-262-8588
Web: None
Hours: 7:00 AM-2:00 PM
Cards: MC V
Dress: Casual
Style: Amer/Ec $$

Menu Sampler:

Breakfast: (served till 2 PM)
All items served with choice of rice, hash browns, country fries or tomato; toast, bagel or English muffin; butter or cream cheese. Bruschetta Poached Eggs $8.75, Spicy Chicken Frittata $8.95, Four Pancakes $4.25, Strawberry Waffle $5.75 (SaSu only), Cheese Blintzes $8.75, Potato Latkes $7.95, Denver Omelet $8.95, Steak & Eggs $10.95, Fresh Mixed Fruit with Yogurt $3.25/$4.95
Lunch:
All served with choice of potato salad, cole slaw, macaroni salad or three-bean salad. Hot Corned Beef, Pastrami, & Swiss cheese with tomato & Russian dressing $9.75, Hot Brisket, Jack cheese, Ortega chili, grilled onion on grilled sourdough with fries $10.95, Meatloaf Sandwich on sourdough toast with grilled onions, gravy & fries $8.25, Hot Corned Beef Thick Deli Sandwich $8.50, Grilled Fresh Ahi or Salmon Club Sandwich w/fries $10.50, Kosher Salami $7.95, Latte $3.00, Cappuccino $2.75, Espresso $2.25, Cheesecake $4.50
Soups: Chicken Matzo Ball Soup (Jewish Saimin) $4.50, Clam Chowder $3.95
Dinner:
N/A

Impressions:

We normally try to highlight places that are easy to locate. That's not Brent's! Naturally this means that most of their patrons are locals. For the rest of us, take Kailua Road into Kailua, and as the road curves right, make a right turn into the driveway between the Ford dealership and First Hawaiian Bank. There in a back courtyard you'll find Brent's. The food served here makes this bit of extra effort worth it. Large servings of delicious mainland style meals are available most of the day. This place bustles. Bring your paper and have a seat indoors or out.

Honolulu

Brew Moon Restaurant & Microbrewery
Ward Center-2nd Level
1200 Ala Moana Blvd.
Honolulu, HI 96814
808-539-0088
www.brewmoon.com
Hours: L/D 11:00 AM-10:00 PM
Cards: AE DC JCB MC V
Dress: Resort Casual
Style: Haw-Reg/Pac Rim $$ Ent Card

Menu Sampler:

Breakfast:
N/A
Lunch/Dinner:
Small Stuff: Ahi Sampler-a trio of blackened, sashimi, and spiked poke $14, Steamed Manila Clams in a white wine garlic broth $11.5, Teri Wings $9
Salads: Spinach Salad w/shiitake mushroom, pecans, bacon, crispy sweet potato, Bermuda onion, with moonberry vinaigrette $9, Ahi Poke Salad $12
Grilled Pizzas: Three Cheese Pizza $14, Barbeque Chicken Pizza $15
Sandwiches: All served with fries or rice. Beer Battered Mahi Burger $9, Crabcake Sandwich w/Cajun mayo $9, Kalua Pork Sandwich $8
Lunch/Dinner Plates: Jambalaya w/spiced meats & seafood, smoked pork, chicken, shrimp, Andouille, ham $15, Chicken Curry w/pineapple, banana, mango, long beans, Jasmine rice $13.50, Manila Clam Pasta $13, Sake Steamed Mahi Mahi with hot sesame oil coconut fried banana, rice & vegetables $14
Dinner Plates: NY Strip Steak w/grilled tomato, green peppercorn sauce, whole grain mustard mashed potatoes $25, Fire Roasted Ribs w/Mardi Gras slaw, mash potato, mustard soy sauce $24, Pacific Bouillabaise in tomato saffron broth $21
Sweet Stuff: Bananas On The Moon with fried bananas, haupia sauce, vanilla ice cream, chocolate sauce, macadamia nuts $6, Ice Cream or Sorbet $4.5
Beers: Handcrafted beers, Happy Hour 3 PM-7 PM Daily.

Impressions:

Up on the second floor of Ward Center you'll find Brew Moon with its Pacific Rim influenced menu. This contemporary restaurant offers dishes that you just won't find elsewhere in Honolulu. Besides Louisiana and island specialties, they offer family favorites like pizza. Look for late night entertainment offering jazz, Hawaiian, contemporary, comedy, etc. Don't forget the house-brewed beers!

Windward

Buzz's Original Steakhouse

413 Kawailea Road (Hwy 61)
Lanikai, HI 96734
808-261-4661
Web: None
Hours: L 11:00 AM-2:00 PM
D 5:00 PM-9:00 PM
Cards: None
Dress: Casual
Style: Sea/Stk $$

Menu Sampler:

Breakfast:

N/A

Lunch:

Burgers: Kiawe Charcoal Broiled Burgers are all served with lettuce and tomato on a sesame seed bun with your choice of a cup of soup or our tempura fries. Buzz Burger Deluxe-a 6 oz. Patty with house dressing and optional Swiss cheese and onions $7.95, Teriyaki/Thai Chicken Burger Thai peanut sauce & sprouts, $7.95 w/marinated beef & mayo dressing $8.95, Fresh Fish Burger char-broiled with Tartar Sauce $8.95, Mushroom Garden Burger $7.95
Salads: All served with French bread & olive oil. Thai Chicken Salad with peanut sauce $8.95, Scampi Salad with tomato, onion bleu cheese, capers, and charbroiled scampi $12.95, BLT Salad $6.00/$7.95, Caesar Salad $6.00/$7.95

Dinner:

Firsts: Tempura French Fries $2.50, Artichoke Surprise $6.95, Escargot $5.95
Soup and Salad Bar: $11.95, Salad Bar $8.95, Soup of the Day $2.50/$4.00
Entrées: Include salad bar, bread & butter. Top Sirloin 10 oz. $17.95, Baby Top $13.95, Ground Sirloin Special w/mushrooms & onions $12.95, Rack of Lamb $25.95, Prime Rib 13 oz. $21.95/Lanikai Cut 17 oz. $26.95, Lobster Tail $31.95, Scampi $22.95, Fresh Fish $Market Price, Chicken Teriyaki $13.95
Desserts: Buzz's Own Ice Cream Pies, Grasshopper Pie or Cheesecake $5.00

Impressions:

Buzz's doubles as both a beachside burger joint and steakhouse. During lunch this weathered wood restaurant serves a casual menu, while in the evening it makes the conversion to supper club fare. Although Buzz's is quite informal, bathing suits are not permitted, so wear a cover-up. Reservations are wise on weekend evenings. There's plenty of parking. Credit cards are not accepted.

Kaimuki

C & C Pasta Company

3605 Waialae Avenue
Honolulu, HI 96816
808-732-5999
Web: None
Hours: L 11:00 AM-3:00 PM Tu-Sa
D 5:00 PM-10:00 PM Tu-Su
Cards: MC V
Dress: Casual
Style: Ital $$

Menu Sampler:

Breakfast:
N/A
Lunch:
Appetizers: Char-Grilled Vegetable Appetizer $9.00, Arugula Salad with pear, pecorino, watercress, and candied walnut salad with red wine dressing $8.00
Sandwiches: Fresh Mozzarella with tomato, sweet basil, drizzled with extra virgin olive oil and topped with cracked pepper $8.50, Roasted Pork Tenderloin & Provolone Cheese with aioli, baby greens, roasted onion and tomato $9.50
Pastas: Fettucine with Roasted Eggplant, tomatoes, smoked mozzarella & basil $10.50, Tagliatelle with Sweet Sausage, peas, and mixed mushrooms in a tomato cream sauce $10.50, Linguine with Clams, white wine, garlic $10.50
Dinner:
Appetizers: Escargot in Pastry with garlic, white wine, parsley & butter sauce $8.50, Warm Shrimp Salad, ricotta salata, green beans, tomatoes $9.00
Pasta: Fettuccine with Chicken, asparagus, porcini mushrooms, prosciutto and cream $17.50, Chef's Signature-Tagliatelle with Roasted Duck, Gorgonzola, pears and arugula $19.00, Fettuccine with Langoustino, beurre blanc $21.50
Entrees: Veal Involtini of pan fried escalope of veal stuffed with fontina and mortadella, fresh asparagus and house potatoes $22.50, House Roasted Pork Rib Florentine w/rosemary, thyme, garlic served with potatoes, grilled pear $25.00

Impressions:

C & C Pasta Company is a fine example of the Kaimuki Dining revolution. The "Build it and they will come" theory works in this part of town. The rustic room has a deli counter in the rear where salame, cheeses, olives and pastry are sold, but those in the know will claim a table in the street side dining area and enjoy a leisurely repast. From appetizers to desserts, the tastes are rich and flavorful.

Diamond Head

Cabanas Seaside Grill

Authors' Favorite

Kahala Mandarin Oriental
5000 Kahala Avenue
Honolulu, HI 96816
808-739-8774
www.mandarinoriental.com

Hours: L 10:30 AM-4:30 PM Mo-Su
D 5:30 PM-9:00 PM Mo-Su
Cards: AE DC DIS JCB MC V
Dress: Resort Casual/Evening Aloha
Style: Pac-Rim $$$

Menu Sampler:

Breakfast:
N/A
Lunch:
The Original Kahala Burger with bacon, avocado, cheddar cheeses, sautéed onions 14.00, Mahi Mahi Sandwich with oven roasted tomatoes, zucchini, wasabi aioli 17.00, Hawaiian Fruit Salad with yogurt or cottage cheese 15.00
Dinner:
To Begin With: Grilled Shrimp Skewers, BBQ Ohelo Berry 14.00, Manila Clams ½ pound 11.00, Crystal Bay Oysters-1/2 dozen 16.00, w/tobiko 28.00
Entrées: Hawaiian Bouillabaise-mahi mahi, clams, mussels, shrimp, ogo, sesame croutons, spicy lilikoi aioli 26.00, Grilled Kona Maine Lobster and Manila Clams with Cabanas Garlic Herb Butter 50.00, Grille "Pulehu" Beef-Maui onions, mushrooms, pineapple garlic sage 20.00, All Day Slow Roast Pork with Granny Smith apple and apricot compote 16.00, Pan Roasted Island Chicken with Maui onion jam 18.00, Fresh Fish Specials $Mkt

Impressions:

On the opposite side of Diamond Head from Waikiki you'll find a hotel all by itself. This is the home of the Kahala Mandarin Oriental and Cabanas Seaside Grill. Dining has always been special at this resort, so it comes as no surprise that their new waterfront venue is a winner. Management has gone outside the box and placed tables under spacious cabanas on the edge of the beach creating one of the most romantic dining settings found in Hawaii. Although the menu isn't lengthy, we had no trouble ordering. Listen for the daily specials. The deck in front of the hotel is very pricey. Get your parking ticket validated!

North Shore

Café Haleiwa
66-460 Kamehameha Hwy
Haleiwa, HI 96712
808-637-5516
Web: None
Hours: B 7:00 AM-12:30 PM Mo-Fr
B 7:00 AM-2:00 PM SaSu
L 11:00 AM-2:00 PM Mo-Sa
Cards: AE MC V
Dress: Casual
Style: Amer/Mex $

Menu Sampler:

Breakfast:
Café Egg Sandwich of a one egg omelet style, cheese, Canadian bacon, toasted English muffin, tomato and sprouts with home fries $5.60, w/avocado $6.70, Huevos Rancheros w/beans & rice, $6.55, Quesadilla with home fries/beans/rice $6.65, Dawn Patrol of two large buttermilk pancakes and two eggs any style-offered between 7 and 8 AM for $3.10, after 8 AM $3.75, ½ papaya $1.10, Homemade Banana Nut Bread $2.50, fruit w/yogurt topped w/granola $4.00
Lunch:
Sandwiches: All served with home fries or potato salad and come with lettuce and tomato, with grilled onion on request. Mahi Mahi-6 oz broiled filet on a poorboy roll $6.95, Kama'aina Burger-1/3# w/cheddar cheese, mushrooms & bacon w/ homefries $8.50, Blue's Chicken Sandwich w/grilled chicken breast, jack cheese, grilled onions & mushrooms w/homefries $7.95, Veggie Sandwich on grilled sourdough bread with melted cheese $4.25 with avocado $5.25
Mexican Lunches-All plates are served with rice & beans or home fries. Fish Tacos with grilled mahi mahi, diced onion, tomatoes, cilantro and a lime on a steamed corn tortilla $6.35, Combination Plates $8.75-$10.50
Dinner:
N/A

Impressions:

Café Haleiwa is the abode of one Duncan Campbell, champion surfer and board designer emeritus. Everything else about the place follows suit. This casual café provides a glimpse into the laid-back North Shore lifestyle. You'll find the food to be good, healthy, and plentiful with daily menu specials and fresh fruits listed on the board inside the front door. Local residents and visitors alike love this place. There is plenty of free parking behind the restaurant.

Kaimuki

Café Laufer

3565 Waialae Avenue #107
Honolulu, HI 96816
808-735-7717, Fax-808-735-2645
www.cafelaufer.com

Hours: BLD 10:00 AM-9:00 PM SuMoWeTh
BLD 10:00 AM-10:00 PM FrSa
Cards: AE DC JCB MC V
Dress: Casual
Style: Amer/Pac-Rim $

Menu Sampler:

Breakfast:

Pastries-All our pastries are made with 100% butter $.65-$1.50

Cakes and Tortes-over a dozen daily to choose from $4.00-$5.75
Fresh Strawberries with Sour Cream & Brown Sugar $6.95
Beverages: Espresso $2.00, Latte $2.75, Cappuccino $2.75, Mocha $3.00, Thai Coffee $3.00, Thai Mocha $3.25, Hot Chocolate $3.00, Hot Tea $1.85

Lunch/Dinner:

Salads: Chinese Chicken Salad of lettuce, sliced chicken topped with sliced almonds, won ton pi, green onion, Chinese parsley, toasted sesame seeds $7.95, Spinach Salad with our own honey mustard dressing, Gorgonzola cheese, craisins and sugar coated almonds $8.75, Orange Seared Shrimp Salad with a warm Orange Balsamic Vinaigrette dressing over Mesclun greens $10.50
Entrees & Sandwiches: Daily Entrée Specials $8.95-$18.95, Bratwurst made from coarse ground pork & spices, grilled, served with sauerkraut and country French bread $9.25, Vegetable Burger with choice of cheese and pasta salad $6.95, Salmon & Pumpernickel of smoked Atlantic salmon, pumpernickel bread, cream cheese, Maui onions, and capers $10.95, Sandwiches with choice of bread, fillings, cheeses, and choice of pasta or green salad with lettuce, tomato and pickle $7.00, Brie served with a mini-baguette and fruits $7.50

Impressions:

A quick glance into Café Laufer's front window reveals what appears to be a small bakery, but then they open for the day's business. The tables in front are soon packed with patrons noshing on simple but tasty deli fare. Management insists that only the finest ingredients are used. The light-dining menu is brief yet creative. You can enter the building street side or from the parking lot in the rear. This restaurant is a definite asset in Kaimuki's restaurant row.

Honolulu

Café Sistina **Authors' Favorite**

1314 S. King Street
Honolulu, HI 96814
808-596-0061
www.cafesistina.com
Hours: L 11:00 AM-2:00 PM Mo-Fr
D 5:30 PM-9:30 PM
Cards: AE DC DIS JCB MC V
Dress: Resort Casual
Style: Ital $$

Menu Sampler:

Breakfast:
N/A
Lunch/Dinner:
Appetizers: Bruschetta Alle Vongole of grilled bread rubbed with garlic and covered with chopped clam in a wine garlic sauce $5.75, Oven Roasted Red Bell Pepper covered with bagna cauda and served with scamorza cheese $7.50
Salads: Insalata Contadina of mixed greens, grilled vegetables, frittata, feta cheese and balsamic vinaigrette $8.75, Verde Della Casa $4.75, Caesar $7.50
The Classics: Linguine Puttanesca with Kalamata olives, garlic, onions, capers, anchovies in a zesty tomato sauce $12.50, Veal Piccata with scaloppine sautéed in butter, capers and lemon wine sauce $16.75, Veal Piccata $16.75
The Contemporary: Pollo Porcini with a chicken breast sautéed with garlic, onions in an Italian wild mushroom sauce $15.50, Scampi San Remo of shrimp Riviera style with artichoke heart, red bell pepper, olives, and pancetta in a pink sauce with linguine $15.50, Mussels alla Toscana with linguine $13.85
The Cutting Edge: Lobster Ravioli with bay scallops, fresh tomatoes, basil in a dry Vermouth butter sauce $16.50, Spicy Tutto Mare with opakapaka, scallops, shrimp, calamari, shellfish in an exotic saffron prosciutto sauce over risotto $18.00, Gnocchi al Gorgonzola with asparagus and fresh tomatoes $14.50

Impressions:

Not only does he cook, he paints as well! Chef Sergio Mitrotti has decorated the walls and ceiling of this bistro-style restaurant with amazingly accurate frescoes from the Sistine Chapel. The kitchen backs this up with superb Northern Italian cuisine. From classics to cutting edge the food is rich, delicious, and varied. This place bustles with a solid following of neighborhood regulars who like the large portions and reasonable prices. Live entertainment is often featured.

Honolulu

California Beach Rock 'N Sushi

404 Ward Avenue
Honolulu, HI 96814
808-597-8000
Web: None
Cards: AE DIS MC V
Hours: L 11:00 AM-2:00 PM Mo-Fr
D 5:00 PM-10:00 PM Su-Th
D 5:00 PM-11:00 PM FrSa
Dress: Casual
Style: Japan $$ Ent Card

Menu Sampler:

Breakfast:
N/A
Lunch:
Specials: Chicken Teriyaki $5.25, Beef Teriyaki $7.25, Shrimp & Assorted Vegetable Tempura $6.95, Mahi Mahi Katsu $6.95, Fish Combo of broiled salmon or mahi mahi, California roll, croquette, shumai, and a chicken wing $7.95, Lunch Sushi Platter-six pieces of nigiri and a California roll $7.95
Dinner:
Special Rolls: Crunchy Roll-shrimp tempura, cucumber, yamagobo, kaiware & spicy mayo coated with crunchy flakes and smelt roe $8.95, Rattlesnake Roll-baked eel layered over a shrimp tempura roll, kaiware, yamagobo, & cucumber, topped with eel sauce $9.25, Crunchy King Crab Roll with smelt roe $9.50
Appetizers: Edamame $2.25, Agedashi Tofu-deep fried tofu in tempura sauce, topped with daikon and green onions $3.75, Beef or Chicken Gyoza-pan fried dumplings $4.75, Seafood Dynamite baked with a masago mayo sauce $10.95
Entrees & Combos: all include rice, miso soup & salad. Chicken-charbroiled & served w/teriyaki, mustard or ponzu $9.95, Supreme Salmon-pan fried fillets topped w/garlic butter soy sauce $11.95, King Crab Legs w/garlic butter on the side $26.95, Katsu or Miso Katsu-Chicken $9.95, Beef, Salmon, or Mahi $11.95
Salads: Salmon Skin Salad with ponzu dressing $6.95, Ahi Tataki Caesar $9.95

Impressions:

This is what you would call a "happening" Japanese restaurant and sushi bar. While it certainly serves up a good lunch, the fun here really begins at night. That's when you'll find a lively young crowd shouting local kine greetings, wearing colorful fashions, and listening to great tunes. Rock 'N Sushi! Park behind the restaurant or across the street at Sports Authority.

Hawaii Kai

Cha Cha Cha Salsaria

377 Keahole C-1A
Honolulu, HI 96825
808-395-7797
www.chachachasalsaria.com
Hours: B 8:30 AM-12:00 PM Su
LD 11:00 AM-10:00 PM Mo-Sa
LD 11:00 AM-9:00 PM Su
Cards: MC V
Dress: Casual
Style: Car/Mex $

Menu Sampler:

Breakfast/Lunch/Dinner:
Soups: Black Bean, Cilantro, & Sour Cream or Tortilla, Chicken, Avocado and Cheese $3.75
Salads: Tostada Salad with chicken, beef or pork $6.50, add fish $7.95, add fresh grilled veggies $6.75, Black Bean, Corn & Bell Pepper Salad $5.95
Entrées: Nachos with chicken, refried beans, cheese, salsa, cilantro, black olives, sour cream, jalapeños $7.25, Beef Tamales served with rice and chips $6.95, Pork Enchiladas with tomatillo salsa, served with beans, rice, chips $7.75, Tacos-crispy, soft corn or soft flour with jerk chicken, refries 1-$3.50, 2-$6.25, Blackened Fresh Fish Taco with pickled cabbage, sour cream, cilantro 1-$4.25, 2-$6.75, Burritos Carne Asada $7.95, Fresh Fish & Veggies Quesadillas on Spinach Tortilla $7.25 or with Chicken and Fresh Papaya Salsa $6.25, Tamales-steamed masa topped with black beans, tomatillo salsa, cilantro, and sour cream with chicken, beef, pork, or grilled veggies, with rice and chips $6.95, Enchiladas-topped with tomatillo salsa, cheese, sour cream & cilantro, chicken, beef, pork or cheese, beans, rice and chips $7.75.
Sweet Endings: Coconut Custard, Chocolate & Jamaican Rum Flan $3.50

Impressions:

Cha Cha Cha Salsaria is a bit hard to define. On one hand, you place your order at the counter a la fast food. On the other, you dine overlooking the water. The menu takes the same tack. Your first impression might be that it's Tex-Mex, but then you notice the Caribbean influences. Regardless, this place prides itself in serving a fresh, healthy cuisine. The extensive fresh condiment bar is an added plus allowing diners to customize their selections. Save room for dessert.

Honolulu

Chai's Island Bistro

Authors' Favorite

Aloha Tower Marketplace
Honolulu, HI 96814
808-585-0011
www.chaisislandbistro.com
Hours: L 11:00 AM-4:00 PM XSaSu
D 4:00 PM-10:00 PM
Cards: AE DC JCB MC V
Dress: Resort Casual
Style: Haw-Reg/Pac-Rim $$$$

Menu Sampler:

Breakfast:
N/A
Lunch:
Appetizers, Soups & Salads: Crispy Duck Lumpia with spicy hoisin sauce & fresh mango tomato salsa $7.95, Combo Platter for Two of king crab cake, ahi katsu, crispy duck lumpia, and kaffir mac-nut encrusted jumbo prawns $26.95
Entrées: Grilled Breast of Chicken Sate with Thai peanut sauce with greens and toasted Asian flat bread $11.95, Crunchy Potato Seared Ahi Sandwich with caramelized pearl onion ponzu demi glace, greens and smashed potato $14.95, Seafood Risotto with heart of palm with prawns, scallops and crab meat $15.95
Dinner:
Appetizers: Honey & Hoisin Marinated BBQ Baby Back Ribs $9.95, Soft Shell Crab Tempura w/chili miso beurre blanc $11.95, Lobster Potstickers $10.95
Entrées: Long Island Duck Bistro Style with spicy port demi glace $33.95, Pan Fried Crispy Whole Moi with sun dried tomato citrus beurre blanc and Asian stir fried vegetables $36.95, Grilled Mongolian Style Lamb Chops with brandy demi glace $37.95, Grilled Garlic & Pepper Crusted Veal Chop with caramelized pearl onion demiglace, mashed taro & Asian stir fried vegetables $38.95

Impressions:

Chai's Island Bistro gives patrons a unique look at the local dining scene. Here at his Aloha Tower location Chef/owner Chai Chaowasaree draws upon his Thai background to create Pac-Rim cuisine that is both exciting and comforting. The resulting preparations are a feast for the senses. This is one of the few places of this caliber where lunch is an option. If you'd like to try fine Pac-Rim dining but are watching your budget, schedule a mid-day meal at Chai's. But then you miss the nightly performances by some of Hawaii's best musicians!

Honolulu

Champion Malasadas **Authors' Favorite**

1926 S. Beretania
Honolulu, HI 96826
808-947-8778

Web: None
Hours: 6:00 AM-9:00 PM Tu-Sa
6:30 AM-7:00 PM Su
Cards: None
Dress: Casual
Style: Spec $

Menu Sampler:

Breakfast/Lunch/Dinner:
Malasadas $.50 each. Coffee, tea, soda and bottled water are offered. Other pastries are also available.

Impressions:

This local establishment specializes in making a Portuguese treat called a malasada. For those new to Portuguese cooking, malasadas are loosely defined as fried sugary donuts without a hole. The similarity to the standard donut shop offering ends there. Joc Miw, the Chinese owner, certainly improved upon the original recipe. His heavenly concoction is more of an egg-rich popover than a donut. Champion Malasadas' sweets are so moist and rich that all it takes is a cup of tea or coffee and you've got breakfast. But have we mentioned that they are addictive? No tables are available, but who cares? The malasada sack is empty before the car starts anyway. Parking is available in front of the store.

Waikiki

Chart House Honolulu Lounge

1765 Ala Moana
Honolulu, HI 96815
808-941-6669
www.charthousehonolulu.com
Hours: D 5:30 PM-9:30 PM
Lounge 4 PM-2 AM
Cards: AE DC DIS JCB MC V
Dress: Resort Casual
Style: Amer/Isl $$$

Menu Sampler:

Breakfast/Lunch:
N/A
Dinner:
Appetizers: Oysters Rockefeller $11.50, Sizzling Szechuan Shrimp $12.95, Escargot Bourguignonne with garlic, basil and bleu cheese butter and French rolls $8.75, Garlic Chicken $7.50, Fried Calamari $6.95, Steamed Clams $11.25
Soups and Salads: New England Clam Chowder $3.95, Seafood Salad on Nalo greens with jumbo shrimp, fried scallops, fried calamari, Maui onion and ripe tomato $14.50, Chart House Salad with Bay Shrimp $5.75/$8.25, Caesar $5.75
Shellfish: Abalone Dore dipped in egg and sautéed in olive oil $Market Price, Seafood Linguini with jumbo shrimp, fresh fish, sweet clams, ocean scallops, asparagus, onions, carrots, & shiitake mushrooms in a tomato garlic cream sauce served over linguini $26.95, Live Maine Lobster 1¼ # $34.50, 2-6# $29.95/#
House Specialties: Dinners are served w/squaw bread & New England Clam Chowder or green salad, & choice of steamed white rice, garlic mashed potatoes or ranch fries. Chinese Steamed Opakapaka w/ginger, cilantro, green onions, sesame oil & soy sauce $30.75, Prime Grade Beef-Prime Rib $25.95, $33.50, $39.50, Filet Mignon $26.95/$36.95, Mac Nut Crusted Mahimahi with mango salsa and white rice $28.95, JJ's Famous Garlic Steak $37.95, Shrimp Scampi $25.50, BBQ Paniolo Baby Back Ribs $21.50, Chicken Piccatta $19.95

Impressions:

If hanging out at the yacht club is one of your feel-good memories, you will enjoy the atmosphere at the Chart House. Although the address is listed as Ala Moana Boulevard, the restaurant actually faces the marina opposite that address. This airy dining spot has been serving good food and drinks for about 35 years. For a late night meal the Chart House offers a satisfying menu along with live entertainment until 12:30 AM.

Waikiki

Cheeseburger In Paradise
2500 Kalakaua Ave
Honolulu, HI 96815
808-923-3731
www.cheeseburgerwaikiki.com
Hours: B 7:00 AM-11:00 AM
L/D 11:00 AM-11:00 PM
Cards: AE DC DIS JCB MC V
Dress: Casual
Style: Amer $$

Menu Sampler:

Breakfast:
Three Egg Omelets served with wheat toast and home fries or rice $7.95, Eggs Benedict $8.95, Spam & Eggs $7.25, French Toast $5.95, Macadamia Nut Pancakes $5.95,Three Pancakes 4.95, Pineapple Boat $4.95, Half Papaya $3.95
Lunch/Dinner:
Sandwiches: All burgers use Meyer Natural Angus beef and are served with 1000 Island dressing, fresh tomatoes, lettuce and sautéed onions on sesame seed or whole-wheat buns. Cheeseburger in Paradise with a blend of jack and cheddar cheeses or swiss $7.25, Best Burger $6.75, Kalakaua Cajun Chicken Sandwich $8.25, Polynesian Chicken Salad Sandwich of grilled chicken blended with celery, cashews, pineapple bits, ginger sauce and topped with toasted coconut on a whole wheat bun $8.25, Fresh Fish Sandwich w/a red Provencal sauce $8.95, Calamari Steak Sandwich w/pineapple mac-nut slaw $8.25, Tofu Burger $7.50
Sides: Ono Onion Rings $4.75,Our Famous Seasoned Fries $3.75, Cheese Fries $5.50, Chili Cheese Fries $6.00, Pineapple Mac Nut Cole Slaw $3.50
Salads: Caesar Salad $7.95, Chinese Chicken Salad with Oriental dressing $10.95, Mandarin Shrimp Salad with a tangy ginger dressing $10.95
Entrées: Coconut Shrimp and Fries with pineapple mac-nut cole slaw $10.95

Impressions:

Legend has it that two girls arrived on Maui back in the 80's and didn't want to leave. After looking around and realizing that they needed to earn some money and finding that they couldn't get a good cheeseburger on the island, they started a small restaurant. The rest is history. Cheeseburger's serves a casual menu with something to please every member of the family. Be aware that the portions are quite large! This is a fun place to listen to DJ tunes or enjoy live entertainment in the evening while having a cold beer and a good meal.

Honolulu

Chef Mavro

Authors' Favorite

1969 S. King St
Honolulu, HI 96826
808-944-4714
www.chefmavro.com
Hours: D 6:00 PM-9:30 PM Tu-Sa
Cards: AE DC JCB MC V
Dress: Evening Aloha
Style: Fre/Haw-Reg/Pac-Rim $$$$

Menu Sampler:

Breakfast/Lunch:
N/A
Dinner:
Appetizers: Kahuku Shrimp, warm lemongrass jelly, confit Hamakua tomatoes, Hirabara's baby greens 16.00, Osetra Caviar from Caspian Sea, served with blinis and crème fraiche $89, Sautéed Hudson Valley Foie Gras, red currant-balsamic glaze, li hing mui-caramelized Maui onions, brioche crisp 20.00
Entrées: Day Boat Hawaiian Catch Provencale "Raite" Sauce, jumbo asparagus duet, sea urchin accents puffed white rice 37.00, Onaga, Marseille Bourride, garlic foam, tarragon glazed baby fennel 39.00, Keahole Lobster, Garam Masala, green apple-celery root puree with shiso accents 42.00, Black Angus Beef "Onglet" sautéed with olive oil balsamic sauce, artichoke barigoule 37.00, Roasted Breast of Barbary Duckling, Yuzu Glaze, leg & thigh served with quinoa, sesame-sweet potato puree 32.00
Cheese: Brie de Meaux, baked Brie dome, red grape-star anise coulis 12.00
Desserts: Lilikoi Malasadas, guava coulis, pineapple-coconut ice cream 10
Three course 56/79, **four course** 66/105, and **six course** menus 93/134 are available, with/without wines.

Impressions:

At the corner of King and McCully food enthusiasts will discover a fine dining experience that ranks among the best in Honolulu. Owner Chef Mavro began his career in Provence, France and has brought those influences to Hawaii Regional Cuisine. His world-class nightly selections are expertly paired with wines by the glass from the restaurant's extensive collection. Those looking for the ultimate should consider one of the multi-course menus. Plan on devoting your evening. Chef Mavro's is an easy drive from Waikiki. Valet parking is available onsite.

North Shore

Cholo's Homestyle Mexican

North Shore Marketplace
Haleiwa, HI 96712
808-637-3059
Web: None
Hours: B 8-11 AM
L/D 11 AM-9 PM
Cards: None
Dress: Casual
Style: Mex $$

Menu Sampler:

Breakfast:
Chillaquillas (Tortilla Casserole) topped with two eggs with rice, beans and tortillas $5.95, Two Soft Corn Tortillas filled with scrambled eggs, cheese, tomato, chile, onion and cilantro with chips $4.95, Pancakes (3) $3.75, Huevos Rancheros $5.95, Mexican Breakfast Sandwich of grilled sourdough bread, cheese, green chili, sliced tomato & omelet style egg, served w/potatoes $4.95

Lunch/Dinner:
Everything comes ala carte, plate, or dinner. Plate includes beans and rice; dinner includes salad, beans, rice, chips and salsa. Taco a la carte $3.00, plate $5.25, dinner $7.50, Enchilada $4.00/$6.75/$9.25, Chimi Changa $6.50/$9.25/$11.50, Gordita $4.95/$7.75/$10.25, Tostada $4.00/$6.75/$9.25, Nachos-homemade chips, fresh salsa, cheddar, jack and jalapenos $4.00, Side Orders of Guacamole $2.00, Sour Cream $1.00, Beans $2.00, Black Beans $2.25 Special Quesadillas-Spinach Quesadilla, black beans, spinach, tomatoes, cheese $5.25/$7.75/$10.25, Cholo's Fish Tacos Plates of local ahi or mahi grilled and spiced $6.75/$9.25/$10.00/$12.50, Shrimp Taco Plates $6.75/$9.25/$10.00/ $12.50, Chicken, Shrimp or Steak Fajitas plates and dinners $9.95-$17.50

Impressions:

When you're up on the North Shore watching killer waves and suddenly feel the need for a Mexican food fix, give Cholo's a try. This open-air storefront eatery is located in the back tier of the North Shore Marketplace in Haleiwa. Cholo's serves large portions of homemade traditional Mexican fare for breakfast, lunch, and dinner. This popular spot always manages to have room for another diner. The bustling North Shore Marketplace serves as the hub for the entire area and makes an interesting stop while touring.

Waikiki

Ciao Mein

Hyatt Regency
2424 Kalakaua Ave
Honolulu, HI 96815
808-923-2426
www.ciaomein.com
Hours: D 6:00 PM-10:00PM
Cards: AE MC V
Dress: Evening Aloha
Style: Chi/Ital $$$

Menu Sampler:

Breakfast/Lunch:
N/A
Dinner:
Appetizers: Spring Rolls with shrimp, bamboo shoots $9.75, Carpaccio-slices of beef tenderloin with capers, olive oil, lemon and pepper $10.75, Focaccia with sautéed plum tomatoes, fresh oregano, and smoked mozzarella $9.00
Soups & Salads: Hearty Minestrone Soup with braised sausage $5.50, Soup Ciao Mein-a clear chicken broth w/lobster won tons $6.75, Chinese Salad $7.50
Entrées: Risotto $7.75, Fried Rice with egg, char siu pork, peas and choice of shrimp or Chinese sausage $9.25, Honey Walnut Shrimp-shrimp with snap peas and honey glazed walnuts $22.75, Seafood Funn Lasagna of assorted seafood, Boursin cheese, smoked mozzarella, spinach, eggplant, look funn noodles and marinara sauce $21.75, Mongolian Sizzle (Beef) $21.25, Bistecca Di Manzo Alle Erbe-marinated sirloin of beef in olive oil, basil, garlic herbs and pine nuts $26.75, Roast Duck Breast w/steamed buns, green onions & hoisin sauce $25.00
Desserts: Tiramisu Sculptures with espresso and sambuca $5.75, Marco Polo Frozen Delight of Napolitan spumone and espresso ice cream rolled in chocolate shavings, lychee sorbet, and white chocolate and ginger ice cream $5.75

Impressions:

H-m-m…Chinese and Italian prepared in the same kitchen and then combined on the same plate? Yes, and it works! In fact, things work extremely well. On the third floor of the Hyatt Regency there's a sleek yet fun restaurant that has been winning awards and pleasing diners with culinary adventures for a number of years. When the wait staff suggests interesting pairings of the delicious foods and beverages, follow their lead. If your decisions waver exotic set dinners are available for $30.00, $36.00 and $42.00 per person.

Windward

Cinnamon's Restaurant **Authors' Favorite**
315 Uluniu Street
Kailua, HI 96734
808-261-8724
www.cinnamonsrestaurant.com
Hours: B 7:00 AM-2:00 PM
L 11:00 AM-2:00 PM
D 5:30 PM-8:30 PM Th-Sa
Cards: DC DIS JCB MC V
Dress: Casual
Style: Ecl/Pac Rim $$

Menu Sampler:

Breakfast:
Omelettes with 3 eggs, choice of country home fries, rice, biscuit, pancakes, or hash browns $7.95-$9.95, Mahi Mahi Benedict $6.75/$8.75, Traditional Benedict $6.95/$8.95 w/home fries or hash browns, Frittata w/basil pesto, artichoke hearts, spinach, onions, olives, melted parmesan cheese $9.25, Carrot Pancakes w/Cream Cheese Sauce $3.95/$5.95, Broiled Prime Rib & Eggs $9.75
Lunch:
Salads: Mandarin-char siu pork, Chinese roast chicken, won ton chips, peanuts, greens, mandarin oranges, Oriental dressing $8.75, Spinach & Bacon $8.50
Sandwiches: Curried Chicken Salad on grilled Portuguese sweet bread with cashew nuts $8.70, Mahi Mahi broiled or dipped in egg and sautéed $8.25
Entrees: Roast Beef with choice of starch, gravy, fresh vegetables $8.25, Stir Fry with mahi, chicken or beef, fresh vegetables, teriyaki sauce, rice $7.95
Dinner:
Specialties of the House: choice of starch and cole slaw garnish-Shrimp Curry with mango chutney $18.95, Mahi Mahi Scampi-sautéed in dairy butter, fresh garlic, vermouth, parmesan cheese $14.50, Chicken or Mahi Mahi prepared picatta style, marsala, chateau in a rich wine sauce, and fantasy-using fresh spinach, broccoli, Swiss Cheese and the house hollandaise sauce $14.95

Impressions:

Those looking for something special and not afraid to read a map should enjoy this island favorite. Just off the main highway near McDonalds in Kailua you'll find Kailua Square and Cinnamon's. This quaint but upscale dining spot serves an ambitious menu of well-executed selections regardless of time of day. This is a great stop for those taking the circle island tour. Park in the courtyard lot.

Oahu Dining

Windward

Crouching Lion Inn

51-666 Kamehameha Hwy
Ka'a'awa, HI 96730
808-237-8511

Web: None
Hours: L 11:00 AM-3:00 PM
D 5:00 PM-9:00 PM
Cards: AE DIS MC V
Dress: Resort Casual
Style: Amer/Isl $$/Ent Card

Menu Sampler:

Breakfast:

N/A

Lunch:

Appetizers: Honey Garlic Shrimp with a light tempura batter and sauce $9.25, Gourmet Sautéed Mushrooms in a butter, garlic and sherry sauce $7.50
Salads: Oriental Chicken Salad $9.25, Shrimp Parmesan Salad $10.25
Sandwiches: All served with fries. Kalua Pork $8.95, Mahi Mahi Melt $8.50
Gourmet Burgers: All served with fries. Cheeseburger Deluxe $8.00
Entrées: Various entrees served with fries, rice or mashed potatoes, vegetables and homemade buns. Kalua Pork Plate with sweet steamed cabbage $10.25, Sautéed Mahimahi $10.95, Chicken Macadamia $10.95, Teriyaki Steak $10.95

Dinner:

Appetizers: Steamed Clams $9.50, Escargot Bourgignonne $9.25
Specialties: Slavonic Steak (Signature Dish)-marinated tenderloin, charbroiled, and served from a sizzling platter of garlic butter $Market Price, Kalua Pork with steamed cabbage and poi bread pudding $14.95, Mahi Mahi sautéed in garlic butter $14.95, Teriyaki New York Steak (8 oz) $19.50, Chicken Macadamia-dipped in an egg and brandy batter, deep fried and served with sweet and sour sauce and macadamia nuts $15.75, Peppersteak $21.50

Impressions:

Whether you are traveling around Oahu or staying on the north shore, stop along the Windward Coast and enjoy the timelessness of the surroundings. Here you'll find a quaint stone building housing the Crouching Lion Inn. This famous Oahu landmark serves comfort food with island influences. Customers will find The Livingston Galleries downstairs for after-meal browsing. The Crouching Lion Inn is located near a curve. Watch the address numbers so you don't miss it.

Waikiki

Diamond Head Grill Authors' Favorite

W Hotel
2885 Kalakaua Ave
Honolulu, HI 96815
808-922-3734
www.diamondheadgrill.com
Hours: D 6:00 PM-10:00 PM
Cards: AE DIS DC JCB MC V
Dress: Evening Aloha
Style: Haw-Reg/Pac-Rim $$$$

Menu Sampler:

Dinner:

Pupus: Sweet Potato Gnocchi, mascarpone cream, Hamakua mushrooms 12, DHG Crabcakes 13, Sugar Cane Skewer Petite Lobster Tempura, spicy Nalo greens, daikon, ponzu 15, Seared Foie Gras, baby beets, crouton 18
Greens & Soup: Waimanalo Arugula, Stilton blue cheese, macadamia nuts, Fuji apples, white wine vinaigrette 9, Housemade Buffalo Mozzarella, Hau'ula vine ripened tomatoes, Waimanalo greens 9, Hau'ula Tomato Gazpacho, fresh island ceviche 8, Caesar of Waimanalo Romaine, white anchovies $9
Entrées: Grilled Mahi Mahi, roasted fennel couscous, roasted carrot jus, Asian vegetable medley 28, Seared Island Ahi, duck hash, caramelized apple demi glace 32, Macadamia Nut Crusted Lamb Chops, potato gratin, roasted garlic sauce 39, Beef Tenderloin, Yukon gold puree, Hamakua Big Island mushrooms 35, Cioppino, seafood assortment, prawns, lobster and clams, tomato basil broth 28, Grilled Pork Chop, savory Kahuku corn pancetta pudding, maple jus 26
Desserts: Warm Kula Strawberry and Candied Ginger Cobbler with white chocolate gelato 8, Warm Lava Cake with Honey Gelato, coffee and vanilla crème Anglaise, assorted fruits 9, Piña Colada Cake, rum, shredded coconut, piña colada crème Anglaise 7.50, Dessert of the Day 8

Impressions:

This upscale restaurant can be found on the second floor of the sophisticated W Hotel at the quiet Diamond Head end of Waikiki. Their dinner selections are an intriguing fusion of island flavors and classic techniques. Expect to find depth and complexity in all the preparations. Chef David Paul had a hand in creating this menu, and it shows. The wine collection backing things up earned a Wine Spectator award in 2004. However, the Diamond Head Grill is more than just a dining spot—it's a night scene. If you like your cocktails made with top shelf liquor that you can actually taste and smell, you've come to the right place.

Diamond Head

Diamond Head Market & Grill

3158 Monsarrat Ave.
Honolulu, HI 96815
808-732-0077
Web: None
Hours: 7:30 AM-9:00 PM
Cards: AE DIS JCB MC V
Dress: Casual
Style: Isl/Pac-Rim $

Menu Sampler:

Breakfast/Lunch/Dinner:
Bakery: Selections very daily. Whole Pies and Tarts- Chocolate Raspberry 9" $24.00, Fresh Fruit Tart 9" $25.00, Lemon Crunch Cake $20.00, DHM Torte-chocolate cookie crust, peanut butter cheesecake, fresh sliced bananas, peanut butter chocolate pudding, whipped topping $24.00. Individual servings of brownies, lilikoi bars, apple-blueberry crisp, butter mochi, blueberry and cream cheese scones, Mango Macadamia Nut Biscotti $1.50, Espresso Bar, Okazuya
Market: Deli carryout meals-selections vary daily-Prime Rib, Kalbi Ribs, Osso Bucco, Garlic Braised Pork Roast, Kalua Pork, Potato and Rice Dishes, Hot Vegetables, Salads, Sushi, Appetizers, Entrees-Thai Red Curry Beef, Jambalaya, Shrimp Linguine, Black Bean Shrimp Stir Fry, Eggplant Parmesan, Beef Stew
Grill: Sandwiches offered alone, as a mini-plate, or as a plate lunch-Char Siu Pork $4.50/$5.75/$6.75, Teriyaki Chicken $4.50/$5.75/$6.75, Grilled Ahi Steak $6.50/$6.75/$8.75, Portobello Mushroom $4.75/$5.75/$7.00
Specials: BBQ Pork Rib plate $9.00,NY Steak plate $9.50, Chicken Eggplant sandwich $6.75, Chicken Eggplant plate $8.00, Kal Bi Beef Rib plate $8.50

Impressions:

Carryout dining is very popular in Hawaii. Most island family members work, including Mom, so dinner often gets picked up on the way home. Local style restaurants many times get the nod, but the Diamond Head Market & Grill takes things up a notch. At the outside service window, you can order a good selection of sandwiches and upscale plate lunches cooked to order. However, the culinary fun really begins inside the store. The bakery counter offers tasty pies, cakes and confections in single servings or entire displays. In the gourmet case, you'll find a particularly nice assortment of prepared entrees and side dishes. Then there's a pantry section with many choice coffees, sauces, chutneys, relishes, and party foods to accompany it all. This bountiful array of foods is perfect for that picnic in Kapiolani Park or a special stay-at-home meal in your condo.

Honolulu

Dixie Grill BBQ & Crab Shack
404 Ward Avenue
Honolulu, HI 96814
808-596-8359
www.dixiegrill.com
Hours: B 8:00 AM-11:00 AM SaSu
L/D 11:00 AM-10:00 PM
Cards: AE DC DIS MC V
Dress: Casual
Style: Amer $$

Menu Sampler:

Breakfast:
Cajun Biscuits/Gravy $3.5, Smokehouse Scramble $8.5, Blueberry Cream Cheese Stuffed French Toast $7, Crab Shack Omelette w/spinach, crab, mushrooms, cheese, hollandaise sauce, hashbrown casserole $12
Lunch/Dinner:
Appetizers: Pile 'O' Rings with BBQ aioli $5, Jumbo Coconut Shrimp $9, Southern Fried Okra $6, Nacho Fries $8, Snow Crab Starter-1/2 # $9
Soup/Salad: Big Daddy's Crab & Shrimp $9.50, BBQ Chop Chicken Salad with cheese & avocado $9, Gulf Coast Gumbo $7/$4, She-Crab Soup $7/$4
Sides: Mashed. Fries, Hush Puppies, Rice, Baked Beans, Co' Slaw, Corn on the Cobb, Garden Green Salad, Garlic Bread, Mac Salad $3, all tasty!
BBQ: Served w/beans and a choice of one side. Baby Back Ribs $19/$13, Hawaiian BBQ Glazed Smoked BBQ Chicken $11, Dixie Mixed Grill of baby back ribs, fresh sausage, pulled pork & chicken $18, T-Bone Steak (20 oz) $24
Meals: Beer Battered Fish Basket with slaw & Dixie fries $9.50, Southern Fried Catfish with rice & corn $13, Fried Shrimp Platter (7) with fries, corn & hushpuppies $14, Mama's Meatloaf with mashers & gravy, onions & corn $12
Sandwiches: Pulled BBQ Chicken, Beef Brisket, or Pork Sandwich with fries or mac salad $6.95, Fresh Fish Sandwich grilled or beer battered $9
Desserts: Pecan Pie topped with ice cream $5.00, Jack Daniels Mousse Pie with Oreo cookie crust $5.00, Key Lime Pie with a granola & graham crust $4.85

Impressions:

Dixie Grill has an atmosphere that would fit right in on the Tamiami Trail. All that's missing is the guy wrestling the rubber alligator. But then, "Hey, these folks make great southern barbeque!" That's a hard commodity to come by in Hawaii. If you are looking for a change of pace, be sure to visit the Dixie Grill.

Oahu Dining

Waikiki

DK Steakhouse
Waikiki Beach Marriott Resort & Spa
2552 Kalakaua Avenue
Honolulu, HI 96815
808-931-6280
www.sanseihawaii.com
Hours: D 5:30 PM-10:00 PM
Cards: AE DC DIS JCB MC V
Dress: Resort Casual/Evening Aloha
Style: Stk/Sea $$$$

Menu Sampler:

Breakfast/Lunch:
N/A
Dinner:
Appetizers: Sweet Maui Onion Soup $6.95, Monster Shrimp Scampi $11.95, Monster Shrimp Cocktail with house made cocktail sauce $11.95, Crispy Asian Seafood Raviolis stuffed with lobster, shrimp, crab, pancetta with a soy wasabi butter sauce $7.95, Sansei Style Crab Cakes w/citrus pesto $10.95. Crispy Chicken Wings $6.95, Bacon Wrapped Scallops $9.95
Side Dishes: Creamed Spinach $6.95, Sansei's Asparagus Milanese $7.95, Baked Potato-1# and fully loaded $5.95, Sautéed Garlic Mushrooms $6.95, Steamed Asparagus $4.95, Sautéed Sweet Maui Onions $3.95
From The Sea and The Butcher: For a Complete Meal add $4.95-adds vegetable du jour and cottage fries or steamed white rice. Fresh Atlantic Salmon with a dill hollandaise sauce $22.95, Fresh Catch of The Day $22.95, Rib-eye on the bone (22oz) $32.95, Filet Mignon $23.95/$28.95, Sansei Filet Mignon topped with a Shiitake Mushroom demi glaze $27.95, Gomadare New York Strip in our special house Sesame Seed Miso Sauce $28.95

Impressions:

If we had to come up with a term to describe D.K. Kodama, multi-faceted would be on top of our list. This contemporary sushi chef turned restaurateur manages to cross culinary divides that others might never approach. His latest venture takes him into the world of traditional steak and seafood. Of course, nothing this man does is ordinary, so why should his new restaurant be any different? The meats, fishes, seafood, and wines are of the highest caliber. Expect to see Japanese influences discreetly appear throughout the menu.

Manoa Valley

Donato's

Manoa Marketplace
2756 Woodlawn Drive, Suite 6-203
Honolulu, HI 96822
808-988-2000
http://donatosrestaurant.com

Hours:	D 5:30 PM-Closing Tu-Su Sunset Menu 5:30 PM-6:30 PM Tu-Su
Cards:	AE DIS JCB MC V
Dress:	Resort Casual
Style:	Ital $$$

Menu Sampler:

Breakfast/Lunch:

N/A

Dinner:

Antipasti: Bruschetta Rustica-toasted Asiago rustic bread topped w/roasted eggplant, tomatoes, basil & ricotta salata $4.95; Mozzarella Farcita-fresh homemade mozzarella stuffed w/roasted peppers, arugula, and Soppressata salami $9.95, Sautéed Black Mussels & a white wine tomato broth $10.95
Insalate: Fresh local grown arugula salad with toasted walnuts, crispy pancetta, & imported Gorgonzola tossed with lemon & olive oil $6.95
Pizzette: Pizzetta with tomato sauce, mozzarella, sautéed mushrooms, Italian sausage $9.25, Margherita- sauce, cheese and fresh basil $6.00
Pasta & Risotto: Risotto con Funghi w/white truffle oil $15.95, Ribbon pasta w/roasted duck breast, prosciutto, capers, & tomato white wine sauce $16.00
Specialita' Della Casa: Saltimbocca di Vitello- sautéed veal scaloppini topped with sage, prosciutto, and fresh mozzarella, served with sautéed spinach $23.95, Filetto di Pesce Moi in Padella-pan sautéed fresh Moi fillet served with Hauula tomato Puttanesca relish, rock shrimp, and asparagus risotto $18.95
Sunset Dinner Menu: 5:30-6:30-Starter, Entrée, Dessert $19.95 + tax/person
Sunday Evening Family Style: 3 courses-$19.95/people, 4 courses-$24.95
Tasting Menus: 3-5 courses $25.00/person-$60.00/person

Impressions:

Not long ago Donato Perfido moved his fine dining restaurant into the misty world of the Manoa Valley. Here he serves a classic Italian menu defined by bold flavors and complex preparations. Those with lighter appetites will find something to like among the tapas and pizza are offered during cocktail hour. Everyone will appreciate the contemporary, genteel atmosphere.

Chinatown

Duc's Bistro
1188 Maunakea
Honolulu, HI 96817
808-531-6325
Web: None
Hours: L 11:30 AM-2:00 PM XSaSu
D 5:00 PM-10:00 PM
Cards: AE DC DIS JCB MC V
Dress: Evening Aloha
Style: Asian/Fre $$$

Menu Sampler:

Breakfast:
N/A
Lunch:
Appetizer: Crab Cake w/herb thermidor sauce $7.95, Shrimp Spring Roll $7.95
Salad: Duck Beaulieu-seared breast of duck with a raspberry vinaigrette $13.95
Entrée: Lamb Chops with Bordeaux Chivry Sauce $19.95, Spicy Lemongrass Chicken $12.95, Fresh Catch sautéed with a fresh tomato dill sauce $14.95
Dinner:
Appetizer: Chesapeake Bay Crab Cakes w/herb flavored thermidor sauce $7.95, Cha Goi Tom-fried spring rolls filled w/shrimp, taro and mushrooms $6.95
Soup: Bisque of Tomato and Lobster $5.95, Asparagus Princess $5.95
Salad: En Bataille of organic baby greens, mushrooms, goat cheese, walnuts, apples, balsamic vinaigrette $5.95, Avocado & Papaya w/greens $5.95
Entrée: Soup or salad included w/main course. Seafood Feuillete Joinville of prawns, scallops, morels, shiitakes folded in crayfish sauce and served in a puff pastry shell $21.95, Steak Aux Poivres-NY Steak flambé with VSOP Cognac, served with pink, green, and black peppercorn sauce $22.95, Spicy Lemongrass Chicken $12.95, Spinach Fettuccini- sautéed with strips of chicken breast, prosciutto and julienne of fresh vegetables in an herb supreme sauce $14.95

Impressions:

Duc's Bistro is a cool oasis of sophistication, which is an interesting contrast to the street scene outside in Chinatown. Those who stop by will find a menu that blends French recipes with Vietnamese influences with Cajun attitude just for spice. This is all complemented by an adequate wine list. Duc's is a wonderfully relaxing dining spot. We were pleased to find live entertainment, even at lunch. Ask the waiter to take care of your parking tab in the lot across the street.

Waikiki

Duke's Waikiki
Outrigger Waikiki Hotel
2335 Kalakaua Ave
Honolulu, HI 96815
808-922-2268
www.dukeswaikiki.com
Hours: B Buf 7:00 AM-10:30 AM
L 11:00 AM-5:00 PM
D 5:00 PM-10 PM
Cards: AE DC DIS MC V
Dress: Casual
Style: Sea/Stk $$

Menu Sampler:

Breakfast:
Buffet of traditional and island favorites, omelet station & juice $10.50
Lunch:
Fresh Fish Tacos $8.95, Roast Turkey and Avocado Sandwich $7.95, Thai Chicken Pizza $7.95, Fisherman's Chowder $3.95, Beachside Burger $6.45
Dinner:
Pupus: Mac Nut and Dungeness Crab Won Ton with mustard plum sauce $9.95, Poke Rolls w/raw ahi, Maui onions, sautéed in rice paper $8.95, Sashimi $6.95
Entrées: Include salad bar and muffins and sourdough bread. Huli Huli Chicken-breast of chicken marinated in garlic, ginger, shoyu sauce and brown sugar $15.95, Fresh Island Fish of the Day prepared five ways $19.95-$25.95, Shrimp Scampi-shrimp sautéed in garlic butter on linguine with mushrooms, fresh tomatoes and capers $19.95, Prime Rib $19.95/$26.95, Big Island Pork Ribs glazed with a mango barbecue sauce & grilled $19.95

Impressions:

This Waikiki favorite was named after famed Olympic athlete and surfer Duke Kahanamoku. You'll find it on the beach at the Outrigger Waikiki Hotel. The breakfast buffet is a tremendous value and a great way to start the day. On the other end of the spectrum, the Barefoot Bar serves a light menu from 5 PM-12 AM and often has live local musicians performing. In between times people wander through for lunch and dinner or to enjoy their favorite adult beverages. While you're there checkout the surfing memorabilia on the walls. And yes, the "Beachboys of Waikiki" really do hang out here. They're just a little older now.

Honolulu

Eastern Garden

98-150 Kaonohi St
Aiea, HI 96701
808-486-8882
Web: None
Hours: LD 10:30 AM-10:00 PM Mo-Fr
LD 8:30 AM-10:00 PM SaSu
Cards: AE MC V
Dress: Resort Casual
Style: Chi $$

Menu Sampler:

Dim Sum: Egg Tartlet, Coconut Haupia Cake, Chinese Donut with Red Sugar $1.95, Barbecued Pork Bun, Steamed Minced Pork Dumpling (Pork Hash), Braised Chicken Feet with Black Pepper, Spring Roll, Deep Fried Shrimp Puff, Pan Fried Taro Cake, Chicken w/Black Mushroom Dumpling, Pan Fried Shrimp & Chive Dumpling $2.45, Fresh Shrimp Dumpling (pepeau), Barbecued Pork, Minced Beef, Steamed Scallop w/Spinach Dumpling, Seafood Bundle $3.25

Lunch/Dinner:

Appetizer: Deep Fried Gau Gee (8 pcs) 4.50, Szechuan Pickle 3.50, Salt and Pepper Fried Tofu 6.95, Cold Jelly Fish 7.95, Spring Rolls (3 pcs) 4.50
Soup: Imperial Scallop Soup 8.95, Won Ton Soup 5.95, Braised Shark's Fin Soup with Crab Meat 9.95/person, Abalone with black mushroom soup 16.00
Entrées: Scalded Live Prawns with Dipping Sauce $Seasonal, Kung Pao Shrimp 8.95, Sliced Abalone with Vegetable 23.50, Baked Lobster with Ginger and Green Onion $Seasonal, Crab with Curry Sauce $Seasonal, Pan Fried Squid with Spicy Salt 6.95, Sautéed Scallop in Wine Sauce 8.95, Oyster with Black Bean Sauce 8.95, Clams with Supreme Sauce 8.95, Sautéed Fish Fillet with Chinese Green 8.95, Mongolian Beef 7.95, Mu Shu Pork 8.95, Orange Chicken 6.95, Eight Treasure Hot Pot 8.95, Broccoli with Tofu in Wine Sauce 7.50

Impressions:

Eastern Garden has a reputation for serving one of the best Chinese menus on Oahu. Things start out mid-morning when the dim sum carts come rolling up to your table. Afterwards, those looking for lunch or dinner can choose from a wide variety of upscale preparations. Live seafood is the specialty here, but those preferring meat or poultry won't be disappointed. Pearl Harbor is just around the corner making this a good choice after visiting the memorial.

Waikiki

Eggs'n Things

Authors' Favorite

1911-B Kalakaua Ave.
Honolulu, HI 96815
808-949-0820
www.eggsnthings.com
Hours: B 11:00 PM-2:00 PM XMoTuWe
B 6:00 AM-2:00 PM MoTuWe
Cards: None
Dress: Casual
Style: Amer/Isl $$

Menu Sampler:

Breakfast:

Eggs: All orders served with 3 buttermilk pancakes or rice or potatoes and 2 eggs any style. Vienna Sausage & Eggs, Spam & Eggs, Corned Beef Hash & Eggs, Link Sausage & Eggs, Portuguese Sausage & Eggs, Ham & Eggs $7.00
Omelettes: 3 eggs, w/3 pancakes, rice or potatoes-toast extra. Cheese, Fresh Mushroom, Green Onion, Canadian bacon, Vegetarian, Corned Beef Hash $8.00
Crepes Suzettes: Sprinkled w/powdered sugar; choice of Sour Cream, Fresh Lemon, Banana, Strawberry, Blueberry $7.25, Choice of Sour Cream Lemon, Sour Cream Banana, Sour Cream Blueberry, Sour Cream Strawberry $8.00
Pancakes: Buttermilk $5.00, Choice of Banana, Blueberry, Coconut, Chocolate Chip, Bran, Buckwheat $6.00, Choice of Macadamia Nut, Pecan $7.00
Waffles: Plain $5.50, Choice of Blueberry, Coconut, Bran, Banana $6.25, Choice of Macadamia Nut, Pecan $7.00, Strawberry or Banana Whip Cream $8
Early Riser Special: 5 AM-9 AM-3 pancakes and 2 eggs $3.75
Late Riser Special: 1 PM-2 PM/1 AM-2 AM-same as Early Riser Special
Juices: Orange/Guava/Pineapple/Apple/Grapefruit/Passion/Carrot/Papaya $3/$6

Impressions:

The first thing that hits you about Eggs'n Things is the odd hours. This place doesn't open until late and then serves all night straight through to the next afternoon. As you can imagine the crowd changes with the clock! Around midnight, expect to find the late night party crowd finishing off their revelry with a stack of pancakes. Then, in the wee hours, the local characters take the stage. Finally, come morning, a steady stream of visitors parades through the door. But regardless of who they are, they all come for the excellent breakfast menu. This is the kind of place where you're not only asked how you want your eggs cooked, you're asked how you want your waffle—soft, medium, or crisp. Don't be put off if there's a wait. Take a seat outside and watch the world go by.

Honolulu

El Burrito
550 Piikoi St
Honolulu, HI 96814
808-596-8225
Web: None
Hours: LD 11:00 AM-8:00 PM Mo-Th
LD 11:00 AM-9:00 PM FrSa
Cards: None
Dress: Casual
Style: Mex $

Menu Sampler:

Breakfast:
N/A
Lunch/Dinner:
Ala Carta: Tamales $3.50, Chile Relleno $4.00, Chicken Chimichanga (2) $7.00, Cheese Quesadilla on Flour Tortilla $4.00, Beef Enchilada with red, green, or mole sauce $4.25, Tacos al Carbon $3.75, Guacamole Tostada $5.00, Cono Loco (Crazy Cone)-Crispy Cone Shaped Corn Tortilla filled with beans and cheese, garnished with lettuce, guacamole, sour cream $3.50, Bean Burritos $4.50, Tostada Nachos $6.25, Cheese Nachos $3.25, Lamb Taquitos (3), Beef Taco Salad $5.50, Gorditas-thick corn tortilla stuffed with choice of chicken, beef, lamb, or beans, then garnished with lettuce, cheese and guacamole $6.50, Menudo, Lamb Consommé, Chicken Soup or Posole $5.00/$6.00
Platillos de Combinacion: served with rice & extra cheese, $8.00-$10.50
Platillos Especiales: served with rice, beans, and 1-2 corn tortillas. Bethany "Special"-Marinated Chicken in our own special sauce $12.50, Beef, Chicken, or Lamb Chile Colorado $12.00, Steak or Chicken ala Mexicana $12.50, Camarones Mexicanos $12.50, Carne Asada $13.00, Pollo con mole $12.50
Platillos de Huevo: Huevos con Chorizo, rice, beans & 1-2 corn tortillas $10.50
Postres: Flan $3.00, Sweet Tamal $2.00

Impressions:

Visitors to the Ala Moana Shopping Center are presented with many dining options. One of our favorites is across the street at the corner of Piikoi and Kapiolani. There in a cubbyhole, you'll find some of the best Mexican food served in Honolulu. The menu is more traditional than trendy. Much of what is served here would be perfectly at home on a village plaza. This isn't Taco Hell!

Honolulu

Elena's Filipino Foods
94-300 Farrington Highway
Waipahu, HI 96797
808-671-3279
Web: None
Hours: B 5:00 AM-10:00 AM
LD 10:00 AM-8:45 PM Su-Th
LD 10:00 AM-9:00 PM FrSa
Cards: AE DIS MC V
Dress: Casual
Style: Fil $

Menu Sampler:

Breakfast:
Omelette Specials: Fried Rice Omelette (Bacon, Spam, Portuguese Sausage, Ham) $6.00, Pork Adobo Fried Rice Omelette $ 6.00, Chicken Fried Rice Omelette $ 6.00, Stuff Fried Rice Omelette $ 6.00, French Toast made with sweet bread $3.00, 3 Hotcakes $3.50, Waffle $3.00, Longaniza (pork & garlic sausage) with 2 eggs, rice, toast, or hotcake $5.00
Lunch/Dinner:
Adobo-pork marinated with vinegar & soy sauce 7.50, Dinugan-pork with blood 7.50, Gisantis-pork with green peas & tomato paste 7.50, Pinakbet-pork with mixed vegetables, eggplant, bitter melon, beans 7.50, Monggo Beans with Pork 7.50, Pansit-noodles & fresh vegetables (noodles imported from the Philippines) 7.50, Mixed Plate-any 4 listed above 7.75, Oxtail Soup 7.95, Sari-Sari of mixed vegetables, eggplant, squash, onchoi, crispy pork 7.50, Shrimp Sarciado-sautéed with tomato, onion, egg 8.95, Fried Bangus (milkfish) 9.50, Bangus Sinigang (soup) 9.75, Kare-Kare- oxtail sautéed with peanut butter 7.95, Beef Asada-filet beef steak 7.95, Lechon-crispy pork 8.50
Desserts: Banana Lumpia, 3 for 3.50, ArrozCaldo 7.00, Halo-Halo 3.50

Impressions:

When you feel the need to immerse yourself in local culture, drive on out to Waipahu and experience Elena's. This is a largely Filipino neighborhood, so guess what? Elena's is a Filipino restaurant with a largely Filipino clientele! Although some of the dishes may be unfamiliar, the friendly staff is always willing to help with explanations and suggestions. A luncheon buffet is also offered for those with big appetites or curiosities. After 30 years in business, this island favorite has become a local institution.

Kapahulu

Genki Sushi

900 Kapahulu Ave
Honolulu, HI 96816
808-735-8889
Web: None
Hours: L/D 11:00 AM-9:00 PM Su-Th
L/D 11:00 AM-10:00 PM FrSa
Cards: AE DC DIS JCB MC V
Dress: Casual
Style: Japan $

Menu Sampler:

Breakfast:

N/A

Lunch/Dinner:

Nigiri Sushi-2 pc $1.20-$4.00, 5 pc $3.10-$5.60, choices include ocean salad, ika (squid), tako (octopus), tamago (egg), shiokara (salted squid), tobikko (caplin roe), seafood salad, tako poke, abalone salad, maguro (ahi), hotate (scallop), ebi (shrimp), salmon, unagi (freshwater eel), iwashi (sardine)
Makimono: California roll (2 pcs.), Canadian roll (2 pcs.), Nishiki roll (2 pcs.)$1.20, Tekka Maki $1.70, 8 pcs. California Roll or Canadian Roll $4.80
Temaki-Handrolls: Tuna Salad Maki or Negitoro Maki $1.20, Seafood Temaki, Spicy Tuna Temaki, California Temaki $1.70, Salad/ Miso Soup $1.20
Party Platters to go $7.40-$38.65, Beer, Wine & Sake available now.
Chicken Kara'age $2.20, Ebi Fry $3.25

Impressions:

If you would like to try sushi in a friendly fast-food atmosphere, try the Kaiten sushi service at Genki Sushi. In the Kaiten system, the sushi is rolled past your counter seat on a conveyor belt. You select what you want to eat and are billed by the number and color of plates chosen. Reasonable prices, a fun experience, and a chance to experiment with Japanese specialties draw many to their doors. This style of sushi service has become global in its popularity. Other locations include the Ala Moana Center, Windward Center, Pearl City, and Waikele Center. Alcoholic beverages are available only at Kapahulu.

Waikiki

Golden Dragon Authors' Favorite

Hilton Hawaiian Village Hotel
2005 Kalia Road
Honolulu, HI 96815
808-946-5336
www.hawaiianvillage.hilton.com

Hours: D 6-9:30 PM XMo
Cards: AE DIS JCB MC V
Dress: Evening Aloha
Style: Chi $$$$
Ent Card

Menu Sampler:

Breakfast/Lunch:
N/A

Dinner:
Appetizers: Golden Phoenix Shrimp $8.95, Crispy Crab Meat Won Ton $7.50, Spicy Roast Duck Salad $8.95, Chicken & Black Mushroom Potstickers $9.95
Soups: Hot and Sour Soup with diced tofu $5.50, Fresh Scallop Soup with pork loin & shiitake mushrooms $5.95, Shark Fin Soup $12.50, Won Ton Soup $5.50
Entrées: Mongolian Loin of Lamb with ginger and scallions $25.50, Cashew Nut Chicken w/water chestnuts & Chinese vegetables $16.50, Cantonese Roast Duck $15.75, Kung Pao Shrimp sautéed w/red chili-Szechuan style $19.50
Signature Selection: $36.00 per person, two-person minimum. Ten items.
The Lotus Dinner: $43.00 per person-Island Pork Char Siu, Chicken Egg Rolls, Crispy Won Tons, Fresh Scallop Soup, Kung Pao Chicken, Szechuan Tenderloin of Beef w/hoisin sauce & fresh tomatoes, Lobster in Curry Sauce w/Haupia, Stir Fried Shrimp w/snow peas & cashew nuts, Duck Fried Rice, Chilled Almond Float, Selection of Chinese Teas and Fortune Cookies

Impressions:

Golden Dragon is one of those places that is almost too good to be true. They have a beautiful setting, the food is outstanding, and the service impeccable. Now that we've got your attention, let's take things in detail. First, reservations are a must. This restaurant tailors it's evening around serving a certain number of diners and you don't want to be disappointed. Next, if there ever was a time to order a complete fixed price dinner, this is it. The dishes Chef Steve Chiang prepares are truly superb. The set menus have been selected to create a complete experience. Finally, this is a dinner to linger over. Don't eat and run!

Oahu Dining

Honolulu

Gordon Biersch Brewery Restaurant

Aloha Tower Marketplace
Aloha Tower Drive
Honolulu, HI 96813
808-599-4877
www.gordonbiersch.com

Hours: L 10:00 AM-4:00 PM
D 4:00 PM-10:00 PM Su-Th, 5:00 PM-11:00 PM FrSa
Cards: AE DC DIS JCB MC V
Dress: Resort Casual
Style: Amer/Pac-Rim $$

Menu Sampler:

Breakfast:
N/A
Lunch:
Pupus: Sweet Chili and Ginger Glazed Chicken Wings $8.50, Cornmeal Dusted Crab Cakes w/Asian Slaw $9.95, Spicy Ahi Spring Rolls w/sriracha aioli $9.95
Salads: Chopped Salad of chicken, pepper jack cheese, artichoke hearts, pepperoni in an Olive Lemon Vinaigrette $10.95, Asian Chicken Salad $10.95
Sandwiches: Marzen Barbecue Burger w/bacon, cheddar cheese, garlic fries $9.50, Blackened Mahi w/Cajun remoulade and garlic fries $9.50
Entrées: Goat Cheese Ravioli w/mushrooms, pine nuts, rosemary $9.95
Dinner:
Pastas: Cajun Fettucine w/grilled chicken & shrimp, Andouille sausage $14.95
Pizzas: $9.95-$11.50-Italian Sausage w/basil $10.95, Classic Pepperoni $10.95
Pupus: Crispy Artichoke Hearts w/Parmesan & lemon aioli $8.25, Gordon Biersch Garlic Fries $4.95, Quick Fried Calamari w/spicy marinara $8.95
Salads: Hummus Salad with peppers, goat cheese and flat bread $9.95
Entrées: Hanger Steak in teriyaki marinade, mashed potatoes $16.95, BBQ Salmon w/grilled red onion, arugula, sweet ginger rice $18.50, Fresh Catch $Market, Lemon Ginger Crusted Salmon with sweet ginger rice and julienne vegetables $17.50, Chicken Marsala with shallots & mushrooms over linguini $14.50, Half Roasted Chicken, garlic mashed potatoes, rosemary au jus $14.50

Impressions:

Find a seat overlooking the harbor and watch the ships go by. With a glass of house brewed beer, exotic pupus, and interesting menu items to accompany the dockside atmosphere, you can't help but relax and enjoy yourself.

Hawaii Kai

Greek Marina

Koko Marina
7192 Kalanianaole Hwy
Honolulu, HI 96825
808-396-8441
Web: None
Hours: L 11:00 AM-3:00 PM Mo-Sa
D 5:00 PM-9:00 PM Su-Th
D 5:00 PM-10:00 PM FrSa
Cards: MC V
Dress: Casual
Style: Greek $$

Menu Sampler:

Breakfast:
N/A
Lunch:
Appetizer: Greek Style Fries with garlic mayo sauce $2.95, Spanokopita $2.95, Fried Eggplant with Greek Marina Dip $5.95, Falafel $5.95, Marides $5.95, Hommus $4.95, Tarama Salata $5.95, Appetizer Platter (for 3 or more) $4.95
Sandwiches: Gyros $5.95-with fries or salad $7.95, Fish $5.95-with side $7.95
Salads: Tabbouleh Salad $4.95, Classic Greek Salad $6.95, Gyros Salad $7.95
Greek Specialties: Gyros with salad & pita $10.95, Moussaka $11.95
Dinner:
Appetizers: As above plus Saganaki flambé tableside $7.95, Dolmades $6.95
Greek Specialties: Gyros Chicken with salad & pita $12.95, Kalamari Steak with garlic sauce, rice, salad, pita $13.95, Lamb Souvlaki with rice, salad & pita $13.95, Lamb Rack broiled Athenian Style with rice, salad & pita $16.95

Impressions:

One of the newest additions at the Koko Marina is a restaurant serving all the Greek specialties. The menu is traditional with fun extras like tableside flambé. We tried a combination platter and found everything to our liking. Portions are quite generous, so don't over order. This attractive café style restaurant offers diners a choice of indoor or outdoor seating. In the evening parking can be scarce, so you may have to look around the complex.

Oahu Dining

Waikiki

Hakone
Hawaii Prince Waikiki Hotel
100 Holomoana St
Honolulu, HI 96815
808-944-4494
www.princeresortshawaii.com
Hours: D 6:00 PM-8:30 PM Ala Carte WeTh
D 5:30 PM-9:00 PM Buffet & Limited Ala Carte FrSa
D 6:00 PM-9:00 PM Su
Cards: AE DC DIS JCB MC V
Dress: Resort Casual
Style: Japan $$$$ Ent Card

Menu Sampler:

Breakfast/ Lunch:
N/A
Dinner:
Appetizers: Ika Shiokara-salted marinated squid $4.00, Tomato Salad with Oriental dressing $7.00, Shrimp Tempura (5 pcs) $14.00
Nabemono-Chafing dish style "cook your own meal"-includes miso soup, oshinko, rice & veg.- Minimum two-person order. Sukiyaki with choice strip loin and vegetables with sweet sukiyaki sauce $34, Shabu Shabu with choice strip loin and vegetables w/ponzu & sesame sauce $34
Teishoku Combination Dinners: Daily-$39 includes rice, miso soup, kobachi, oshinko, and dessert plus one of the featured entree items-tempura, wafu filet mignon, Panko Fried Shrimp, Chicken, and Vegetables, Lobster Nogarayaki and broiled fish of the day
Hakone Buffet: Sushi Buffet with salads, shabu shabu, shrimp & vegetable tempura, noodles, sashimi, nigiri sushi, temaki, rice, oshinko, specials and dessert station- Adults $42, Child $21

Impressions:

Dining at Hakone is an authentic cultural experience where one can discover classic Japanese cuisine. You can order a nabemono chafing dish, select from the a la carte menu, or enjoy the Hakone Buffet. The buffet features a wide variety of hot and cold dishes such as crispy shrimp, rib eye steak with teri-glaze, steamed Manila clams, salmon, butterfish, and Alaskan crab legs. The Prince is a lovely hotel with dining rooms overlooking the marina. Parking is readily available either by valet, in the adjoining deck, or along the marina.

North Shore

Haleiwa Joe's Seafood Grill

66-001 Kamehameha Hwy
Haleiwa, HI 96712
808-637-8005
Web: None
Hours: L 11:30 AM-4:15 PM Mo-Sa
L 11:30 AM-3:45 PM Su
D 5:30 PM-10:30 PM FrSa
D 5:30 PM-9:30 PM Mo-Th
D 5:00 PM-9:30 PM Su
Cards: MC V
Dress: Casual
Style: Isl/Sea $$$

Menu Sampler:

Breakfast:

N/A

Lunch:

Small Plates: Ahi Spring Rolls $9.95, Thai Fried Calamari $6.50, Sweet Kalbi Ribs with a scoop of white rice $8.95, Peel & Eat Fire Shrimp $8.75
Soups & Salads: Tropical Grilled Shrimp Salad on greens with our lilikoi vinaigrette $12.25, Roasted Garlic Bread $4.25, Fish Monger Soup $4.25
Lunch Plates & Sandwiches: Haleiwa Joe's Hamburger on a poppy seed bun with toppings & fries $7.25, Crunchy Coconut Shrimp with steamed rice $14.95

Dinner:

Small Plates: Island Ceviche with cilantro, tomato and jalapeno $6.95, Joe's Tempura Crab Roll $9.25, Luau Lumpia with Kahlua pig and taro leaf $8.25
Soup, Salads & Other Stuff: Ginger Peanut Chicken Salad on greens with a spicy ginger dressing $9.75, House Salad with a sesame-miso dressing $3.95
Big Plates: Seared Fresh Ahi with spicy seasonings, on a bed of sautéed noodles and ginger glazed baby carrots $20.75, Chinese Style Steamed Fish in Ti leaves with sesame oil, fresh ginger, cilantro, and green onion $19.95, Prime Rib roasted bone-in with creamy horseradish sauce & garlic mashed potatoes $27.75
Desserts: Key Lime Pie $5.50, Mango Sorbet $4.25, Love Cake $6.25

Impressions:

Offering an eclectic island menu, a marina in front, the quaint village of Haleiwa behind, and the Pacific Ocean all around, this casual full-service restaurant has what every visitor imagines in a Hawaii dining experience. Visitors and locals alike appreciate Haleiwa Joe's and patronize this establishment heavily.

Kaimuki

Hale Vietnam

1140 12th Avenue
Honolulu, HI 96816
808-735-7581
Web: None
Hours: LD 11:00 AM-10:00 PM
Cards: DIS MC V
Dress: Casual
Style: Viet $$

Menu Sampler:

Breakfast:
N/A
Lunch/Dinner:
Appetizers: Summer Rolls-boiled shrimp, seasoned pork, fresh mint, bean sprouts and rice noodles rolled in rice paper with special peanut sauce $4.75
Salads: Green Papaya of shredded papaya, roast pork, boiled shrimp, mint leaves $8.25, Lemon Beef-char-broiled beef slices, romaine, cucumber, tomatoes, toasted peanuts, onion flakes, Chinese parsley $8.25
House Specials: Pho-Famous Beef Noodle Soup of Vietnam-Medium Bowl $6.00, Large Bowl $6.50-your choice of rare steak, brisket, flank, tendon, tripe, chicken balls, beef balls, lean cooked chicken. Side plate of bean sprouts, fresh basil, chili pepper, and a lemon wedge. Oxtail Soup with noodle or rice $7.50
Vietnamese Sour Soup: Popular soup in Vietnam with fresh lemon grass, bean sprouts, bamboo shoots, celery, tomatoes, and fresh herbs-Catfish $11.75, Shrimp $11.75, Chicken $10.50, Vegetarian $9.50
Seafood Soup $6.95, Long Rice Soup $6.75, Vegetarian Long Rice Soup $6.75, Spicy Beef and Pork Noodle Soup $7.95, Fried Egg Noodle $8.95
Vietnamese Plate: Includes consommé, steamed rice, lettuce, cucumber and tomato slices $8.50-choices of BBQ Pork Chop, Shredded Pork, Chicken, BBQ Shrimp, Sautéed Lemongrass Shrimp or Beef, BBQ Beef
Entrees: Vietnamese Fondue $15.95-$17.95, Sautéed Beef, Chicken, Shrimp, or Tofu with Vegetables, or Lemongrass, Peanut Sauce, Black Beans $9.50-$11.75

Impressions:

Looking at the patrons sitting around the dining room of Hale Vietnam you'll find a wonderful cross-section of the cultures found in Honolulu. People from every background gather here to enjoy the healthy, fresh Vietnamese cuisine served in this attractive restaurant. Located in Kaimuki's restaurant row, this busy dining spot has metered parking in a large city lot behind the complex.

Manoa Valley

Hanaki Japanese Buffet
Manoa Marketplace
2756 Woodlawn Drive
Honolulu, HI 96822
808-988-1551
Web: None
Hours: L 11:00 AM-2:00 PM Mo-Fr, XTu
L 10:30 AM-2:00 PM SaSu
D 5:00 PM-9:00 PM
Cards: AE DC DIS MC V
Dress: Casual
Style: Japan $$

Menu Sampler:

Lunch:

Buffet: Seating at 11:00 AM and 12.30 PM, Monday-Friday, Miso Soup & Soba Noodles, Shrimp & Vegetable Tempura Station, Contemporary Sushi Bar, Sashimi and Assorted Cold Salads, Yaki Soba, Chicken Teriyaki, Traditional and Creative Chef's Specials, Shaved Ice and Dessert Bar $12.95, Seniors 55+ $10.95, Kids under 4 ½ feet tall $4.95

Buffet: Monday through Friday Dinner Buffet and Saturday and Sunday Lunch Buffet features the above items with more sushi, poke and dungeness crab legs $17.95, $8.95 Kids under 4 ½ feet tall, Seniors 55+ $15.95 Monday-Friday Dinner, no special seniors price Saturday and Sunday Lunch Buffet

Buffet: Saturday and Sunday Evenings features a seafood extravaganza, including Dungeness Crab Legs, Miso Butterfish, and the Chef's Seafood Creations and tender Prime Rib carved to order plus the above items $24.95 for adults and $11.95 for Kids under 4 ½ feet tall. No senior specials.

Impressions:

Back in the Manoa Valley behind the University of Hawaii, culinary adventurers will discover a special dining experience. There around the corner from Safeway in the Manoa Marketplace you'll find Hanaki Japanese Buffet. The first things that strike you when you walk through the door are the clean lines and civilized atmosphere of this traditional establishment. Then, after being escorted to one of the simple tables, you'll have the opportunity to experience a variety of Japanese centered cuisine. The hallmark here is quality. Everything from the selections offered to the levels of preparation and presentation exceed one's expectations. The staff is very helpful to all, but as local people and Japanese visitors favor this place, expect your visit to be a cultural encounter.

Oahu Dining

Honolulu

Hard Rock Café
1837 Kapiolani Blvd.
Honolulu, HI 96814
808-955-9383
www.hardrock.com
Hours: L/D 11:30 AM-12:30 AM
Cards: AE DIS JCB MC V
Dress: Resort Casual
Style: Amer/Ec $$

Menu Sampler:

Breakfast:
N/A
Lunch/Dinner:
Starters: Santa Fe Spring Rolls with fresh salsa and guacamole dressing $7.19, Classic Chicken Wings with choice of dipping sauce $7.99, Southwest Nachos w/roasted corn, cheeses, salsa $8.49, Jumbo Combo (all kine goodies!) $14.29
Salads: Grilled Chinese Chicken Salad $9.39, Haystack Fried Chicken Salad $9.19, Hard Rock Caesar Salad $7.99, Cobb Salad $9.39, House Salad $7.19
Burger Platters: Each half-pound burger comes with toppings and a full plate of French fries. Char-Broiled Burger $8.39, Cheeseburger $8.99, Bacon Cheeseburger $9.19, Natural Veggie Burger with Cajun mayonnaise, served with cole slaw and baked potato $8.59, Turkey Burger w/mustard-mayo $8.79
Specialties: Grilled Sirloin Steak (9 oz) grilled, topped with a horseradish demi sauce and frizzled onions with a side of "twisted mac n cheese" and fresh seasonal vegetables $15.29, Famous Grilled Fajitas of chicken, beef or fresh veggies, numerous condiments, pinto beans and seasoned rice $12.49
Desserts: Cheesecake $4.79, Dessert Nachos $7.99, Down Home Apple Cobbler $4.99, Seasonal Shortcake $5.99, Thick Shakes & Malts $3.99

Impressions:

You'll find the Hard Rock Café on the downtown side of Waikiki. Not only is this rock-n-roll icon a fun place for great tunes and fabulous memorabilia, but they serve a solid casual dining menu. The burgers are made with high quality ground beef and the entrées add interesting twists to everyday comfort food. Make sure you ask to see the dessert menu! Check the website for a listing of entertainment and upcoming special events. There is a parking lot on site, but it can get crowded. Plan ahead if you drive. Better yet, walk or take a cab.

Oahu Dining

Waikiki

Hau Tree Lanai
The New Otani Kaimana Beach Hotel
2863 Kalakaua Avenue
Honolulu, HI 96815
808-921-7066
www.kaimana.com
Hours: B 7:00 AM-11:00 AM
L 11:30 AM-2:00 PM Mo-Sa
L 12:00 PM-2:00 PM Su
D 5:30 PM-9:00 PM
Cards: AE DIS JCB MC V
Dress: Resort Casual
Style: Haw-Reg/Pac Rim $$$ Ent Card

Menu Sampler:

Breakfast:
Poi or Buttermilk Pancakes 8.50, Salmon Benedict Florentine-seared salmon, spinach, bacon, and poached eggs on a pepper-cheddar scone topped with a dill hollandaise, served with breakfast potatoes 14.50, Asian Breakfast of longanisa sausage, garlic fried rice, two eggs any style, pickled green papaya salad, and sliced Japanese cucumbers 12.00, Corn Beef Hash and Eggs $11.50

Lunch:
Ahi Cobb Salad with seared island ahi, red potato salad, asparagus, Nicoise olives, anchovy fillets, balsamic vinaigrette 16.75, Crab Cake Burger on a whole wheat bun with seasoned fries 14.50, Seafood Omelet with rice or fries 13.75

Dinner:
Appetizers: Escargot Maison 11.25, Pan Smoked Hoisin Duck Breast on a poi-green onion-wild rice pancake 8.75, Seafood Tsunami Supreme 16.25
Soups/Salads: Portuguese Bean Soup 6.50, Warm Lamb Chop Salad 8.50
Entrees: Crab-Avocado Crusted Fresh Mahimahi glazed with garlic aioli with citrus beurre blanc sauce 28.50, Organic Western Ranchers Beef 38.95

Impressions:

Remember the beautiful beach scenes from the Magnum P.I. television series? Many of them were shot in front of this restaurant. Hau Tree Lanai is located on a terrace overlooking San Souci Beach at the quiet end of Waikiki. The setting is lovely at any time, but becomes stunning at sunset. A high level of preparation and presentation is maintained three meals a day.

Kapahulu

Hee Hing Restaurant
449 Kapahulu Ave
Honolulu, HI 96815
808-735-5544
Web: None
Hours: L/D 10:30 AM-9:30 PM
Cards: AE DC DIS JCB MC V
Dress: Resort Casual
Style: Chi $$

Menu Sampler:

Breakfast:
N/A
Lunch/Dinner:
Appetizers: Shrimp Pouches with salad sauce $5.95, Crisp Kau Chee $4.95, Spring Rolls $6.95, Crisp Won Ton $4.95, Golden Fried Spring Rolls $6.95
Soups: Hot and Sour Soup $7.25, Chicken Sweet Corn Soup $7.25, Kup Dai Fish Cake Rice Soup $6.25, Mustard Cabbage Soup $7.25, Egg Flower $7.25
Rice: Yang Chow Style Fried Rice $7.25, Chicken and Salt Fish Fried Rice $9.50, Char Siu and Roast Duck on rice $7.95, Minced Beef Fried Rice $7.25
Noodles: Chicken Lobster Noodles $15.95, Chow Fun w/beef, bell peppers and black bean sauce $7.50, Singapore Rice Noodles $7.50, Beef Chow Fun $7.50
Entrées: Roast Pork and Tofu Casserole in earthen pot $9.25, Scallops with Chinese peas in taro nest $13.50, Curry Lobster $24.95, Sauteed Sea Bass with ginger and onion $11.95, Crabmeat on poached hearts of lettuce $16.95, Shrimp with pineapple $7.95, Abalone with black mushrooms and oyster sauce $27.95, Almond Chicken $7.25, Mongolian Beef Tenderloin $8.95, Sweet and Sour Spare Ribs with pineapple $6.95, Spicy Szechuan Beef $7.95, Steamed Pork Hash $6.75, Sweet and Sour Roast Duck $7.50, Mochi Rice Duck $7.95
Dessert: Almond Float $1.95, Lychee Ice Cream $2.75, Almond cookie (3) $.35

Impressions:

Hee Hing shares a building with Sam Choy's Diamond Head Restaurant on the park side of Kapahulu Avenue. There's parking under the building for the use of both. The Lee family operates this restaurant and serves up an extensive menu of Szechuan, Cantonese, and Northern Chinese delicacies. Besides the ala carte items, Hong Kong style dim sum is served at lunch. They also offer a complete section for vegetarians. No MSG is used in their preparations. This is a good choice for Chinese food lovers who don't want to venture away from Waikiki.

Honolulu

Helena's Hawaiian Foods

1240 North School Street
Honolulu, HI 96819
808-845-8044
Web: None
Hours: LD 13:00 AM-7:30 PM Tu-Fr
Cards: None
Dress: Casual
Style: Isl $

Menu Sampler:

Breakfast:

N/A

Lunch/Dinner:

Ala Carte: Poi 1.75/2.00, Rice .60/.90, Kalua Pig 2.50/3.50/6.95, Kalua Pig & Cabbage 2.75, Laulau 2.75, Tripe Stew 2.75, Beef Stew 2.75, Salt Beef with Watercress 3.00, Luau Squid 2.75, Luau Chicken 2.75, Long Rice Chicken 2.75, Short Ribs Pipikaula Style 3.50/6.95, Lomi Salmon 2.75, Lomi Salmon with Raw Fish & Limu 3.00, Lomi or Poke (Aku or Ahi) 2.75, Opihi 2.75, Poke Fish with Opihi 3.75, Fried Butterfish Collar 3.50, Boiled Butterfish Collar (with stew gravy or plain) 3.50, Fried Aku or Ahi 2.75, Fried Aku or Ahi Bone (when available) 3.00, Haupia 1.25/2.50/9.00, Soda 1.00

Combos: Menu A includes Kalua Pig and Lomi Salmon with two scoops rice 6.15, small poi 7.00, large poi 7.25; **Menu B** includes Kalua Pig and Pipikaula Short Ribs with two scoops rice 6.90, small poi 7.75, large poi 8.00; **Menu C** includes Kalua Pig, Lomi Salmon, and Pipikaula Short Ribs with two scoops rice 9.65, with small poi 10.50, with large poi 10.75; **Menu D** includes Kalua Pig, Lomi Salmon, Pipikaula Short Ribs, Luau Squid with two scoops rice 12.40, with small poi 13.25, with large poi 13.50

Impressions:

Helen Chock is an institution on the Honolulu restaurant scene. She has been cooking and serving great regional food so long that most people have forgotten when it all began. Her North School Street restaurant isn't easy to find, but all the locals know where it's at, so that's "No problem!" The draw here is the traditional Hawaiian food served in a variety of combinations. Luau favorites like kalua pig and lomi salmon are available for workday lunches and dinners instead of only on special occasions. When visiting Helena's be sure to check out the awards on the walls. Even the James Beard crowd is sold on this one! There is parking in front of this modest eatery, but go early to find a spot.

Honolulu

hirOshi

Authors' Favorite

Restaurant Row
500 Ala Moana Blvd.
Honolulu, HI 96813
808-533-4476
Web: None
Hours: D 6:00 PM-10:00 PM
Cards: AE DC DIS JCB MC V
Dress: Resort Casual/Evening Aloha
Style: Asian/Euro $$$

Menu Sampler:

Breakfast/Lunch:
N/A
Dinner:
To Start: Duo of Contemporary Sushi-sweet miso glazed salmon and ginger scallion ahi 9.95, Spinach Salad with crumbled eggs, tsukemono, bacon bits, Hauula tomato and mustard sesame vinaigrette 6.75, Bo Bo Farms Foie Gras Sushi with teriyaki glaze and essence of shiso 7.95
In Between: Seared Sea Scallops with bacon takana ragout, tobiko and kabayaki butter sauce 9.95, Softshell Crab "Ooze" with kabocha puree, wilted spinach and julienned Big Island ginger w/lemon jelee 7.75, Lacquered Salmon with cilantro rice, homemade tsukemono & ume puree 14.75, Sizzlin' Moi Carpaccio w/Big Island ginger, Hauula tomato, Mrs. Cheng's tofu & ponzu vinaigrette, truffled Nalo micro greens 9.95, Bacon Wrapped Jumbo Shrimp 7.95
To Complete: Seared Kanpachi w/Portuguese sausage potstickers "al dente" & chervil clam jus 15.75, Miso Yaki Butter Fish w/wilted spinach & lemon-ume jelee 15.95, Red Wine "Braised" Veal Cheek w/cilantro "pesto" crust, succotash, scallop potato & natural jus 15.95, Pan Roasted Filet Mignon w/seared foie gras, Frankie's peppercorn, Nalo micro arugula foie gras-ponzu sauce 21.95, Moi, Catch of the Day, & Manila Clam "Cioppino" 16.95

Impressions:

Hiroshi Fukui has always had a way with inspired light bites. At this new venue he combines his classic training with eastern influences and locally sourced ingredients to create what he has dubbed "Eurasion" tapas. In keeping with the Spanish origins of this dining style, bold flavors dominate. His partner, master sommelier Chuck Furuya, backs this up with one of the island's finest wine lists.

Diamond Head

Hoku's

Authors' Favorite

Mandarin Oriental Hotel
5000 Kahala Ave
Honolulu, HI 96815
808-739-8780
www.mandarin-oriental.com
Hours: SuBru 10:30 AM-2:30 PM
L 11:00 AM-1:00 PM Mo-Fr
D 5:30 PM-10 PM
Cards: AE DC DIS JCB MC V
Dress: Evening Aloha
Style: Asian/Ec/Haw $$$$

Menu Sampler:

Breakfast:
Brunch Buffet: $44/adults, $22/child. Fresh Oysters, Crab Claws, Smoked Salmon, Ahi, Caesar Salad, Tandoori Chicken Salad, soups and desserts including a choice of a **regular menu entrée:** King Crab Omelet $22.00, Hoku's Eggs Benedict $19.00, Portuguese Sweet Bread French Toast $15.00
Lunch:
Three-Course Business Lunch $29.75, Ala Carte entrees and salads.
Dinner:
Starters: Lobster and Sweet Kahuku Corn Chowder $9.75, Oxtail Soup with chive pancakes $8.00, Hoisin Duck Taco w/pineapple mango salsa $12.00
Salads: Warm Lobster and Baby Spinach Salad w/truffle vinaigrette $21
Main Courses: Herb Crusted Fresh Island Onaga (Signature Dish) w/creamed spinach, red wine shallots and garlic mashed potatoes $37, Grilled Australian Rack of Lamb, Nicoise olive crushed Yukon Gold potatoes, yellow beans and natural jus $34, Mahi-Mahi Baked in Pandan Leaf, Okinawan sweet potatoes, kabocha pumpkin and long beans, w/vanilla orange sauce $29
Desserts: Chocolate Lovers Variation of Melting Chocolate Cake, Frangelico Soufflé, Chocolate Crème Brulee $7.75, Asian Pear & Pistachio Crisp $7.75

Impressions:

This contemporary dining room overlooks the ocean at the Kahala Mandarin Hotel. Chef Wayne Hirabayashi of the Hawaiian Island Chef's group oversees the operation of the display kitchen and its menu of innovative fusion cuisine. The pupus are like mini-entrees and can easily become dinner by themselves. This is truly fine dining in a matching locale. Reservations are recommended.

Honolulu

Hong Kong Harbour View Seafood Restaurant

1 Aloha Tower Drive
Honolulu, HI 96813
808-566-9989
Web: None
Hours: 9:30 AM-10:00 PM
Cards: AE DC DIS JCB MC V
Dress: Resort Casual
Style: Chi $$

Menu Sampler:

Breakfast/Lunch:
Dim Sum: 9:30 AM-2:30 PM-40-50 choices, Lunch 11:30 AM-2:30 PM
Lunch/Dinner:
Appetizers: Fried Bacon with Prawns Scallop Roll (5) $14.95, Minced Seafood in Lettuce $12.95, Cha Sho Pork $9.95, Fried Egg Roll/Crispy Won Ton $6.50
Sizzling Platters: Sizzling Oyster with Black Bean Sauce $16.95, Sizzling Beef w/Satay Sauce $12.95, Sizzling Tenderloin Steak w/Black Pepper Sauce $16.95
Soup: Dried Scallop Soup $14.95, Hot and Sour Soup/Won Ton Soup $10.95
Live Seafood: Live Maine Lobster sautéed with garlic & butter sauce/live Dungeness Crab sautéed with ginger & green onion/ live Hawaiian Prawns scalded with special sauce/ Oysters with black bean sauce in shell (4) $Mkt
Entrées: Braised Abalone with Black Mushrooms $26.95, Kung Pao Prawns $15.95, Hot Pot of Chicken & Tofu with Salted Fish $15.95, Crispy Roast Chicken $10.95, Lemon Sauce Chicken/Mu Shu Chicken $10.95, Pork Chop Peking Style/Sweet and Sour Pork $10.95, Egg Fu Yong $8.95, Fried Ground Tofu and Shrimp with Brown Sauce (5) $12.95, House Special Fried Rice with Assorted Seafood $14.95, Shrimp Pan-Fried Noodle $12.95, BBQ Pork Noodle in Soup $10.95, Duck with Vegetable Noodle in Soup $10.95
Dessert: Almond Pudding $2.50, Sweet Mochi Dumpling in Soup $3.50

Impressions:

The Aloha Tower Marketplace is home to several notable restaurants. Here on the second floor overlooking the water you'll find the Hong Kong Harbour View Seafood Restaurant. Naturally this elegantly furnished establishment specializes in Hong Kong style seafood, but is also known for its dim sum service at lunch. You'll see five dim sum wagons circulating around the room. Each one takes a different culinary approach with the group offering between 40 to 50 items in total. Midday shoppers will find this to be an affordable way of sampling many "delicate bites". Make sure to get your parking ticket validated.

Oahu Dining

Waikiki

House Without A Key
Halekulani Hotel
2199 Kalia Road
Honolulu, HI 96815
808-923-2311
www.halekulani.com
Hours: B Buf 7:00 AM-10:30 AM Mo-Sa
B Buf 7:00 AM-11:30 AM Su
L 11:00 AM-5:00 PM Mo-Sa, Noon-5 PM Su
D 5:00 PM-9 PM
Cards: AE DC DIS JCB MC V
Dress: Resort Casual
Style: PacRim $$$

Menu Sampler:

Breakfast:
Buffet of traditional and Japanese entrees and salads $21.95
Lunch:
Appetizers: Premium Grade Ahi Sashimi w/shredded daikon & ginger $16.00
Salads: Caesar Salad with Poached Shrimp & garlic bread $15.50
Sandwiches: Grilled Lemongrass Chicken Sandwich on a croissant $14.00
Entrees: Sautéed Hawaiian Mahimahi w/lemon pepper basil crab sauce $16.50
Desserts: Almond Float with Seasonal Fruit & Lychee Sorbet $6.50
Dinner:
Cocktail Appetizers: Hot Pupu Assortment of Coconut Shrimp, Teriyaki Beef Brochettes and Vegetable Spring Rolls $14.00, Calamari Fritte $9.00
Salads and Soups: Spicy Chicken Salad with lilikoi mustard emulsion $7.50, Maui Onion Soup Gratinee with Swiss & Gruyere Cheese $8.50
Entrees: Ka'u Orange and Poha Berry Glazed Island Chicken Breast with seasonal vegetables and Lemon Verbano Saffron Rice $17.50, Seared New York Steak with Roasted Mushroom Shallot Sauce and vegetable $22.00
Desserts: Chocolate Macadamia Nut Haupia Tart w/raspberry coulis $6.50

Impressions:

House Without A Key has the relaxed pace and feel of neighbor island resort dining. Yes, it is located in a fine hotel, but no, patrons don't feel the need to dress for dinner. This casual but upscale restaurant overlooks the ocean from the courtyard of the Halekulani. We view it as an oasis in the midst of the hustle and bustle of Waikiki. House Without A Key offers exemplary meals and civilized service throughout the day. Entertainment is offered nightly.

Oahu Dining

Waikiki

Hula Grill Waikiki
Outrigger Waikiki Hotel
2335 Kalakaua Ave
Honolulu, HI 96815
808-923-4852
www.hulapie.com
Hours: B 6:30 AM-10:30 AM
D 5:00 PM-10:00 PM
Cards: AE DC DIS JCB MC V
Dress: Resort Casual
Style: Haw Reg/Sea $$$

Menu Sampler:

Breakfast:
Stack of Traditional Buttermilk Pancakes 6.50, with Bananas & Mac Nuts or Maui Pineapple & Coconut 7.00, Kama'aina Omelet with three eggs, ham, smoked bacon, Portuguese sausage, green onion, cheddar and home style potatoes or rice and toast 8.50, Hula Eggs Benedict with Portuguese sausage and papaya hollandaise 9.00, Loco Moco made with a petite filet and shiitake mushroom sauce 13.00, Spam & Eggs 8.00, Stir Fried Rice & Eggs 8.00
Lunch:
N/A
Dinner:
Pupus and Dim Sum: Shrimp and Mauna Kea goat cheese quesadilla with mac nuts and black bean Maui onion relish 9.50, Waimanalo Vegetable Strudel, filo pastry, roasted vegetables and tomato fondue 8.00, Steamed Clams 9.50
Soups and Salads: Wok Charred Ahi Caesar Salad 12.00
Entrées: Fire Grilled Ono, pineapple salsa on spinach salad with chili lime vinaigrette 24.00, Spicy Shrimp Kung Pao, mac nut garnish, namasu salad 19.50, Filet Steak Kiana-Steak Diane w/shiitake cream & lilikoi butter 26.00

Impressions:

If you're looking for a Maui-inspired experience in Waikiki, go to Hula Grill. There's a style about this place. It's the essence of Hawaii Regional Cuisine. Everything possible from the day-boat fish to the garnish is sourced locally. Then the kitchen takes these riches and combines them in a fusion of local culture and classic techniques. Even the setting fits the neighbor island mood. The second floor waterfront location has been transformed into a beach house restaurant reminiscent of old Hawaii. Waikiki needed Hula Grill.

Waikiki

Hy's Steak House

Authors' Favorite

2440 Kuhio Ave
Honolulu, HI 96815
808-922-5555
www.hyshawaii.com
Hours: D 6:00 PM-10:00 PM Su-Th, D 5:30 PM-10:00 PM SaSu
Cards: AE DC DIS JCB MC V
Dress: Evening Aloha
Style: Sea/Stk $$$$

Menu Sampler:

Breakfast/Lunch:
N/A
Dinner:
Appetizers: Filet Mignon Tartare $11.95, Crab Cake with roasted garlic, pine nuts & basil $12.50, Escargot a la Hy's $12.50, Ahi and Scallops Katsu $14.95
Soups: Onion Soup Gratinee $5.95, New England Clam Chowder $5.95
Salads: Hawaiian Salad a la Hy's $9.95, Caesar Salad $10.95/person, Hy's Seafood and Avocado Salad $12.95, Warm Spinach Salad (tableside prep) $9.95
Entrées: NY Peppercorn Steak glazed with Madagascar peppercorn sauce $33.95, Roast Rack of Lamb $42.95, Filet Mignon $35.95/$42.95, Prime Rib $25.95/$32.95, Steak Teriyaki $30.95, Chateaubriand for Two with a bouquet of fresh vegetables and sauce bearnaise $39.95 per person, Filet of Beef Wellington topped with pate maison and mushroom duxelles baked in a light pastry and served with a cabernet truffle sauce $36.95, Broiled Veal Chop Forestiere with shiitake and oyster mushrooms and Marsala wine sauce $36.95, Scallops charred and served with a Thai style sauce accented with basil, lemon grass and ginger $29.95, Chicken Marsala or Piccata $19.95/Veal choice $22.95
Accompaniments: Sauteed Onions $5.50, Creamed Spinach $5.50, Mushroom and Onion Sauté $6.50, Hollandaise or Bearnaise $1.95, Fresh Asparagus $8.50

Impressions:

Hy's main floor typifies the classic steak house with low lighting, starched tablecloths, and dark woods surrounding an open-hearth grill. However, up a few stairs patrons enter a plush tropical-toned dining room where a quieter experience awaits. Regardless, tuxedoed waiters serve a diverse menu of kiawe grilled meats, seafood, and Continental specialties. Tableside preparation might be a dying art, but not at Hy's. Diners can enjoy wines by the bottle or by the glass from the house's extensive wine list. Valet parking is available at the door.

Honolulu

India House Restaurant
University Square Shopping Center
2633 South King Street
Honolulu, HI 96826
808-955-7552
Web: None
Hours: L 11:00 AM-2:00 PM Mo-Sa
D 5:00 PM-9:30 PM Mo-Sa
D 5:00 PM-9:00 PM Su
Cards: MC V
Dress: Casual
Style: Indian $$

Menu Sampler:

Breakfast:
N/A
Lunch/Dinner:
Appetizers: Samosas-crisp pastry cones stuffed with potatoes, vegetables, and peas (4 pieces) $6.50, Pakoras-spicy vegetable fritters (tempura) $6.50, Paneer Pakoras $8.75, Papdums-delicious spicy crisp wafers $3.00
Soups: Mulligatawny-delicately spiced chicken soup cooked in tandoori oven $2.50, Vegetarian Soup $3.50
House Specialties: All served with naan bread, rice pullao, vegetable curry. Tandoori Chicken-chicken marinated in spices, herbs and yogurt and baked in a tandoori oven $15.95, Boti Kabob-choice cubes of marinated lamb, skewered w/onion, bell pepper and tomato $16.95, Fish Tikka-marinated, skewered $16.95
Ala Carte: Tandoori Specials using fish, chicken, lamb $9.95, Chicken Curry $9.95, Chicken or Lamb Vindaloo-highly spiced chicken or lamb cooked with potatoes in a tangy sauce $10.95, Lamb Spinach-lamb cooked with spinach and fresh Indian spices $10.95, Chana Masala-garbanzo beans cooked with fresh ginger and tomato $8.95, Palak Paneer-cottage cheese and spinach $8.95
Desserts: Halwas-cream of wheat pudding w/raisins, nuts and coconut $4.50

Impressions:

There is an area of South King Street near the University of Hawaii housing some great ethnic and alternative restaurants. This is where you'll find India House with its marvelous Northern Indian cuisine. Tablecloths and gracious service separate this establishment from your run of the mill storefront eatery. Park in the Central Pacific Bank lot on the corner, and get your ticket validated.

Chinatown

Indigo Eurasian Cuisine
1121 Nuuanu Ave
Honolulu, HI 96817
808-521-2900
www.indigo-hawaii.com
Hours: L 11:30 AM-2:00 PM Tu-Fr
D 6:00 PM-9:30 PM Tu-Sa
Cards: DC DIS MC V
Dress: Resort Casual
Style: Euro-Asian $$$

Menu Sampler:

Breakfast:
N/A
Lunch:
Cool Island Buffet: Lobster Potstickers 8.00, Lumpia Wrapped Shrimp w/chipotle aioli 9.00, Buddhist Bao Buns 7.00, Goat Cheese Won Tons 6.00
Starters: Roasted Tomato Garlic Crab Soup w/blue crab & cilantro pesto 6.50, Asian Caesar Salad with fresh poached ahi, grated parmesan 10.95
Entrées: Grilled Island Breast of Chicken with Indigo peanut sauce $13.50
Dinner:
Starters: Chinese Gin Doi w/roasted duck and dried apricots 7.50
Soups & Salads: Toasted Pecan Crusted Chevre and grilled portabella mushrooms w/plum vinaigrette 9.75, Nalo Farms Mesclen Greens with hibiscus mango vinaigrette 6.25, Roasted Tomato Garlic Crab Soup 6.75
Entrées: Grilled Shrimp with Thai macadamia nut pesto and green papaya slaw 21.25, Grilled Rib Eye Beef w/Black Bean Beurre Blanc Sauce & mashed potatoes 22.95, Mongolian Lamb Chops w/minted tangerine sauce 25.75, Cates Ocean Raised Moi Roasted in Banana Leaf & cocoa bean curry 21.50
Desserts: Apple Lemongrass Crisp served with Vanilla Gelato 6.25, Ginger Crème Brulee 5.25, Rich Goat Cheesecake with ginger lime sauce 5.50

Impressions:

Indigo invokes a New Orleans atmosphere with its brick walls, iron balconies, and hanging plants. Located in one of the oldest buildings in Chinatown, this downtown restaurant delivers exotic flavors borrowed with abandon from all around the world. The proprietor calls his offerings Eurasian, but from our viewpoint it looks more like Eclectic Global. This is a lively place in the evening with unique pupus, live music, and interesting crowd.

North Shore

Jameson's By The Sea

62-540 Kamehameha Hwy
Haleiwa, HI 96712
808-637-4336
Web: None
Hours: B 9:00 AM-12:00 PM SaSu
L 11:00 AM-5:00 PM
D 5:00 PM-9:00 PM
Cards: AE DC DIS JCB MC V
Dress: Casual
Style: Amer/Sea $$$

Menu Sampler:

Breakfast:
Saturday and Sunday only from 9AM-12 PM. All menu items under $12.00.
Lunch:
Appetizers: Cajun Chicken Wings $8.95, Thai Shrimp Summer Rolls with avocado, mint, carrots and greens in rice paper w/a spicy dipping sauce $12.95
Entrées: Grilled Crab and Shrimp with cheddar cheese on sourdough bread with choice of fries or cole slaw $13.95, Curried Chicken Salad served in a papaya $13.95, Teriyaki Chicken with sides $14.95, New York Steak with sides $24.95.
Dinner:
Appetizers: Salmon Pate $10.95, Fried Calamari with marinara sauce $10.95,
Entrées: All served with steamed white rice, garlic linguini, Oriental fried rice or potatoes and steamed vegetables in season. New York Steak, broiled to order $26.95, Sweet Australian Lobster Tail, broiled, served with Beurre Blanc Sauce and Drawn Butter $Market Price, Baked Stuffed Shrimp (Great!) stuffed with breadcrumbs, crabmeat and cheese topped with hollandaise $24.95, Teriyaki Chicken, boneless breast marinated and sautéed to a golden brown $17.95, Seafood served Diablo Style or Scampi Style on a bed of linguine $22.95. Note the daily fresh fish specials and their creative preparations.

Impressions:

Jameson's is one of those places that pulls people off the highway. Travelers circling the island will be particularly interested in the weekend breakfast and daily lunch offerings. As things quiet down in the evening, this North Shore beach house goes to a traditional steak and seafood menu. The laid back setting is a perfect fit for most island visitors; it's called sunshine, seafood, and suds!

Honolulu

Jimbo's Restaurant

1936 South King Street
Honolulu, HI 96826
808-947-2211
Web: None
Hours: L 11:00 AM-2:50 PM
D 5:00 PM-9:50 PM
Cards: MC V-Cash Only for Carryout
Dress: Casual
Style: Japan $

Menu Sampler:

Breakfast:

N/A

Lunch/Dinner:

Udon- homemade noodles hot, cold or yaki (stir-fried) with: Fish Cake and Green Onions $5.40, Beef & Vegetable $6.75, Bukkake-Tempura Chip & Vegetable with dark broth $7.40, Udon with dipping sauce $5.40, Stir Fried Udon with tofu & vegetables $6.75, Hot Chicken Udon $6.75 Salad Udon of cold skinny udon w/fresh vegetables & shrimp or chicken $8.25, Katsu or Tako & Vegetable $7.75. All above may be made w/skinny udon or soba $1.50 extra
Donburi: Various toppings of meats, seafood, vegetable or tempura with egg on hot rice- Chicken & Egg $6.95, Pork Katsu & Egg $7.95, Shrimp & Vegetable Tempura with egg $9.45, Tofu & Egg $6.95, Shrimp Tempura $7.95
Curry Rice: Corn Curry w/chicken or beef on rice $7.60,with pork katsu $8.65, Pork Katsu Curry on rice $7.65, Beef or Chicken Curry $6.60, Plain $5.60
Side Orders: Miso Soup $1.50, Green Salad $4.05, Rice $1.10, Hiyayakko-cold tofu $3.50, Ten Mori-mix tempura platter $8.10, Octopus Tempura $3.95, Vegetable Tempura Platter $6.95, Kayaku Musubi $1.85, Potato Salad $1.50,
Dessert: Green Tea Ice Cream with Azuki Beans $2.50, Lychee Sorbet $2.50

Impressions:

Jimbo's is the kind of place local Japanese families and businessmen go to eat. The menu offers dishes that ordinary people enjoy as they get on with their daily lives. Call it Japanese comfort food if you will, but udon and katsu have a lot more in common with hamburgers and fried chicken than they do with sukiyaki or shabu shabu. We were impressed with the relaxed atmosphere, as the small restaurant filled up quickly after they opened, but never seemed overly busy. Parking is limited out front, so plan on arriving early or look along the street.

Honolulu

John Dominis Restaurant Authors' Favorite

Kewalo Basin
43 Ahui St
Honolulu, HI 96813
808-523-0955
www.johndominis.com

Hours: Su Bru 9:00 AM-1:00 PM
D 6:00 PM-9:00 PM
Cards: AE CB DC JCB MC V
Dress: Evening Aloha
Style: Sea $$$$

Menu Sampler:

Breakfast:
Sunday Brunch $31.95 Extensive selection of seafood and traditional foods
Lunch:
N/A
Dinner:
Appetizers: Smoked Salmon w/condiments $9.95, Escargot Dijonaise Style in Puff Pastry $9.95, Caesar Salad in a bread basket $6.95, Oysters Rockefeller with fennel butter and Pernod, topped with hollandaise $10.95
Entrées: Fresh Island Moi steamed with thin slices of ginger, scallions, lemon shoyu, cilantro & hot peanut oil; Szechuan style with a spicy sweet-sour sauce $29.95, Seafood Bouillabaisse $35.00, Grilled Miso Salmon in sake broth with baby bok choy $28.95, Angus Tenderloin of Beef with potato, vegetables, green peppercorn and brandy $29.95, Macadamia Nut Breaded Veal Piccata with lemon butter, capers and Japanese eggplant $22.95, Wok Fried Caramelized Tiger Prawns with fried rice and Oriental vegetables $34.95

Impressions:

In the midst of all the commercial activity between Waikiki and downtown Honolulu, you'll find a jewel of a restaurant. There on the end of a wharf sits John Dominis. Although the area speaks of early industrial revolution, the panoramic view enjoyed by diners is unparalleled. Inside, the salt-water pond winds its way through the restaurant further enhancing the upscale atmosphere, while outside, the surfers give a pre-sunset show. The menu reflects the fresh fish brought into the docks, so inquire about the daily specials. Sunday Brunch is a bountiful feast, and dinner has never disappointed us. Reservations are always recommended.

North Shore

Kahuku Shrimp Trucks
Kamehameha Hwy
Kahuku, HI 96731
Phone: -------
Web: None
Hours: 10:00 AM-6:00 PM
Cards: None
Dress: Casual
Style: Sea $$

Menu Sampler:

Breakfast:
N/A

Lunch/Dinner:
Plate Lunch Style Shrimp includes two-scoop rice and one scoop macaroni salad: Garlic Butter, Tempura, Western BBQ, Cocktail, Hot and Spicy, or Coconut Lemon Sauce $10-$11. Other choices include Whole Head-On Shrimp boiled or fried , Mahi Mahi, Snow Crab. Some have intriguing side dishes to offer as found at Macky's-pineapple slice, steamed Okinawan sweet potato, and a tossed green salad with vinaigrette. These venues begin at Punalu'u and continue counter-clockwise up through Kahuku.

Impressions:

Drive to the north tip of Oahu and you'll find a thriving cottage industry. There along the highway people have set up roadside businesses reminiscent of Route 66. Instead of beaded belts and rubber tomahawks, the specialties of the house revolve around locally produced food products. Fresh prawns and shrimp from the nearby aquaculture farms appear in various preps. Depending on the location you may also find Kahuku corn and various tropical fruits. Besides the usual two-scoop rice and mac salad that comes with plate lunch, soda, bottled water, and plenty of napkins are available. Seating means picnic tables under canvas roofs. Watch for the signs. Stop and talk story on your way around the island.

Honolulu

Kaka'ako Kitchen
Ward Center
1200 Ala Moana Blvd-Bay1
Honolulu, HI 96813
808-596-7488
Web: None
Hours: B 7:00 AM-10:00 AM Mo-Fr
B 7:00 AM-11:00 AM SaSu
L/D 10:30 AM-9:00 PM Mo-Th
L/D 10:30 AM-10:00 PM Fr
L/D 11:30 AM-10:00 PM Sa
L/D 11:30 AM-5:00 PM Su
Cards: AE JCB MC V
Dress: Casual
Style: Haw-Reg $

Menu Sampler:

Breakfast:
Fried Rice 3.95, with one egg add .95, Banana Poi Bread 1.95. All the following served with white rice and a homemade biscuit with lilikoi butter, Pan-Seared Mahimahi and Two Eggs 7.25, Loco Moco 6.75, Kaka'ako Kitchen Omelet with three eggs, bacon, Spam, char siu chicken, Portuguese sausage, kamaboko and green onion 6.95, Corned Beef Hash with two eggs 6.95, French Toast 4.95
Lunch/Dinner:
Local Plates & Sandwiches: Shichimi Seared Ahi Sandwich with tobiko aioli, soy-sake drizzle on taro bun with fries or mac salad $8.75, Tempura Mahimahi on taro roll $7.50, Grilled Pastrami with Swiss cheese, house-made Russian dressing, on whole wheat hoagie bun $7.75, BLT and Crab Sandwich with basil mayonnaise on toasted herb bread $9.75, Chinese Char Siu Chicken Salad 8.50
Gourmet Plates: Crispy Fried Sweet Chili Chicken with rice, greens or mac salad $7.75, Chicken Piccata over Linguine w/lemon caper sauce, taro roll $8.95, Fire Roasted Fillet of Wild Salmon with cilantro butter 10.75

Impressions:

Kaka'ako Kitchen is an affordable fast food outlet for Chef Russell Siu's Hawaii Regional Cuisine. The no-frills approach might look like plate lunch, but it has a gourmet twist. Customers can expect bare floors, plastic chairs, and Styrofoam containers. However, they will also find exciting cuisine at lunch wagon prices. Try to avoid peak meal times. This place is very popular with the local business crowd. Parking is free in the Ward Center deck adjacent to the shop.

Diamond Head

Kapiolani Community College

Ka'ikena Dining Room
Ohelo Building, 2nd Floor
4303 Diamond Head Road
Honolulu, HI 96816
808-734-9499
http://food.kcc.hawaii.edu/kaikena

Hours: L Seating at 11:00 AM, 11:30 AM, Noon
D Seating at 5:30 PM & 6:00 PM
Cards: MC V
Dress: Resort Casual
Style: Fine $$

Menu Sampler:

Lunch:
Menus rotate frequently. Complete lunch includes choice of soup or salad, entrée, dessert, and beverage. Choice of Starters: Mixed Greens with Asparagus Vinaigrette or Tuscan White Bean Soup. Choice of Entrée: Grilled Snapper with Sauce Vierge, saffron spinach, garlic whipped potatoes, vegetables $15.95, Ravioli with Sundried Tomatoes and Ricotta Stuffing, creamy mushroom sauce $13.95, Scampi Style Shrimp with Pasta in Garlic Butter Sauce, vegetables $14.95, Braised Lamb Shanks, polenta, tomato confit, vegetables $15.95, Roast Cornish Game Hen, polenta, grilled vegetables $14.95
Dessert: Your choice of items such as Fresh Baked Apple Pie, Strawberry Shortcake, Chocolate Cream Pie, Orange Passion Chiffon Pie, Assorted French Pastries on a luscious pastry cart.
Beverages: Kona Coffee, Decaf Coffee, Hot or Iced Tea

Impressions:

If you would like to see where some of Hawaii's finest chefs got their start, drive up the side of Diamond Head to Kapiolani Community College and check out their Culinary Arts Program. As part of their education students operate the Ka 'Ikena Laua'e Restaurant. Inside this fine dining room students prepare and present a series of gourmet menus. Reservations are a must for these events so be sure to call ahead. Its also a good idea to check their website as the schedule varies with the school year. BYOB is permitted, so don't forget the wine!

Waikiki

Keo's in Waikiki
2028 Kuhio Ave
Honolulu, HI 96815
808-951-9355
www.keosthaicuisine.com
Hours: B 7:30 AM-11:00 AM
L 11:00 AM-2:00 PM
D 5:00 PM-10:30 PM
Cards: AE DC DIS JCB MC V
Dress: Resort Casual
Style: Thai $$

Menu Sampler:

Breakfast:
Two Eggs with choice of meat and rice or hash brown $6.25, Asian Breakfast of broiled salmon, seasoned seaweed, pickled vegetables, steamed rice, miso soup and one egg $9.95, Buttermilk Pancakes with bananas or strawberries $4.75
Lunch/Dinner:
Appetizers: Golden Triangles (4)-tiger prawns wrapped in pastry triangle shells with shiitake mushrooms, water chestnuts, chives and fresh spices, deep-fried and served with tangerine hot sauce $7.95, Crispy Shrimp or Calamari lightly coated with rice flour, deep-fried, served with a vinaigrette hot sauce $10.95
Soups: Thai Ginger Soup with fresh Thai ginger from our farms, vegetables, coconut milk, green onion, spices, Thai parsley and seafood $4.25
Salads: Glass Noodle Salad with shrimp, onion, mint, lime juice, spices $13.95, Beef Larb-famous spicy salad with fresh lettuce and cabbage $13.95
Entrées: Thai Style Pork Chops marinated in spices $14.95, Hot Basil with chicken or beef $11.95, Honey Glazed Grilled Thai Style Spare Ribs $14.95, Chicken Panang Curry $12.95, Thai Crispy Fish with chili sauce $17.95
Desserts: Thai Tapioca $3.95, Mango Sorbet $5.95, Flan $3.95, Mud Pie $6.95

Impressions:

Twenty-five years ago Keo broke new ground by being the first to serve Thai cuisine in Honolulu. This was a natural success in a market attuned to Asian dining styles. Here you had ingredients people were accustomed to being served with zest like no one had experienced. Today this spacious Waikiki restaurant features tropical café style dining complete with rattan chairs and umbrella-covered tables. Normally Thai restaurants are lunch and dinner venues but Keo opens up for breakfast as well. All three are expertly prepared and fairly priced.

Kaimuki

Kim Chee II
3569 Waialae Ave.
Honolulu, HI 96816
808-737-7733
Web: None
Hours: LD 10:30 AM-9:00 PM
Cards: AE MC V
Dress: Casual
Style: Kor $

Menu Sampler:

Breakfast:
N/A
Lunch/Dinner:
Lunch Special includes Bar-B-Q Chicken, Meat Jun, & Man Doo with vegetables & rice $6.90, **Dinner Special** includes Bar-B-Q Short Rib, Shrimp Tempura, Fried Man Doo & Meat Jun $10.90
Combo Plates: Combo Plate of Bar-B-Q Beef, Chicken & Fried Man Doo with vegetables & rice $6.90, Kal Bee of Bar-B-Q Short Ribs with vegetables & rice $14.90, Chicken Katsu with vegetables & rice $7.50, Bibim Bap-Rice with vegetables, egg, and beef or chicken $7.50, Bibim Kooksoo of noodles with vegetables and beef or chicken $6.30, Fried Man Doo with vegetables & rice $6.30, Spicy Shoyu Chicken with vegetables & rice $7.50, Chicken Tofu with vegetables $7.50, Kim Chee Restaurant Special of Bar-B-Q Short Rib, Beef, Chicken, Meat Jun & Fried Man Doo with vegetables & rice $14.90
Fish: Fried Corvina Fish with rice $8.50, Shrimp Tempura with rice $8.50
Soup: Miso Soup with rice $7.50, Man Doo Kook-dumpling soup $7.50, Oxtail Soup with rice $9.00, Duk Man Doo-rice cake and man doo in soup $7.50
Side Orders: Butterfish $9.90, Mackeral $7.50, Fried Tofu $3.90, Kim Chee $2.00, Squid $7.50, Mahimahi Katsu $7.50, Dried Radish $4.00, Fish Jun $7.50

Impressions:

Kim Chee II is another one of those local favorites that has become an island institution. Kaimuki residents gather in this over-sized diner for the good food, fair prices, and convivial atmosphere. In keeping with tradition, the Korean menu stresses lean meats, fresh vegetables, and healthy preparations. Some items are offered in small portions for children and light appetites. If you've never tried Korean food, this would be a good place to start. You'll find Kim Chee II in Kaimuki's restaurant row. There's a large parking lot in the rear.

Honolulu

Kincaid's Fish, Chop, and Steak House
Ward Warehouse
1050 Ala Moana Blvd
Honolulu, HI 96813
808-591-2005
Web: None
Hours: L 11 AM-5 PM
D 5-10 PM
Cards: AE DC DIS JCB MC V
Dress: Resort Casual
Style: Ec/Stk $$$

Menu Sampler:

Breakfast:
N/A
Lunch:
Starters: Broadway Pea Salad with peas, water chestnuts, sugar snap peas and bacon with white pepper dressing $5.50, Onion Soup baked with cheeses $6.95
Entrées: Sesame Chicken Salad $10.95, Prime Rib French Dip on a garlic butter toasted roll with au jus $11.95, Dungeness Crab and Artichoke Sandwich $11.95, Oven Roasted Chicken Dijon with panko flakes and parmesan $12.95
Dinner:
Appetizers: Warm Brie with Macadamia Nut Crust, seared and drizzled with balsamic-honey glaze $9.50, Coconut Tiger Prawns w/Cajun Marmalade $10.95
Entrées: Almond Crusted Sea Scallops with champagne beurre blanc $21.95, Roasted Chicken Breast Dijon with panko flakes and parmesan $16.95, Filet Mignon grilled, served with steakhouse butter and crispy onion strings $32.50, Baby Back Ribs with Hawaiian Barbecue Sauce, fries, slaw $18.95, Grilled New Zealand Rack of Lamb, in a Hunan Style Barbecue Sauce $25.95
Desserts: Kincaid's Original Burnt Cream $4.50, Roasted Pear Bread Pudding with Bourbon-Custard Sauce $6.50, Island Style Cheesecake $5.50

Impressions:

Beveled glass, multi-level floors, lots of brass, and a glossy wood décor are all part of the pleasant atmosphere you'll find at Kincaid's. Of course the view out over the park to the ocean doesn't hurt either. The menu does a first rate job of combining variety with innovative preparations. Kincaid's is known for their consistent quality, friendly staff, and reasonable prices. This is a favorite with the local business set. There's plenty of free parking in the shopping center lot.

Windward

Kin Wah Chop Suey

45-588 Kamehameha Hwy
Kaneohe, HI 96744
808-247-4812
Web: None
Hours: LD 10:00 AM-9:00 PM
Cards: AE DIS MC V
Dress: Casual
Style: Chi $

Menu Sampler:

Breakfast:
N/A
Lunch/Dinner:
Soup: Bird Nest Soup 10.50, Scallop Soup 8.00, Watercress with Fishcake Soup 5.25, Hot Sour Soup 5.75, Shark Fin Soup19.00, Long Rice with Pork Soup 5.25
Chop Suey: Kin Wah Chop Suey 5.00, Shrimp Chop Suey 5.75
Entrees: Pork or Beef with Ginger & Green Onion 6.00, with Green Pepper & Black Bean Sauce 5.50, with Tomato 5.50, with Eggplant 6.00; Char Siu 4.50, Sweet Sour Pork 5.25, Shrimp Pineapple 7.25, Kun Pao Shrimp 7.50, Lobster with Curry Sauce 14.50, Oyster Roll with Pork 5.75, Pot Roast Chicken with Oyster Sauce 6.00, Chicken with Chinese Peas 6.00, Lemon Chicken 6.00, Crispy Chicken 6.00, Roast Duck with Gravy 6.25, Stuffed Duck 7.75
Chow Mein: Kin Wah Chow Mein 5.50, Pot Roast Chicken Chow Mein 6.50
Gau Gee: Plain Crispy Gau Gee (10 pcs.) 4.75, Soft Gau Gee with Chicken & Vegetables (Gravy) 6.25, Wor Gau Gee Mein Soup 5.50, Gau Gee Soup 5.00
Sizzling Platters: Mongolian Beef 6.50, Stuffed Tofu with Pork 5.75
Plates: "A" -Beef with Broccoli, Gon Lo Mein, Lemon Chicken, Crispy Wun Ton & Rice $5.25, "B"-Pot Roast Pork, Spareribs, Beef Broccoli, Crispy Gau Gee, Fried Shrimp, Rice $6.00

Impressions:

Kin Wah Chop Suey is local party heaven. Visitors will have no problem getting a table for lunch, but watch out for dinnertime! That's when you'll find groups of 30, 45, or 60 residents sitting together celebrating one of life's milestones. This is a chop suey house with the comfort food and reasonable prices we have come to expect from such establishments. Now here's an inside tip you won't see anywhere else; this place has got to have the most reasonably priced top-shelf call drinks in Hawaii. Maybe that's why their functions are so popular! Look for Kin Wah in the shopping building behind the Island Mini-Mart.

Oahu Dining

Honolulu

Kirin

2518 S. Beretania
Honolulu, HI 96826
808-942-1888
Web: None
Hours: L 11:00 AM-2:00 PM
D 5:00 PM-Midnight
Cards: AE DC DIS JCB MC V
Dress: Resort Casual
Style: Chi $$$

Menu Sampler:

Breakfast:
N/A

Lunch:
Appetizer: Deep Fried Bacon Roll with scallop & shrimp $14.95, Drunken Chicken-northern style $7.95, Spring Rolls $6.95, Deep Fried Won Ton $6.95
Entrées: Fried Shrimp with honey glazed walnut $15.95, Fried Fillet of Squid with peppery salt-spicy $9.95, Fried Saucy Spare Ribs "Wu Shi" Style $10.95

Dinner:
Appetizer: Sliced Five Spiced Beef Shank-spicy $9.95, Spring Rolls $7.95
Soup: Each serves 4 people. Hot & Sour Soup-spicy northern style $8.95, Crab Meat with dried fish maw soup $15.95, Shredded Dried Scallop with yellow chive soup $15.95, Eight Treasures & Tofu Soup $9.95, Chicken & Corn $8.95
Entrées: Fried Fillet of Uhu with peppery salt-spicy $14.95, Braised Sea Cucumber with shrimp roe-northern style $16.95, Saute Oyster with Szechuan garlic sauce-spicy northern style $13.95, Peking Duck (whole) with 12 thin pancakes $36.00, Baked Sesame Pocket Buns stuffed Peking style with minced pork and mustard stem $6.95, Maine Lobster $16/#, Dungeness Crab $16/#
Dessert: Sesame Mochi Balls in Red Bean Soup $2.95, Green Tea Ice Cream $3.25, Lychee Sherbet $3.25, Almond Tofu with fruit cocktail $2.95

Impressions:

Entering this cool, dark restaurant after leaving the bright, bustling world of South Beretania is a study in contrast. This traditionally decorated dining spot serves authentic Szechuan, Hunan, Peking, and Cantonese cuisine. Live seafood is king here and would be a wise choice for the discriminating diner. Note the late night dining hours. You can get lost in the Waianae's and still make it back in time for dinner. This is one of those places where valet parking is a must.

Windward

Koa House

46-126 Kahuhipa
Kaneohe, HI 96744
808-235-5772, Fax 808-247-8806
Web: None
Hours: BL 6:30 AM-2:00 PM
Cards: MC V
Dress: Casual
Style: Amer/Isl $

Menu Sampler:

Breakfast:

Eggs: served with choice of rice, toast or home fried potatoes, Corned Beef Hash & Eggs, Vienna Sausage & Eggs, Spam & Eggs, or Hamburger Patty & Eggs 4.95, Portuguese Sausage & Eggs 4.75, Canadian Bacon & Eggs 5.25, Steak & Eggs 6.95, Scottish Bangers & Eggs 5.25, Mahimahi & Eggs 5.95, Kalbi & Eggs 6.95, Eggs Benedict 5.75/6.75, Vinha D'alhos & Eggs-Portuguese marinated pork 6.25, add 1.00 for 3 pc buttermilk pancakes
Griddle: Sweet Bread French Toast 4.50, Banana or Blueberry Pancakes 3.75, Pecan Waffles 3.75, Crepe Suzettes-Sour Cream & Lemon 5.75

Lunch:

Sandwiches & Burgers: choice of tossed salad, potato salad, macaroni salad or home fries, Fried Shrimp, Bacon & Cheese Sandwich 6.25, Chili Burger 4.75, Mushroom Burger 4.95, Shrimp Burger 5.50, BLT 4.45, Steak Sandwich 6.25
Entrees: served with a hot vegetable and choice of French bread or rice, tossed salad, potato salad, macaroni salad, or home fries; Sautéed Shrimp and Mahi 6.95, Mahi Juhn-lightly breaded in egg batter 6.25, Teriyaki Hamburger Steak 5.75, Hamburger Steak with Brown Gravy 5.75, Vinha D'alhos (Portuguese marinated pork) 6.75, Chicken Cutlet 5.75, Chili & Spaghetti served with French Bread 4.95, Chili & Rice or Crackers 3.95, Kalbi 6.95

Impressions:

If you're driving around the island, take the Kahuhipa turn-off from the Kahekili Highway and look on the right hand side for Koa House. This local favorite has been around for a long time as witnessed by the priceless koa wood interior that gives the restaurant its name. The menu has international influences designed to please a wide range of tastes. Locals consider this to be a top budget choice as the pricing is very reasonable. Even the lunchtime entrees come in below six dollars. There's a small lot in front, but be prepared to park along the street.

Hawaii Kai

Kona Brewing Company

Koko Marina Center
Kalanianole Highway
Honolulu, HI 96825
808-394-5662
www.KonaBrewingCo.com
Hours: LD 11:00 AM-10:00 PM Mo-Su
Cards: DC DIS MC V
Dress: Casual
Style: Amer/Isl $$

Menu Sampler:

Breakfast:
N/A

Lunch/Dinner:
Pupu: Roasted Garlic served with toasted spent grain focaccia and warmed creamy Gorgonzola cheese $5.99, Pele's Fire Wings-Fire Rock Marinated Wings with a spicy teriyaki glaze, side of Ranch $6.49, Cheesy Garlic Bread with fresh garlic aioli, mozzarella & Parmesan with a side of marinara $3.99
Salads: Greek Salad with cucumbers, Kalamata olives, Maui onions, pepperoncini, tomatoes & feta cheese atop Kahuku romaine with balsamic vinaigrette $6.49/$9.49, Strawberry Spinach Salad with toasted macadamia nuts, Gorgonzola, Maui onions, and strawberry vinaigrette $7.99/$9.99
Sandwiches: All are served with Kettle Chips, substitute salad for $1.99. Porterhouse Dip of roast beef marinated and cooked in our Black Sand Porter, topped with roasted red onions and melted cheddar & mozzarella cheeses, Porter au jus for dipping $9.99, Imu Style Kalua Pork Sandwich with cabbage, pineapple mesquite BBQ sauce, roasted onions, cheddar & mozzarella $8.99
Gourmet Pizzas: Small 10", Medium 12", and Large 14". All pizzas are available as Calzones. Kona Wild Mushroom Pizza-garlic infused olive oil base, mozzarella & chevre, wild mushrooms, roasted garlic, roasted onions & red peppers, Thai Chicken or Shrimp with spicy peanut Thai base, roasted red peppers, mozzarella, green onions, sesame seeds, $13.99/$17.99/$20.99
Beer: State of the art draught system for twelve full time brews

Impressions:

The Kona Brewing Company has brought its Big Island charm, handcrafted beer and fun food menu to the Koko Marina Center at Hawaii Kai. This dockside bar and grill targets grazers looking for light bites and a party atmosphere. Those returning from Hanauma Bay will appreciate this casual lunch stop.

Oahu Dining

North Shore

Kua 'Aina Sandwich Shop
66-160 Kamehameha Highway
Haleiwa, HI 96712
808-637-6067
Web: None
Hours: LD 11:00 AM-8:00 PM
Cards: None
Dress: Casual
Style: Amer $

Menu Sampler:

Breakfast:
N/A
Lunch/Dinner:
Salads: Tossed Green $2.85/$3.75, Tuna or Turkey Salad $5.30
Kua Aina Burgers-Choice of bread or rolls- ⅓lb/ ½ lb- Hamburger $5.70/$6.10, Cheeseburger $6.00/$6.40, Bacon Burger $6.10/$6.50, Ortega Burger $6.00/$6.40, Avocado Burger $6.40/$6.75, Pineapple Burger $6.00/$6.40, Kiddie Burger $3.60, Extra toppings available.
Sandwiches: Mahi Mahi $6.20, Teri Chicken $6.20, BLT $5.40, Hot Roast Beef $5.65, Cold Roast Turkey $5.65, Mahi, Ortega & Cheese $6.85, Roast Beef & Avocado $6.60, Grilled Eggplant & Peppers $5.75, Turkey & Avocado $6.60
Sides: French Fries $1.80/$2.60, Cole Slaw $.60, Pickle $.25, Pepperoncini $.60
Cold Drinks: Small $1.05, Medium $1.25, Large $1.40, BYOB Free

Impressions:

There are times when only a burger will do. If that mood strikes you, go for the best. Cruise on up to the North Shore to the small village of Haleiwa and try Kua'Aina Sandwich Shop. The food here has always been top-notch but until recently was difficult to get because of diminutive premises. Kua 'Aina has moved into new digs a couple hundred yards down the street. Now they have plenty of seating outside on the porch or yard and in the dining room. Just step inside and place your order at the counter before finding a table. When your name is called pick up your food. Your burgers will come with ⅓# or ½# patties served medium unless otherwise requested on a choice of Kaiser roll or breads and a variety of toppings. The fries are great. A single basket easily shares for two. Gourmet sandwiches are also available. There's free parking in the rear of the building. Take note that no credit cards are accepted, so bring cash!

Waikiki

Kyoya
2057 Kalakaua Ave.
Honolulu, HI 96815
808-947-3911
Web: None
Hours: L 11:00 AM-1:30 PM XSu
D 5:30 PM-9:30 PM
Cards: AE DC DIS JCB MC V
Dress: Resort Casual
Style: Japan $$$$

Menu Sampler:

Breakfast:
N/A
Lunch:
Teishoku-All include by kobachi, salad, tsukemono, misoshiru & rice. Shrimp Tempura & Butterfish Misoyaki $14, Chicken Katsu $12, Tonkatsu $13, Sashimi $20, Cha Soba $9, Tempura Soba or Udon $11, Sushi & Sashimi
Nabemono-Shabu Shabu or Beef Sukiyaki, Udonsuki-min. two $25/person
Dessert: Papaya $4, Ice Cream $3, Iced Coffee $5
Dinner:
Teishoku-All accompanied by salad, tsukemono, misoshiru, rice & dessert. Sashimi $28, Butterfish Misoyaki $24, Tonkatsu $24, Beef Teriyaki $25,
Nabemono-Shabu Shabu-slices of beef, fresh vegetables, and long rice simmered in a kobu broth and served with two dipping sauces, Sukiyaki-slices of beef & fresh vegetables cooked in a tasty Sukiyaki sauce, or Udonsuki-thick udon noodles, chicken, shellfish & vegetables all simmered in a light broth-Prepared at your table w/accompanying dishes and dessert- $35/$45/$55
Ala Carte: Beef Teriyaki $18, Soft Shell Crab $17, Shrimp and Vegetables Tempura $15.00, Edamame $7, Tsukemono $7/$12, Sunomono $8, Wafu Steak $20, Chicken Karaage $10, Salmon Shioyaki $14, Maguro Poki $6
Sake Samplers: Reishu or Atsukan-three samples in each group $10.00

Impressions:

Everything about Kyoya is classic Japanese. This Waikiki tradition has been around for fifty years, so you know it works. The menu offers patrons a choice of dining styles as well as dining rooms. Different moods and different times of day call for different approaches. This upscale restaurant does it all well.

Honolulu

La Mariana Sailing Club

Authors' Favorite

50 Sand Island Access Road
Honolulu, HI 96817
808-848-2800
Web: None
Hours: L 11:00 AM-3:00 PM
D 5:00 PM-9:00 PM
Cards: AE MC V
Dress: Casual
Style: Isl/Sea $$

Menu Sampler:

Breakfast:
N/A
Lunch:
Salads: Salad Platter with Tomato & Hard Boiled Egg & Garlic Bread $5.25, topped with Shrimp, Turkey, or Chicken $8.75, Tuna $7.75, Avocado $7.50
Sandwiches: Bacon or Bay Shrimp & Avocado on wheat bread with alfalfa sprouts, tomato $7.75, Mahi Mahi Fish & Chips $8.25, Club Special $8.25
Entrees: 6 oz NY Steak Sandwich with cole slaw $9.50, Linguini in Garlic Butter, Parmesan Cheese & Garlic Bread $7.25, French Dip au jus $8.25
Specials: All are served with vegetable & choice of starch. Mahi Mahi Sautéed, Broiled or Cajun Style $9.00, Shrimp Curry with Vegetables $9.00, Ahi or Calamari Steak-choice of prep $Mkt, Eggs Benedict with Ham & Turkey on English Muffin $5.00/$9.25, Sautéed Island Chicken Linguini $9.00
Dinner:
Appetizers: Mushrooms sautéed w/garlic & white wine $8.75, Tako Poke $9.50
Seafood Specialties: Shrimp Scampi $16.25, Seafood Brochette of shrimp, scallop, mahi mahi, onion, green pepper, tomato $17.00Ahi Cajun Black & Blue New Orleans Style $Mkt, Stuffed (with seafood) Eggplant au Gratin $17.00
Meat & Poultry: Prime Rib $16.75/$17.75, Garlic Steak w/Anchovies $16.75

Impressions:

Have you ever wondered where the objets d'art migrate to after a legendary Honolulu hot spot closes? La Mariana has often been the answer. This kitschy, comfortable collection of bamboo, fish tanks and Hawaiiana is located in the midst of the commercial/industrial bustle on Sand Island. The menu offers a variety of fare, but we favor the very reasonably priced fresh fish. Ask about the daily specials before ordering. Parking is tight at lunch. Go early.

Oahu Dining

Waikiki

La Mer

Authors' Favorite

Halekulani Hotel
2199 Kalia Road
Honolulu, HI 96815
808-923-2311
www.halekulani.com
Hours: D 6:00 PM-10:00 PM
Cards: AE DC DIS JCB MC V
Dress: Formal
Style: Fre $$$$

Menu Sampler:

Breakfast/Lunch:
N/A
Dinner:
Starters: Tartare of Hamachi, Ahi and Salmon with Three Caviars and Three Coulis 23.00, Soup of Mussels and Moano Fillets with saffron and chanterelles 14.00, Escargot in the manner of Provence 18.00, Gourmand Selection 36.00
Entrées: Lobster "Galette" of Basmati Rice and Roasted Opakapaka Sausage 43.00, Crispy Skin Fillet of Onaga with Truffle Jus, Tomato Confit and Fried Basil 39.00, Roasted Salmon and Salmon Tartare with a Meaux Mustard Sauce and Bouquet of Greens 36.00, Bouillabaise La Mer Style in a Puff Pastry 40.00, Kobe Style Filet of Beef Three Ways-Beef Carpaccio with a Parmesan Shaving, Tournedos of Beef with Bone marrow and Bordelaise Sauce, Sliced Filet of Beef on a Truffle Jus with Provencale Vegetables 48.00, Rack of Lamb with a Dijon Mustard Crust, Provencale Style Vegetables and Creamy Potatoes 43.00, Barbary Duck Breast Roasted with Lavender Honey, thigh Confit, Thyme and Garlic, Braised Belgian Endives 38.00, Selection of French Cheeses 14.00
Desserts: Painter's Palette with Almond Florentine, five sorbets, seasonal fruit and freshly pureed coulis: Pineapple Crème with lilikoi jaconde and sorbet $15

Impressions:

This restaurant is the premier venue in the Halekulani's dining collection. The hotel complex is an oasis in the heart of bustling Waikiki Beach, and La Mer is positioned to take advantage of all the grounds have to offer. Here Chef Yves Garnier combines classic techniques with French, Mediterranean, and island influences to create stellar results. No attention to detail is spared in presenting these masterpieces. Service at La Mer is second to none. This has long been the ultimate fine dining spot on Waikiki Beach. Reservations are imperative.

Niu Valley

Le Bistro

Authors' Favorite

Niu Valley Shopping Center
5730 Kalanianole Hwy
Honolulu, HI 96821
808-373-7990
Web: None
Hours: D 5:30 PM-9:00 PM XTu
Cards: AE MC V
Dress: Resort Casual
Style: Cont/Ec $$$

Menu Sampler:

Breakfast/Lunch:
N/A
Dinner:
Appetizers: Escargot De Bourgogne 7.8, Fricassee of Fresh Manila Clams 8.8, Today's Soupe 3.9, French Onion Soupe 5.8,Caesar Salade 5.8
Takanohana Grill: Takanohana Grilled Chicken w/white rice 14.8/16.8, Black Angus Beef skewers w/a light red wine sauce, white rice 14.8/16.8
Le Bistro Pastas: Gorgonzola Spaghettini with slivered almonds & cracked black pepper 13.8, Penne Pasta with Italian Sausage, spinach 14.8
Les Entrées: New Orleans "Miro Street" Style Scallops seared with a rich black pepper sauce 16.8/19.8, Classic French Bistro Steak-Rib Eye w/cognac, Roquefort Butter 21.8/25.8, Barbequed Lamb Chops glazed with Balsamic Vinegar 25.8, Seabass in Morels 25.8, Opakapaka Prossecco 25.8, Grilled Paillard of Chicken, Mushroom & Bacon w/garlic roasted potatoes 14.8/16.8, Salmon Grenobloise, North Atlantic, with white wine and capers 19.8, Lemon, Rosemary & Thyme Grilled Chicken with garlic roasted potatoes 14.8/16.8
Weekly Specials: Sunday-Osso Bucco, Monday-Surprise, Wednesday-Veal w/ wild mushrooms, cognac sauce, Thursday-Live Maine Lobster

Impressions:

On the mauka side of the highway between Diamond Head and Hawaii Kai there's a small shopping venue that houses a couple of great little restaurants. There in the Niu Valley Shopping Center you'll find Le Bistro serving upscale, eclectic continental cuisine to an equally upscale and eclectic crowd. Although the menu isn't extensive, it is well rounded, and everyone in your party should be able to find something to please. This is a chef owned and operated restaurant which accounts for the consistency in the quality of food and service.

Oahu Dining

Chinatown

Legend Seafood Restaurant
Chinatown Cultural Plaza
100 N. Beretania Street
Honolulu, HI 96817
808-532-1868
www.legendseafood.com
Hours: BL 8:00 AM-2:00 PM SaSu
BL 10:30 AM-2:00 PM Mo-Fr
D 5:30 PM-10:00 PM
Cards: AE DC JCB MC V
Dress: Casual
Style: Chi $$

Menu Sampler:

Breakfast/Lunch:
Dim Sum Service-Prices per Plate $2.15-$4.75
Dinner:
Appetizer: Chinese Chicken Salad with Jellyfish $11.95, Deep Fried Sliced Squid with Spicy Salt $7.95, Drunken Chicken $7.25, Crispy Spring Rolls $5.95
Soup: Shark's Fin Soup with Seafood $16.95, Conpoy Thick Soup $9.95
Entrées: Sautéed Sliced Beef with ginger & green onion on sizzling platter $8.95, Braised Tenderloin Chinese Style $11.95, Baked Live Lobster with butter $Mkt, Sautéed Seafood in Taro Basket $13.95, Sautéed Scallop Szechuan Style $13.95, Stir Fried Shredded Chicken with Spicy Sauce $8.50, Roast Duck (1/2) $11.50, Deep Fried Chicken Stuffed with Minced Shrimp (half) $18.00
Vegetable & Tofu: Stir Fried Ong Choy with Shredded Pepper & Preserved Bean Curd $7.50, Steamed Tofu w/shrimp, shrimp roe and shrimp sauce $9.50
Funn/Noodle/Rice: Stir Fried Look Funn with Beef and Black Bean Sauce $7.50, Fried Rice, Yong Chow Style $7.50, Malaysian Style Chow Funn $7.50

Impressions:

Imagine a bustling, Asian crowd filling a large dining room where English is definitely a second language, and you'll get a pretty close feel for the scene at Legend Seafood Restaurant. This is even more obvious on Saturday and Sunday mornings when the dim sum service starts at 8 AM. When the food carts come around, just point! Not only will the friendly staff help you make selections, but fellow diners will also offer their recommendations. We view this as the perfect lunch spot after spending a morning in the Chinatown markets. Be sure to use the parking deck IN the Chinese Cultural Plaza and get your ticket validated.

Kapahulu

Leonard's Bakery
933 Kapahulu Ave
Honolulu, HI 96815
808-737-5591
Web: None
Hours: 6:00 AM-9:00 PM
Cards: None
Dress: Casual
Style: Spec $

Menu Sampler:

Breakfast/Lunch/Dinner:
Malasadas $.66, Pastries such as Fruit & Custard Danish $.70, Donuts $.48-$.82 each, Pies-whole-Custard, Pumpkin, and Apple $5, Cream Pies $6.75, Cookies in packages $1.30-$3.50, Coffee, Tea, Bottled Water

Impressions:

Leonard's Bakery is a Honolulu institution. Besides their wonderful pastries, cakes, and pies they are renowned for making great malasadas. It seems that everyone in Hawaii needs a malasada fix now and then, and at a price of just sixty-six cents no one should go without! This treat can be compared to a rich donut minus the hole that is deep-fried and then sprinkled with sugar. Malasadas eaten hot with a cup of coffee or tea make a great breakfast.

Honolulu

Like Like Drive Inn Restaurant

745 Keeaumoku Street
Honolulu, HI 96816
808-941-2515
Web: None
Hours: BLD 24/7
Cards: None
Dress: Casual
Style: Amer $

Menu Sampler:

Breakfast:
Two eggs, choice of meat, choice of white rice, brown rice, hash brown potatoes, or toast $6.40, Ham & Cheese Omelette with choice of starch $6.90, Shrimp Omelette with choice of starch $7.65, Fresh Banana Hotcakes $5.45, Golden Brown French Toast $5.05, French Pancakes rolled with guava jelly $5.40, Thick Malted Waffle $5.15, Fresh papaya $3.00, Juice $2.35
Lunch/Dinner:
Salads: Chef's Salad $8.70, Shrimp Salad $8.65, Fruit Salad $7.75
Sandwiches: Hot Roast Beef with mashed potatoes & brown gravy $6.55, Hamburger $3.30, Grilled Mahi Mahi $4.65, Clubhouse w/French fries $6.55, Manhattan with bacon, turkey, tomato, lettuce and served with French fries $6.55, Fried or Deviled Egg Sandwich $3.15, Hot Dog $2.10
Entrées: US Choice Rib Steak with sautéed onions $12.00, Butterfish $9.00, Italian Spaghetti with meat sauce $6.85, Pork Chops with banana fritter $8.65, Hamburger Steak with sautéed onions and brown gravy $7.35, Shrimp Curry $8.95, Teriyaki Tenderloin of Beef (5 PM-5-AM) $8.35, Lamb Chops $8.65
Desserts: Our Famous Lemon Chiffon Pie $2.75, Carrot Cake $2.65, Peach Melba $4.10, Milk Shakes $3.30, Malts $3.45, Ice Cream Float $3.20

Impressions:

Like Like Drive Inn is no longer on the Like Like Highway. In fact, it's not even a drive inn! This popular Honolulu institution has grown into an expansive, full-service restaurant. Only the original sign remains to remind today's patrons of what once was. That doesn't mean the owners have forgotten their roots. One look at the menu will tell you that casual dining is still the rule. Expect large portions of island and mainland favorites at reasonable prices.

Chinatown

Little Village Noodle Shop Authors' Favorite

1113 Smith Street
Honolulu, HI 96817
808-545-3008
Web: None
Hours: LD 10:00 AM-Midnight
Cards: AE MC V
Dress: Casual
Style: Chi $

Menu Sampler:

Breakfast:
N/A

Lunch/Dinner:

Specialty: Shrimp Won Ton Mein $5.25, Duck Noodles Oahu Style $6.75
Traditional Northern Style: Hot & Sour Soup $6.75, Soft Noodles in hot peanut sauce $5.25, Chicken Chives Potstickers (8) $5.95, Sweet Crepe w/red beans $4.75, Shanghai Fried Noodles $7.25, Sesame Pancakes (2) $4.75
Greens & Healths: Steamed Ong Choy with bean curd sauce $6.75, Eggplant w/garlic sauce $7.95, Mu Shui Vegetables w/pancake $7.50, Ma Po Tofu $7.95
Canton Style: Boneless Chicken Noodle w/black bean sauce $6.75, Salted Fish w/chicken fried rice $7.25, Seafood Congee $5.75
Chef's Specialty: Chili Shrimp Sizzling $12.95, Stir-Fried Clams with lemon grass $9.95, Szechuan Spicy Chicken $7.95, Beef w/black pepper sauce $7.95, Orange Chicken $7.95, Stir-Fried Lamb with leek and chili $10.95, Mu Shu Pork $7.50, Hunan Steamed Fish (spicy) $12.95, Honey Walnut Shrimp $12.95
Hong Kong Style: Grilled Chicken Wings (8 pcs) $5.25, Roasted Duck ½ $10.95, Whole $18.00, Pupu Samplers $6.95, Roasted Pork $5.95
Dessert: Sweet Mango Pudding $1.95, Tapioca with Taro $1.50

Impressions:

Through the years many of the Chinese eateries in Honolulu's Chinatown have given way to people from other parts of Asia as the original proprietors moved on to other pursuits. Not so up on Smith Street. Here the Little Village Noodle House keeps the old traditions alive serving a very reasonably priced mixed Chinese menu. We like the simple yet pleasant décor. Then, there's the waiter who stood ready to make sure that two visitors from another island ordered a balanced lunch. Finally, of course, comes the food, which is tasty, light, and plentiful. Parking is available on the street or in a lot behind the shop.

Honolulu

Longhi's Ala Moana
1450 Ala Moana Blvd.
Honolulu, HI 96814
808-947-9899
www.longhis.com

Hours: B 8:00 AM-11:00 AM Mo-Fr
B 7:30 AM-11:00 AM SaSu
L 11:00 AM-5:00 PM
D 5:00 PM-10:00 PM
Cards: AE DIS JCB MC V
Dress: Resort Casual
Style: Ital/Med $$$

Menu Sampler:

Breakfast:
Baked Italian Frittata with Meat & Vegetables or Vegetables with hollandaise on toasted French bread 10.00, Today's Quiche 9.00, French Toast with Grand Marnier, powdered sugar butter and maple syrup 9.25

Lunch:
Appetizers: Grilled Portobello Mushroom w/basil goat cheese pesto, roasted red bell peppers & imported goat cheese 9.00, Ahi Carpaccio on Bruschetta 15.00
Entrees: Belgian Endive Salad with gorgonzola cheese, caramelized macadamia nuts and scallion mint vinaigrette 10.25, Peking Duck Sandwich with hoisin sauce on our scallion roll 10.00, Chicken Picatta Open Faced Sandwich 13.00, Fresh Island Fish Longhi Style sautéed in butter, white wine & lemon with diced tomatoes & basil over garlic toast 14.00, Lobster Cannelloni w/béchamel 14.50

Dinner:
Appetizers: Frutti Di Mare-Poached Shrimp, Scallops, and Calamari, marinated in extra virgin olive oil, garlic, fresh herbs, roasted Mancini peppers, & Kalamata olives-served chilled 16.50, pacific Manila Clams in broth 14.50
Entrees: Prawns Amaretto-sautéed in Amaretto, brandy, fresh orange juice and cream 29, Seared Ahi Au Poivre with shiitake mushrooms in a garlic, green peppercorn, and brandy sauté 30, Lamb Chops (2) w/a raspberry-mint sauce 31
Desserts: Hot Chocolate Soufflé, flowing chocolate center, Haagen-Dazs 12

Impressions:

Bob Longhi has brought his formula of old world style and new world cuisine to the Ala Moana Shopping Center. Looking for an upscale breakfast or lunch in an open-air setting? You'll find it here. Then stop by later for tapas and cocktails or make reservations for a romantic dinner. Celebrity watching can be a plus!

Windward

Lucy's Grill N' Bar Authors' Favorite

33 Aulike Street
Kailua, HI 96734
808-230-8188
Web: None
Hours: B SuBru 9:30 AM-1:30PM
D 5:00 PM-10:00 PM
Cards: MC V
Dress: Resort Casual
Style: Ec/Pac Rim $$$

Menu Sampler:

Breakfast:

Sunday Brunch: Fresh Fish Benedict with spinach, poached egg, English muffin, papaya hollandaise $15, Sweet Bread Mac Nut French Toast $6

Dinner:

Appetizers: Crispy Kalua Pig Triangles with mascarpone & sweet sour Mandarin orange plum sauce $6, Coconut Crusted Shrimp w/sweet Asian chili beurre blanc $10, Pulehu Style Baby Lamb Chops, green papaya chutney $12
Pizza: Kalua Pig Pizza w/red onions, hoisin sesame, mozzarella $11
Salads: Grilled Caesar Salad with fresh papaya, Reggiano, and crouton $8, Pick-It Salad with hearts of romaine, gorgonzola, caramelized walnuts, oil and vinegar $8, Romaine, rock shrimp, crab, avocado, egg, bacon, tomato $18
Entrées: Includes starch and vegetable. $3 charge for splits and special orders. Pan Seared, Pepper Crusted Ahi with wasabi miso beurre blanc $24, Lemongrass Crusted Scallops with green papaya salad, yellow Thai curry $23, Pulehu Style Baby Lamb Chops (6), green papaya chutney, lilikoi demi $24, Crispy Gingered Chicken w/Lucy's Hong Kong style noodles $16
Sides: Brown & White Rice Mix $2, Lucy's Mash Potatoes $3
Desserts: Crème Brulee $6, Dark Chocolate Soufflé Cake with chocolate truffle center and vanilla ice cream $8, Raspberry or Mango Sorbet $4, Gelato $4

Impressions:

Just behind McDonald's on the main highway coming into Kailua, you'll find Lucy's Grill N' Bar. This casually upscale dining spot offers tables inside and out and features a display kitchen preparing an eclectic island menu. We found the tastes to be complex to the point of addiction. Lucy's is quite the hangout for local patrons of all ages and can get busy. The creative fusion menu and upbeat atmosphere are conducive to good dining and lots of fun. This is a great place for an early dinner before heading back across the Pali. Check out the fish tanks!

Honolulu

L'Uraku
1341 Kapiolani Blvd
Honolulu, HI 96814
808-955-0552
www.luraku.com
Hours: L 11:00 AM-2:00 PM
D 5:30 PM-10:00 PM
Cards: AE DC JCB MC V
Dress: Resort Casual
Style: Euro/Japan $$$

Menu Sampler:

Breakfast:
N/A
Lunch:
Baby Spinach & Garlic Shrimp with crispy bacon & mustard sesame vinaigrette $9.50, Panko Shrimp Katsu $12.75, "Crunchy" Soft Shell Crab BLT with avocado, Japanese cucumber and citrus aioli on foccacia $13.00, Pork Loin Rack sautéed & served with stir fried vegetables, tomato lomi, rice $15.00
Weekender Lunch served on Saturday, Sunday & certain holidays only: Four-course meal for $16 includes three courses (choice of entrée) plus dessert.
Dinner:
Starters: Bento Box Sampler of baked oyster, ahi tartare, crab cake, salmon sushi $12.95, Ahi Tartare $8.95, Sizzlin' Moi Carpaccio w/Big Island ginger, tofu, tomato concasse, peppered ponzu vinaigrette & julienned nori $6.95
Entrées: Miso-Yaki Butterfish served on 'Nalo pea sprouts & pickled red ginger $19.25, Pan Roasted Pork Chop & "Crunchy" Shrimp w/garlic mashed potato, Hauula tomato lomi & wasabi ketchup $20.50, Garlic Ribeye Steak with roasted garlic, steamed vegetables, light teriyaki sauce $24.00, Pan roasted Onaga served w/Manila clams & spicy clam broth $26.25, Filet Mignon $28.50

Impressions:

The high ceilings of this upscale restaurant are adorned with hand-painted umbrellas for a whimsical East meets West atmosphere that carries all the way through the menu. This is pupu heaven. The tastes at L'Uraku are exquisite. The chef starts with high quality ingredients and gives all of the preparations a pronounced Japanese twist. Their take on fusion cuisine has won many awards. The one-way streets can make driving a challenge so consider taking a cab.

Honolulu

Maple Garden

909 Isenberg St
Honolulu, HI 96826
808-941-6641
Web: None
Hours: L 11:00 AM-2:00 PM
D 5:30 PM-10:00 PM
Cards: AE DC DIS JCB MC V
Dress: Casual
Style: Chi $$

Menu Sampler:

Breakfast:
N/A
Lunch/Dinner:
Appetizers: Fried Won Ton $5.25, Spring Roll-House Specialty-$5.95, Wonderful Taste Chicken (hot)-House Specialty-$6.95, Szechuan Cabbage (hot) $2.95, Jelly Fish $6.50, Shredded Chicken w/sesame sauce (hot!) $6.50
Soup: Sour Hot Soup $6.50, Tofu & Oyster Soup $7.95, Winter Melon Soup $5.75, Shredded Pork with Szechuan Cabbage $5.75, Egg Flower Soup $5.75
Vegetables: Creamed Tientsin Cabbage $6.75, Sautéed Crispy String Beans-House Specialty-$6.95, Fried Soft Tofu Ala Maple Garden $7.95
Entrées: Shrimp Maple Garden $8.75, Shrimp with Hot Peppers $8.25, Oysters with Ginger Sauce-House Specialty-$9.50, braised Salmon $9.95, Fish with chili sauce (hot) $8.25, Diced Chicken with Chili (hot) $7.95, Beef & Squid Szechuan Style-House Specialty-$8.25, Hot Garlic Chicken $8.50, Shredded Pork with Dry Tofu-House Specialty-$7.75, Singing Rice with Pork & Vegetables $8.75, Fried Soft Tofu Ala Maple Garden $7.95, Curried Beef $7.75
Dessert: Almond Beancurd $1.75, Pearl Dumplings-House Specialty- $2.50

Impressions:

Maple Garden is a small neighborhood restaurant located on Isenberg between Kapiolani Boulevard and South King Street. This family-owned establishment serves excellent Szechuan cuisine at reasonable prices. Some of the dishes are mildly zesty, while others are best described as peppery hot. Regardless, this is substantial food that satisfies. Besides the ala carte items they offer daily lunch specials at prices under $8.00. Although the clientele are mainly local residents, you'll find akamai visitors dining at Maple Garden as well. There's a small lot next to the building, but you may have to park along the street.

Honolulu

Marbella Authors' Favorite

1680 Kapiolani Blvd.
Honolulu, HI 96814
808-943-4353
Web: None
Hours: L 11:30 AM-2:00 PM Mo-Fr
D 5:30 PM-10:00 PM
Dress: Resort Casual
Style: Med $$$

Menu Sampler:

Breakfast:
N/A
Lunch:
Pizzas: Artichoke Tuscan with Spinach, Chicken and garlic cream sauce 9.00
Pastas: Fettucine with Calamari and Prawns in a Putanesca sauce 9.75
Sandwiches: Eggplant red pepper & zucchini w/spiced goat cheese 7.50
Dinner:
Soups: Lentil Soup with cumin essence and garlic chips 6.50
Salads: Spanish Composed Salad with oranges, goat cheese & cherry tomatoes 6.75, Mixed Green with granny smith apple brulee and Gorgonzola 7.00
Appetizers: Caramelized Onion Tart with goat cheese, olive tapenade and arugula 8.00, Marbella Spanokopita Filo Pastry with spinach, feta cheese & leek with yogurt sauce 7.50, Grilled Salmon stuffed in grape leaves 8.50
Main Course: Grilled Balsamic Chicken with red wine potato puree and ratatouille 16.00, Saffron Risotto with Daily Fresh Medley Fish, basil oil & garlic shrimp pil pil 18.50, Salmon Wellington with parmesan crusted sea scallops, red wine and beurre blanc 19.00, Oven Baked Cumin Crusted Whole Moi with roasted garlic potatoes and green beans 18.00
Desserts: Chocolate Ganache Stuffed Beignet 8.50, Granny Smith Apple Galette w/Gelato 7.00, and Molten Center Chocolate Cake w/vanilla gelato 5.50

Impressions:

Marbella has brought an intriguing blend of Mediterranean flavors and casual sophistication to the Honolulu dining scene. The ambitious menu draws from numerous Southern European sources and provides diners with choices not normally found in this Asian cuisine dominated city. Another big plus is the pricing, which is really quite reasonable for a dining experience of this level. Parking can be a problem in this busy area, so consider taking a cab.

Honolulu

Mariposa

Neiman Marcus
Ala Moana Shopping Center
Honolulu, HI 96814
808-951-3420
www.neimanmarcus.com

Hours: Su Bru 11:00 AM-3:00 PM
L 11:00 AM-3:00 PM XSu
D 5:00 PM-9:00 PM
Cards: AE DC JCB MC V
Dress: Casual
Style: Ec/Euro-Asian $$$

Menu Sampler:

Breakfast:
Brunch: Caesar Salad $12.00, with chicken $15.00, Housemade Corned Beef Hash & Eggs $10.00, Char Siu & Eggs with Fried Rice $9.00
Entrées: Sautéed Opakapaka with seasonal vegetables, Yukon Gold potatoes and a three pepper vinaigrette $Market Price, Thai Yellow Seafood Curry $18
Lunch:
Entrées: Steamed Manila clams in an herbed miso broth with toasted baguette $15.00, Barbecued Beef Brisket with cole slaw, garlic mashed potatoes and crispy tobacco onions $17.00, Kahuku Corn Chowder $5.00/$6.00
Sandwiches: Slow Smoked Beef Brisket w/tomatoes, lettuce, herb aioli $11.00
Dinner:
Appetizers: Vegetarian Lumpia with Nuoc Cham dipping sauce $8.00, Lobster Katsu w/mango-chile-lime sauce $14.00, Sesame Ahi Tartare w/tobiko $13.00
Entrées: Pan Seared Sea Scallops with herb and garlic pappardelle, sautéed spinach and Portobello mushrooms $25.00, Pulehu Steak Alae, mashed potatoes, seasonal vegetables and red wine demi glace $29.00,Almond-Herb Risotto in roasted garlic vegetable stock, crimini mushrooms, tomato concasse, Olde Amsterdam Gouda and Maui onion jus $18.00, Braised Duck Leg $24.00

Impressions:

Chef Douglas Lum presides over this highly regarded restaurant. Here on the third floor of Neiman Marcus in the Ala Moana Shopping Center, he serves an intriguing menu of fusion cuisine. Besides the wide variety of ala carte items, High Tea is served on Sunday afternoons from 2-5 PM ($16) with English tea, sandwiches, and pastries available for a special treat while shopping.

North Shore

Matsumoto Store

66-087 Kamehameha Hwy
Haleiwa, HI 96712
808-637-4827
www.matsumotoshaveice.com
Hours: 8:30 AM-6:00 PM
Cards: AE DC DIS JCB MC V
Dress: Casual
Style: Spec $

Menu Sampler:

Breakfast/Lunch/Dinner:

Shave Ice in a large selection of local and traditional flavors:
Small Shave Ice $1.30, Large Shave Ice $1.50. Shave Ice with ice cream: Small $1.80, Large $2.00. Shave Ice with Azuki beans: Small $1.80, Large $2.00. Shave Ice with ice cream and azuki beans: Small $2.00, Large $2.20.

Impressions:

Haleiwa is a quaint beachside village on the north shore of Oahu. Here you will find the Matsumoto Store serving that island favorite--shave ice. Since 1951 the Matsumoto's have served this local treat that is similar to a snow cone but with a finer texture. After shaving the ice off a block, they stack it high in a paper cone and add your choice of flavored syrups. For those with more experienced tastes, they offer sweet azuki beans or premium ice cream as add-ons. It can get busy here, but the line moves quickly. There's plenty of parking alongside the store.

Waikiki

Matteo's
364 Seaside Ave
Honolulu, HI 96815
808-922-5551
Web: None
Hours: D 5:30 PM-11:00 PM
Cards: AE DC DIS JCB MC V
Dress: Evening Aloha
Style: Ital $$$$
Ent Card

Menu Sampler:

Breakfast/Lunch:
N/A
Dinner:
Antipasto: Escargots-baked in a garlic Dijon & fresh herb butter $10.95, Calamari Fritti $7.95, Artichokes alla Matteo's in a garlic butter with white wine and lemon $7.75, Seafood Medley Vinaigrette w/vegetables and noodles $12.95
Salads and Soups: Parma Onion Soup topped with French bread croutons, Italian cheeses & prosciutto $7.50, Salad Caprese with fresh buffalo mozzarella, Roma tomato, grilled fennel, greens and balsamic-basil vinaigrette $7.95, Zuppe Di Clams $10.95, Minestrone Milanese $5.25, Seasonal Soup $5.50
Entrées: Grenadine of Beef Tenderloin topped with a red wine sauce and mushrooms $26.95, Veal Osso Bucco Milanese braised in a rich red wine sauce with saffron risotto and topped with a citrus gremolata $29.50, Cioppino alla Livornese with lobster, clams, mussels, shrimp, scallops, calamari and fresh fish poached in an Italian saffron, tomato and vegetable broth $32.50, Chicken Florentine on spinach with a chardonnay-garlic butter sauce $22.95, Eggplant Parmigiana Dinner $19.95, Veal Saltimbocca $26.95, Fresh Fish Dore Style-battered in egg and topped with a lemon-butter caper sauce $Market Price.
Pasta: Four Cheese Ravioli with Marinara drizzled with roasted garlic cream and macadamia nut pesto $17.95, Seafood Puttanesca on linguine$22.95
Dessert: Pastry & Dessert Tray $6.95, Bananas Foster "Frank Sinatra" with Curacao, rum over ice cream $10.95, Espresso, Cappuccino, Coffees $2-$5.50

Impressions:

Matteo's has been a local favorite for so long it's hard to remember when it opened. This restaurant serves classic Italian cuisine in a traditional atmosphere and does it well. Besides the fine menu, they offer an excellent wine list. It's a little congested in this part of Waikiki, so it would be wise to walk or take a cab.

Chinatown

Mei Sum Dim Sum

Authors' Favorite

65 N. Pauahi St.
Honolulu, HI 96817
808-531-3268
Web: None
Hours: BLD 7:00 AM-9:00 PM
Cards: MC V
Dress: Casual
Style: Chi $

Menu Sampler:

Breakfast/Lunch/Dinner:
Dim Sum-wonderful variety and quality-Sweet Sesame Ball $1.95, Mochi Puff $1.95, Shrimp Dumpling $2.35, Shrimp Pork Hash $2.35, Custard Tart $1.95, Mochi Rice in Lotus Leaf $2.35, Lotus Sugar Bow $2.35, Beef Ball $2.35, Steamed Look Funn w/BBQ Pork $3.15, Steamed Look Funn w/ Scallop $3.15
Appetizer: Shrimp Canton $8.50, Pepper Salt Squid $7.95, Drunken Chicken $6.95, Spring Rolls (4 pcs) $3.95, Deep Fried Stuffed Tofu $6.95
Soup: Seaweed Tofu Soup $5.95, Egg Drop Soup $4.50, Won Ton Soup $4.25, Seafood Rice Soup $6.95, Meat Ball Rice Soup $4.95, Rice Soup $2.50
Entrées: Jumbo Scallop with Black Bean Sauce $8.95, Seabass w/Ginger Onion $8.50, Szechuan Style Shrimp $8.50, Seafood Tofu Casserole $8.95, Oyster & Shredded Pork w/Szechuan Sauce $9.50, Beef w/Satay Sauce $7.95, Roasted Duck $6.95, Chicken w/Black Mushroom $7.95 Pork Ong Choy w/Shrimp Paste or Pork Kau Yuk w/Mui Choy $6.95, Scallop Fried Rice $9.50
Vegetables: Chinese Broccoli w/Dried Flounder $6.95, Choy Sum w/Garlic Sauce $5.25, Dried Tofu w/Bean Sprout $5.95, Black Mushroom w/Vegetables $6.95, Steamed Stuffed Tofu $6.95, Braised Mixed Vegetables $5.95
Look Funn: Seafood Noodle in Soup $6.95, Wor Won Ton Mein $4.95, Roast Duck with noodle in soup $5.95, Beef Brisket Noodle in soup $4.95

Impressions:

If you're looking for great dim sum or a Hong Kong style menu served in an authentic yet quieter setting, head up to the corner of Smith and Pauahi in Chinatown. There you'll find Mei Sum Dim Sum. This simple eatery doesn't make a show of things, but the kitchen consistently delivers. Where most places only serve dim sum as a late breakfast, lunch, or teatime treat, Mei Sum offers these delicacies throughout the day. Make sure to look under the glass top on your table for the day's specials. After deciding we couldn't pass any of them by, we ordered way too much, but that was part of the fun of it!

Honolulu

Mekong II

1726 S. King
Honolulu, HI 96826
808-941-6184
Web: None
Hours: L 11 AM-2 PM XSaSu
D 5-9:30 PM
Cards: AE DC JCB MC V
Dress: Casual
Style: Thai $$

Menu Sampler:

Breakfast:
N/A
Lunch:
Appetizers: Spring Rolls $6.50, Bangkok Wings $6.95, Fish Patties $6.95
Salads: Green Papaya Salad-papaya /tomatoes, chilis, spices, lime $5.95
Soups: Spicy Seafood Soup $4.50, Spicy Chicken Soup $3.75, Spicy Fish $3.95
Entrées: Thai Noodles with Chicken-Pad Thai-$6.95, Evil Jungle Prince $7.50
Vegetarian Entrees: Mixed Vegetable Thai Curry w/Thai red curry, $7.25
Rice and Noodles: Water Chestnut Fried Rice $6.95, Shrimp Fried Rice $8.95
Dinner:
Appetizers: Bangkok Wings $7.95, Fish Patties $7.95, Fried Calamari $8.95
Salads: Thai Beef or Chicken Salad $7.95, Calamari Salad $8.50
Soups: Spicy Shrimp Soup $4.25, Ginger Chicken Soup $4.25
Entrées: Evil Jungle Prince w/Chicken $8.50, Thai Ginger Shrimp $10.50
Vegetarian Entrees: Thai Noodles with Tofu and Bean Sprouts $7.50
Rice & Noodles: Spicy Beef Fried Rice $8.50, Vegetable Fried Rice $7.50
Desserts: Lychee or Mango Sorbet $3.95, Thai Apple-Banana Coconut with Tapioca $3.25, Thai Iced Tea $1.50, Thai Tapioca Pudding $2.95

Impressions:

This small neighborhood restaurant is part of Keo's family of Thai eateries. Although the atmosphere at Mekong II might be a little more basic than some, it's hard to beat the prices. In this part of Honolulu everyone has to keep their overhead down, so if you are trying to do the same this would be a good call. Mekong II offers a good selection of quality Thai specialties including a tasty vegetarian menu. Parking can be a problem here. There's a small lot behind the building, but if that's full you'll have to look along the street.

Waikiki

Michel's Authors' Favorite
2895 Kalakaua Ave
Honolulu, HI 96815
808-923-6552
www.michelshawaii.com
Hours: Su Bru 9:00 AM-Noon, D 5:30 PM-9:30 PM
Cards: AE DC DIS JCB MC V
Dress: Evening Aloha
Style: Fre $$$$

Menu Sampler:

Breakfast/Lunch:
Sunday Brunch 10 AM-1 PM (Last Seating)-Eggs Benedict with artichokes and Dungeness crab meat $36, Lobster, Shrimp, Scallop Omelette $34
Dinner:
Appetizers: Ahi Carpaccio off bigeye tuna in a truffle vinaigrette w/a slaw of cucumber, tomato, & daikon $14, Burgundy Escargot in herb garlic butter $13, House Smoked Salmon w/warm potato pancake & grilled apple, greens and Waldorf salad $16, Fresh Oysters with shallot vinaigrette $16
Soups & Salads: Creamy Lobster Bisque with fresh Maine lobster meat flamed in Cognac at your table $9, Sweet Maui Onion soup with caramelized Maui onion with three cheeses under a crisp puff pastry crust $9, Belgian Endive Shrimp Salad w/ gorgonzola, toasted almonds & tomato w/vinaigrette $14
Entrées: Filet "Rossini" style-grilled beef tenderloin on sautéed spinach & fresh foie gras terrine, truffled mashed potato, mango-papaya chutney & Madeira sauce $48, Duckling a l'Orange with red cabbage, mashed potatoes & classic duck-orange jus $34, Goat Cheese-crusted Rack of Lamb with au gratin potatoes, bacon wrapped haricot verts & zinfandel sauce $38, Crab-Stuffed Maine Lobster baked & served w/saffron pilaf, black bean & white wine sauce $48, Potato Crusted Onaga on sautéed orzo & spinach, sweet rock shrimp, tomato coulis, garlic cream $28, Chateaubriand for Two $42/person
Dessert: Chocolate or Grand Marnier Souffle-20 minute preparation

Impressions:

Located in the Colony Surf Condominiums at the quiet Diamond Head end of Waikiki, you'll find one of Honolulu's long time favorite restaurants. This gracious dining room sits on the beach and provides fabulous views all the way down to its sister restaurant, John Dominis. Michel's presents classic French Continental cuisine at its finest with standards of service to match. Reservations are a must at this popular dining spot. Take a cab and avoid the parking hassle.

Waikiki

Miyako

The New Otani Kaimana Beach Hotel
2863 Kalakaua Ave
Honolulu, HI 96815
808-923-1555
www.kaimana.com
Hours: 5:30 PM-9:00 PM
Cards: AE DC DIS JCB MC V
Dress: Resort Casual
Style: Japan $$$
Ent Card

Menu Sampler:

Breakfast/Lunch:
N/A
Dinner:
Appetizers: Edamame 3.00, Mozuku-seaweed in a shoyu vinaigrette 6.00, Maguro Yamakake-fresh island tuna with Japanese yam 8.00
Grilled Dishes: Sirloin Steak Miyako Style 18.00, Chicken Kushiyaki 12.00, Oyster Platter w/butter herb sauce, special mayonnaise topping 9.50
Vinegared/Fried Dishes: Assorted Sunomono 9.50, Lobster Tempura 18.00
Sashimi: Maguro 15.00, Amaebi 16.50, Beef Tataki with ponzu sauce 14.50
Steamed Dishes/Tofu/Salad: Chawan Mushi-steamed egg custard with shrimp, chicken and mushroom 8.50, Cold Tofu with condiments 4.25, Hot Tofu with condiments 6.50, Wafu Salad of green with sesame dressing 6.50
Rice/Soup: Ume Chazuke-pickled plum over rice in soup 7.50, Sake Chazuke-salmon over rice in soup 8.00, Cha Soba-cold green tea buckwheat noodle 7.25, Clear Soup 3.50, Soybean Soup 2.50, Red Soybean Soup 3.00, Rice 1.50
Sushi: Ala Carte-Tuna 3.00, Salmon Roe 3.50, Eel 2.50, Fatty Tuna Mkt $, Rainbow Roll 12.50, California Roll 11.50, Tekka Roll 5.00, Kappa Roll 4.00
Special Kaiseki Dinner: includes appetizer, soup, entrees, dessert $28.00/$38.00/$43.00/$65.00, Special Nabe Dinners-Sukiyaki $30.00, Shabu Shabu $33.00, Udonsuki $38.00-Minimum of two orders

Impressions:

Miyako is located on the quiet Diamond Head end of Waikiki overlooking San Souci Beach. It would be easy for diners to get caught up in the lovely views, but the excellent food and service rule here. This dignified restaurant offers a wide-ranging menu of Japanese specialties served by kimono-clad waitresses. Plan on spending your evening enjoying this gracious cultural experience.

Waikiki

Momoyama

Sheraton Princess Kaiulani Hotel
120 Kaiulani Ave
Honolulu, HI 96815
808-922-5811
Web: None
Hours: D 5.45PM-9:30 PM
Cards: AE DC DIS JCB MC V
Dress: Resort Casual
Style: Japan $$$$
Ent Card

Menu Sampler:

Breakfast/Lunch:
N/A
Dinner:
Appetizer Specials: Edamame $3.95, Ahi Shioyaki $7.95, Deep Fried Oyster $4.95, Deep Fried Octopus $4.95, Sashimi $5.95, Marinated Pork $4.95, Asari Soup $5.95, Ohitashi $3.95, Agedashi Tofu $5.50, Tako Sunomono $4.95, Soft Shell Crab Karaage $7.95, Tsukemono $4.50, Hiyayakko $3.95
Sushi: Omikase Deluxe Combination $32.00, Chirashi-sushi rice topped with assorted seafood $27.95, California Temaki-crabmeat and avocado $6.95, Toro Temaki $6.95, Firecracker-spicy tuna $6.95, Hamachi Nigiri $7.95, Rainbow Maki $10.95, Shrimp Tempura Maki $7.95, Ume Shiso Maki $4.50
Golden Combinations: served with wafu salad, zensai, tsukemono, rice, miso soup and ice cream-Ikizukuri Lobster or Steamed Lobster w/seafood sashimi & NY steak or fish Misoyaki $62.00, Momoyama Royal-Lobster tail, traditional style w/broiled NY steak $42.00, Matsutake Kamameshi Teishoku- w/salad, tsukemono, tako sunomono, sashimi, tempura, miso soup & ice cream $45.00 Chef Yamada's "Kaiseki Special"-check with your server!

Impressions:

Momoyama is owned by Kyoya, which is a signal to veteran Honolulu foodies that it has got to be good. This venerable establishment offers a wonderful list of set dinners complemented by fine appetizers and sushi. Diners new to the world of Japanese cuisine need not be concerned. The menu translates very well both in language and selection. A professional wait staff is on hand to assure that your experience will be memorable. Watch for promotional discounts as they are often available and can place Momoyama within many budgets.

Honolulu

Morton's The Steakhouse, Honolulu
Ala Moana Center
1450 Ala Moana Blvd.
Honolulu, HI 96814
808-949-1300
www.mortons.com
Hours: D 5:30 PM-11:00 PM Mo-Th
D 5:00 PM-11:00 PM FrSaSu
Cards: AE DC JCB MC V
Dress: Evening Aloha
Style: Stk $$$$

Menu Sampler:

Breakfast/Lunch:
N/A
Dinner:
Appetizers: Smoked Pacific Salmon $14, Jumbo Lump Crabmeat Cocktail with mustard mayonnaise $14, Broiled Sea Scallops wrapped in Bacon with apricot chutney $14, Sautéed Wild Mushrooms $10, Lobster Bisque $13
Salads: Morton's Spinach Salad $9, Sliced Beefsteak Tomato $9
Entrées: Double Filet Mignon, Sauce Béarnaise $40, Porterhouse Steak $44, New York Strip Sirloin $44, New York Steak Au Poivre, five peppercorn cognac cream sauce $46, Rib Eye Steak Cajun or Broiled $35/$34, Domestic Double Rib Lamb Chops $35, Colossal Shrimp Alexander with Sauce Beurre Blanc $34, Chicken Christopher, Garlic Beurre Blanc Sauce $24, Broiled Salmon $26, Jumbo Lump Crab Cakes, mustard mayonnaise sauce $34
Vegetables: Sautéed Fresh Spinach & Mushrooms, Creamed Spinach, Sautéed Wild Mushrooms, Sautéed Onions, Baked Idaho Potato, Lyonnaise Potatoes, Mashed Potatoes, Steamed Fresh Broccoli with Sauce Hollandaise $55
Desserts: A wonderful selection including the house specialty of a Chocolate, Raspberry, Grand Marnier or Lemon Soufflé $15, Espresso or Cappucino

Impressions:

Morton's of Chicago is known for its top quality prime USDA beef, but the menu doesn't stop there. Excellent veal, lamb, chicken, and seafood dishes are available as well. But this is a steak house, and the steak had better be done right. Morton's answer to that is broiling the carefully aged meat at 1200 degrees to sear it and seal in its juices. Drive up to the second level of the Ala Moana Shopping Center on the ocean side and you will find the entrance located between Neiman Marcus and Sears. There is a valet, but parking is no problem.

Kapahulu

Mr. Ojisan

Kilohana Square
1018 Kapahulu Ave
Honolulu, HI 96816
808-735-4455

Hours: L 11:00 AM-2:00 PM Mo-Fr
D 5:30 PM-11:00 PM Mo-Th
D 5:30 PM-1:00 AM FrSa
Cards: MC V
Dress: Casual
Style: Japan $$

Menu Sampler:

Breakfast:
N/A
Lunch:
Appetizer: Assorted Sashimi $16.95, Tako Wasabi $3.95, Tako Sashimi $8.25, Yamakake (wild yam) $6.95, Kimpira Gobo-fried seasoned burdock $4.50, Clam with butter $6.75, Broiled Salmon $6.95, Fried Tofu $5.95, Gyoza $3.25
A la Carte: Wafu Steak $12.95, Shrimp Tempura $10.95,Vegetable Tempura $7.95, Chicken Katsu $6.95, Pork Ginger $7.25, Soft Shell Crab $6.25
Side Dishes: Oshinko Mori $3.95, Musubi-Plain $1.95, Miso Soup $1.75
Special Combination Dinners include miso soup, oshinko, kobachi, rice & dessert $15.95, choice of two items-Assorted Sashimi, Shrimp & Vegetable Tempura, Tonkatsu, Chicken Katsu, Chicken Teriyaki, Beef Teriyaki, Broiled Saba, Broiled Salmon, Broiled Sanma, Deep Fried Soft Shell Crab.
Sukiyaki $18.95, $34.00 for two, includes kobachi, rice, oshinko, dessert
Yose-Nabe $18.95, $34.00 for two-one pot cooking with seafood, chicken, vegetables & kobachi, rice oshinko, dessert, Teishoku dinners $8.95-$16.95
Dinner:
All the above selections plus Udon $7.25-10.95, & Wafu Steak Teishoku $14.95

Impressions:

If you'd like to experience the Honolulu version of a Japanese neighborhood tavern, take a ride out Kapahulu to Mr. Ojisan. True to its roots, this place has the comfort of a well-worn pair of shoes. Inside, the small tables are continually being rearranged to suit the needs of the upbeat crowd. The menu does a great job covering the Japanese culinary waterfront. The only thing missing is a sushi bar. Although taking a cab always makes sense when visiting the Kapahulu restaurants, there is a parking lot in the courtyard behind the building.

Honolulu

Murphy's Bar & Grill
2 Merchant St
Honolulu, HI 96817
808-531-0422
www.gomurphys.com
Hours: L 11:30 AM-2:30 PM Mo-Fr
D 5:00 PM-10:00 PM Mo-Su
Cards: AE DC DIS MC V
Dress: Casual
Style: Irish $$

Menu Sampler:

Breakfast:
N/A
Lunch:
Appetizers: Salmon Pâté with minced onion, capers, sour cream, toasted rounds crackers $7.00, Spicy Fried Chicken Wings, ranch dressing $8.00
Salads: Oriental Chicken Salad $9.75, Murphy's "Big" Salad $8.50
Entrées: Fish & Chips-fresh cod and French fries served with malt vinegar $8.25, Crab & Shrimp grilled on sourdough $9.50, Gaelic Steak-NY Steak with green peppercorn sauce, mashed potatoes and vegetable $12.50, Corned Beef & Cabbage (Th) $10.50, Sweet Potato Crusted Catfish w/rice, corn relish $10.50
Dinner:
Beverages: A rack of single malt scotches and draught beers.
Appetizers: Edamame $5.00, Jalapeno Poppers $6.50, Fried Calamari $7.75
Sandwiches: Served w/fries or potato salad. Hamburger $7.50, Chicken $9.50
Dinners: Fresh Island Ahi (grilled or blackened) served with rice and vegetables $13.00, Fresh Atlantic Salmon w/sweet chili sauce, rice & veg./Caesar $11.50
Saint Patrick's Day: 10,000-12,000 people attend Murphy's Block Party. Over 1,000 # of corned beef are served that day. Lamb Shank, Gaelic Steak, Salmon.

Impressions:

Between Chinatown and the financial district you'll find a wonderfully authentic Irish pub. This is the kind of place you go when you feel the need to drink beer, talk loud, throw darts, or play a round of shuffleboard. The menu offers classic pub food with meat and potato dishes heading the list. For the purist, fish and chips are available as well. There's seating in an attractive dining area at the front of the building or in the bar toward the back. If you've had enough sun, sand, and surf to hold you, this is a pleasant place to while away some time.

Oahu Dining

Waikiki

Musashi
Hyatt Regency Waikiki & Spa
2424 Kalakaua Ave
Honolulu, HI 96815
808-923-1234
www.hyatt.com
Hours: B 5:30 AM-10:30 AM
D 6:00 PM-10:00 PM
Cards: AE DC DIS JCB MC V
Dress: Evening Aloha
Style: Japan $$$$

Menu Sampler:

Breakfast:
Meals: Yakizakana-scrambled eggs, chilled tofu, broiled salmon, miso soup, rice, pickled vegetables $16.00, Zosui-rice soup served with Japanese pickled plum, pickled vegetables and Hawaiian fruit with kani (crab) $12.95, tamago (egg) $11.95, yasai (vegetables) $10.95
Lunch:
N/A
Dinner:
Appetizers: Hamachi Yellow Tail flown in daily from Japan served in a traditional manner $Mkt, Assorted Sashimi of fish & seafood $12.50, Cold Tofu w/grated ginger, bonito flakes & spring onions $6.50, Maguro Sashimi $12.00
Soups & Salads: Miso Soup with spring onions, mushrooms, and seaweed $3.00, Egg Custard with chicken, shrimp, and Japanese vegetables $6.25
Sushi Bar: Matsu $33.00, Ume $23.00, Chirashi $27.00, TekkaJyu $24.00
Dinners: Assorted Fish Tempura $27.00, Shabu Shabu w/Prime Sirloin-cooked tableside $29.00, Sukiyaki $29.00, Kaiseki Style Dinner-Steak & Lobster $75.00
Teppanyaki Dinners served from 6-9PM with seating on the hour. Musashi special of Filet Mignon, Lobster and Scallop $47.00, Steak & Prawns $37.00

Impressions:

On the third floor of the Hyatt Regency you'll find a Japanese restaurant where 99% of the patrons come from Japan. That could be intimidating or exciting depending on one's point of view. We prefer the later and see Musashi as an adventure not to be missed. The room isn't particularly large, but the menu covers the traditional Japanese dining styles with grace and style. Let the hostess know what you are interested in so she can seat you properly.

Waikiki

Neptune's Garden

Authors' Favorite

Pacific Beach Hotel
2490 Kalakaua Ave
Honolulu, HI 96815
808-921-6112
www.pacificbeachhotel.com

Hours: D 5:30 PM-9:30 PM Tu-Sa
Cards: AE DC DIS JCB MC V
Dress: Evening Aloha
Style: Cont/Sea/Stk $$$$
Ent Card

Menu Sampler:

Breakfast/Lunch:
N/A

Dinner:
Starters: Phyllo Prawns wrapped in ribbon pastry crust & crisp fried with a starfruit & Ewa watermelon "Lacquer" $10.95, Steamed California Artichoke with lemon-garlic butter sauce, topped with fre4sh Parmigiano Reggiano cheese $9.00, Togarashi Pepper Seared Scallops, grilled polenta cake, greens $9.75
Soups & Salads: Fresh Lehua Taro Vichyssoise with lomi tomato puree $7.75, Kona Lobster Bisque with mushroom fricassee $6.75, Hirabara Farms Baby Romaine Caesar with parmesan crisp $7.75, Tropical Seafood Cobb with shrimp, scallops, & lobster claw, avocado, mango, hearts of palm, tomato, crisp plantain chips, served with Mai Tai Louie Dressing $12.00, Baby Greens $6.50
Entrées: Pan Fried Big Island Moi with rice cracker riso and light shiso butter nage $31.50, Seafood Bouillabaisse with aioli and garlic crostini $29.50, Thai Salmon Shioyaki with green curry, kaffir lime, & lemongrass $25.00, Steamed or Grilled One and One Half Pound Live Lobster with steamed rice & Ponzu Wasabi Butter Sauce $33.50, 12 Oz, Prime Filet Mignon $36.50, Chinese Style Roast Duck with Pohaberry and Mango Sauce $25.50, Fish Trilogy $38.00
Degustation Menus: $65.00, $75.00, and $85.00 per person

Impressions:

There is no such thing as a bad table at Neptune's. The entire dining room is built around the hotel's beautiful three-story 280,000-gallon aquarium. As one might expect, in this fine restaurant seafood holds center stage. However, just so all tastes are covered, Neptune's also offers a variety of superlative meat and poultry dishes. It would be hard to find a more tranquil dining setting anywhere.

Waikiki

Nick's Fishmarket Waikiki
2070 Kalakaua Ave
Honolulu, HI 96815
808-955-6333
www.nicksfishmarketwaikiki.com
Hours: D 5:30 PM-10:00 PM
Cards: AE DC DIS JCB MC V
Dress: Evening Aloha
Style: Sea $$$$
Ent Card

Menu Sampler:

Breakfast/Lunch:
N/A
Dinner:
Appetizers: Coconut Shrimp served with a mango cocktail sauce $11.45, Oysters Rockefeller $11.25, Calamari Fritti $10.45, Scampi in garlic butter $11.25, Crab Seafood Cake served with an Oriental cole slaw & a spicy red bell pepper sauce $11.45, Blackened Sashimi sliced rare served with a shoyu mustard sauce $13.95, New Zealand Pacific Oysters, fresh, on ice $11.45
Entrées: Fresh Shellfish Bouillabaisse with spiny lobster tail, king crab legs, shrimp, mussels, clams and fresh Hawaiian fish in a saffron broth $39.45, Norwegian Salmon marinated in honey and sake wine, grilled and served with white rice, tomato confit and chili butter $30.95, Hawaiian Mahi Mahi grilled and glazed with a sweet chili, cilantro, sesame marinade and served with a tropical salsa and roasted yellow pepper sauce $30.95, Mixed Seafood Grill of shrimp, scallops, salmon, Caribbean lobster tail and island fish served with oven roasted tomato and basil mashed potatoes and pesto butter $38.95, Lobster Thermidor $48.95, Filet Mignon (8oz) rolled in cracked black pepper and served with au gratin potatoes and a cognac cream demi glace sauce $31.45
Watch for the **Chef's Specials** of complete dinners for $29.95(4 course) or $35.00 (5-course) Early Dining Specials $19.99, 2-For-1 Coupons, Keiki Menu

Impressions:

This fine dining restaurant has been a Waikiki landmark for over 30 years. Success speaks for itself as diners return to enjoy the excellent menu and fine service. As the name would suggest, the specialty of the house is seafood. The approach is Pacific Rim with island flair. Besides their dinner selections, they also offer a late night menu as well as half-price pupu and drink specials in the lounge. Live entertainment is a regular feature. Reservations are recommended.

Waikiki

Oceanarium Restaurant

Pacific Beach Hotel
2490 Kalakaua Ave
Honolulu, HI 96815
808-921-6111
www.pacificbeachhotel.com

Hours: Su Bru Buf 10:00 AM-2:30 PM
B 6:00 AM-11:00 AM, XSu 6:00 AM-8:30 AM
L 11:00 AM-2:00 PM XSu
D 5:00 PM-9:30 PM
Cards: AE DC DIS JCB MC V
Dress: Casual
Style: Amer/Isl $$

Menu Sampler:

Breakfast:
Sunday Brunch: prime rib & fresh seafood bar including oysters & sashimi, salad & appetizer bar, entrees and desserts bar- adults $20.95/children $10.50
Weekday Breakfast Buffet: Wide selection plus Fried Rice $12.95
Continental Breakfast: $7.50 a la carte/$9.50 buffet or A la Carte Menu
Lunch:
Thin Sliced Roast Prime Rib of Beef and melted cheddar cheese on sourdough with au jus and fries, garlic fries or onion rings $7.95, Saimin Noodles and Oxtail in broth with ginger and cilantro $7.95, Caesar Salad $6.75
Dinner:
Prime Rib & Seafood Nightly Dinner Buffet 5-9:30 PM: Fresh Oysters and Mussels on the half shell, shrimp, sashimi, poke, salads, kim chee, tsukemono, cheese, fruit, crackers, clam chowder, carved prime rib, steamed snow crab legs, fresh fish of the day, chef's specials, mahimahi with chef's sauce, chef's chicken, roasted pork loin, vegetables, salads, rice, potatoes, seafood pasta station, pastry dessert selections $29.95 for adults, $15.25, children 5-10 years

Impressions:

One wall of this popular family restaurant is a huge three-story aquarium. That might be enough to capture an audience but the Oceanarium works to keep them by providing a solid menu of quality selections at reasonable prices. Buffet style breakfasts are served daily. However, Sundays are special, so the Sunday brunch takes things up a notch. For added affordability early bird specials and a 10-and-under children's menu are available. This is a good stop on the way to the zoo.

Diamond Head

Olive Tree Café
Kahala Mall
4614 Kilauea Ave
Honolulu, HI 96816
808-737-0303
Web: None
Hours: D 5:00 PM-10:00 PM Mo-Su
Cards: None
Dress: Casual
Style: Greek $$

Menu Sampler:

Breakfast:
N/A
Lunch/Dinner:
Soup: Avgo Lemeno-Chicken broth with egg and lemon flavors $2.88, Fresh Pumpkin and Mung Bean $2.88, Lamb Lentil & Vegetable $3.84
Appetizers: Hommus-ground garbanzo, tahini, garlic spread $3.84, Mussel Ceviche-mussels with lemon/lime, capers, olive oil, herbs $4.80, Bean Salad-bean (Yeegantes), mixed with fresh herbs, diced tomatoes & pita bread $4.80, Dolmatakia-stuffed grape leaves with rice, herbs, olive oil with tzatziki $4.80, Baba Ghanoosh-pureed broiled eggplant, takini, garlic with pita $4.80
Salads: Greek Salad with Kalamata olives and feta cheese $6.72, Tabule Salad of cracked bulgar wheat, diced tomatoes, cucumbers, onions with lemon-mint dressing on mixed greens $4.80, Feta Cheese & Kalamata Olives $4.80
Entrées: Souvlaki-(kebabs) served in pita bread with tzatziki (mint, cucumber, yogurt sauce-Fresh Fish $9.60, Chicken $7.68, Lamb $9.60, Falafel of ground vegetables and garbanzo beans, deep fried in pita bread w/tahini $7.68.
Dessert: Baklava $1.92, Galatoboriko-Lemon Custard layered with Filo $1.92 Various gelatos & sorbets (such as uzou sorbet) $1.92
Specials: Daily; Tues.-Chicken Saffron, Wed.-Lamb Shank Plaki,, Thurs.-Imam Biyaldi, Fri.-Variety such as Pastitsio, Lamb Okrar, etc., Sat/Sun-Spanokopita

Impressions:

Located at the Kahala Mall this indoor/outdoor café might be a bit small in size, but it's long on good food and friendly atmosphere. The authentic Greek cuisine is fresh and flavorful, and the self-service is fast and efficient. This is a popular dining spot with local residents so go early or late to get a table. You can BYOB without a corkage fee. If the lot is full, park your car down the side street.

Honolulu

OnJin's Café

401 Kamake'e St
Honolulu, HI 96814
808-589-1666
Web: None
Hours: L 11:00 AM-10:00 PM Mo-Sa
D 5:00 PM-10:00 PM Mo-Sa
Cards: AE DIS MC V
Dress: Resort Casual
Style: Eurasian $$$

Menu Sampler:

Breakfast:
N/A
Lunch:
Starters: Ahi Karaage in a sweet sour chili sauce $7.50, French Onion Soup with melted Swiss cheese and crouton $4.50, Crab Cakes with two tomato sauce and momiji aioli $9.00, Korean Style Potato and Shrimp Pancake made with mochi-ko and kochijon $7.50, Crispy Chicken Wings with spicy aioli $6.75
Entrees: Open Face Crab and Cheese Melt on onion bun $7.50, Boolgogi and Kimchi Sandwich-grilled Korean style beef and kimchi on a bun $6.25, Crispy Snapper drizzled with lemon caper beurre blanc $6.95, Baby Back Ribs-4 piece $9.50, 7 piece $18.00, Curried Chicken Salad lightly spiced with raisins and apples $6.75, Shrimp and Couscous Salad-semolina tossed in a light dressing of herbs $7.95, Grilled New York Steak w/garlic mashed 6 oz-$9.50, 10 oz $16.00
Dinner:
Appetizers: All of the above plus Escargot En Croute-French snails in a puff pastry $6.75, Charred Ahi-spicy ahi with soy lilikoi beurre blanc $6.75
Entrées: All of the above plus Bouillabaise de Chef Onjin flavored w/saffron, lemon grass, & plum tomatoes $20.95, Rack of Lamb-Dijon & rosemary $21.00
Desserts: Cheesecake with Fruit Sauce $3.75, Caramel Custard $3.25

Impressions:

Chef OnJin has been part of the Honolulu fine dining scene for quite some time now. Her spins on Eurasian cuisine lead to plate lunch combinations you won't find on a kau kau wagon! Recently she extended her hours and realigned her menu so patrons can partake of her creations throughout the day. A few special items are added during dinner hours to enhance an already enticing menu. We view OnJin's as an exceptional value in a market where exceptions are the rule.

Kapahulu

Ono Hawaiian Foods Authors' Favorite

726 Kapahulu Ave.
Honolulu, HI 96815
808-737-2275
Web: None
Hours: L/D 11:00 AM-7:45 PM XSu
Cards: None
Dress: Casual
Style: Haw $

Menu Sampler:

Breakfast:
N/A
Lunch/Dinner:
Ono Hawaiian Foods Special Plates: All plates include Pipikaula, Lomi Salmon, Haupia, Rice or Poi. Kalua Pig Plate $9.15, Laulau Plate $9.15, Chicken Long Rice Plate $9.15, Combination Plate w/Kalua Pig & Laulau $12.00. No substitutions except for rice or poi. Take out boxes available.
Ala Carte: Kalua Pig $5.35, Laulau or Chicken Laulau $4.75, Squid, Chicken, or Butterfish Luau $4.75, Pipikaula $5.40, Hua Kai (Egg Soup) $3.20, Chicken Long Rice Soup $4.55, Salt Meat Luau or Salt Meat Watercress $8.50, Sardine Watercress $4.75, Chicken Watercress Soup $4.75, Chop Steak (Monday only) $6.80, Plain Butterfish (boiled) $4.75, Beef Stew (except Tuesday) $5.40, Beef Curry $4.40, Tripe Stew $5.50, Lomi Salmon $3.25/$4.75, Poke Squid (Tako) $7.30, Portuguese Sausage $2.70, Spam $2.70, Poi $2.25/$2.50, Rice $1.75, Sweet Potato (2 pcs) $1.75, Haupia (3 pcs) $0.85, Kim Chee $1.55, Opihi $4.90, Fried Fish, Lomi Fish & Onion, or Poke Fish $Prices Vary
Sodas $1.20

Impressions:

Would you like to try authentic Hawaiian food without attending an expensive luau? Then take a ride out Kapahulu to Ono Hawaiian Foods. This diminutive eatery is popular with locals and visitors alike. Out in front you'll see a sign that states, "Aloha-Please Wait Outside-Form A Line To The Right-Be Cool-No Get Mad." That pretty well tells you that you'll have to wait for a seat during busy times. However, it becomes obvious that the extra time invested is well spent after the waitress covers your table with bowls and plates. Parking in this area is dicey so we'd recommend taking a cab. Then, after "eating until you're tired", you'll appreciate the walk home!

Waikiki

Orchids

Authors' Favorite

Halekulani Hotel
2199 Kalia Road
Honolulu, HI 96815
808-923-2311
www.halekulani.com

Hours: SuBruBuf 9:30 AM-2:30 PM
B 7:30-11:00 AM XSu
L 11:30 AM-2:00 PM XSu
D 6:00 PM-10:00 PM
Cards: AE DC DIS JCB MC V
Dress: Evening Aloha
Style: Cont $$$$

Menu Sampler:

Breakfast:

Sunday Brunch Buffet: Bountiful variety of hot & cold sushi, poke, sashimi vegetable and meat salads, fruit, smoked fish, traditional breakfast items, roast meats, pastas, popovers, crepes, soup and desserts $39.50/adults, $24/children
Regular Menu: Eggs Benedict $13.00, with Scottish smoked salmon $14.50, with Alaskan king crab cake $16.00, Poi Pancakes $9.00, Haupia Bread French Toast $9.00 **American Breakfast:** $20.50 **Japanese Breakfast:** $24.50

Lunch:

Soups, Salads & Appetizers: Maryland Jumbo Lump Crab Cake with a chili yogurt and chive dressing $10.50, Portuguese Bean Soup $6.00, Caesar $9.00
Entrées: Seared Ahi Nicoise Salad $20.00, Madras Seafood Curry over jasmine rice with pineapple chutney $18.00, Ahi over macadamia nut fried rice $19.00

Dinner:

Appetizers: Crispy Soft Shell Crab with wasabi cream $8.50, Sautéed Jumbo Sea Scallops topped with Osetra caviar and butter-chive sauce $16.00, Ahi seared with Cajun spices, sesame seeds and lilikoi aioli $14.00
Entrées: Steamed Onaga Oriental Style with shiitake mushrooms $33.00, Filet Mignon or NY Steak with a portobello mushroom sauce $29.50
Desserts: Hazelnut Dacquoise with a chocolate cream and mocha sauce $8.00

Impressions:

Orchids combines a beautiful setting, wonderful service, and an exceptional menu to create one of the finest dining experiences in Hawaii. This is a must.

Oahu Dining

Waikiki

Padovani's Restaurant & Wine Bar
DoubleTree Alana Waikiki Hotel
1956 Ala Moana Blvd
Honolulu, HI 96815
808-946-3456
www.padovanirestaurants.com
Hours: B 6:30 AM-10:00 AM
L 11:30 AM-2:00 PM
D 6:00 PM-9:30 PM
Cards: AE DC DIS JCB MC V
Dress: Evening Aloha
Style: Fre/Med $$$$

Menu Sampler:

Breakfast:
Upside Down Pancakes (Pineapple, Blueberry, Banana, Macadamia Nut) $7.95, Continental Breakfast $12, Full American $17.95
Lunch:
Appetizers: Mesclun Salad with Jerez vinaigrette $10, Onion Soup Gratinee $9, Sweet Corn Clam Chowder $10, Risotto of Shrimp & Asparagus $18
Entrées: Hawaiian Salad & Sautéed Shrimp w/avocado, papaya, mango & mac nuts w/ sweet & sour vinaigrette $16, Crispy Confit of Duck Leg w/ragout of vegetables vinaigrette $22, Fresh Baked Pizza du Jour $12, Fresh Catch $26/35
Dinner:
Appetizers: Vichyssoise of kiawe smoked salmon & crab $16, Sautéed Portabella & Polenta, marmalade of onions, truffle oil vinaigrette $15, Parfait of Avocado & Dungeness Crab in fresh artichoke hearts $15
Main Course: Roasted Muscovy Duck Breast, sautéed endive, ginger jus & grapes $32, Roasted Quail stuffed with mushrooms & marmalade of onions, garlic jus $30, Grilled John Dory, fresh asparagus, tomatoes, capers & Nicoise olive vinaigrette $32, Pan-Fried Scallops with creamy cilantro curry sauce $33
Desserts: Strawberry Sunburst $14, Chocolate Mousse $14

Impressions:

Padovani's has a dual identity. The downstairs dining room offers an amazing collection of Continental dishes. Then, upstairs in the Wine Bar you'll find a lighter, less expensive menu accompanied by over 570 different wines, 64 of them available by the glass. This very Continental restaurant provides some of the finest dining of its type in the islands. Proper attire is de rigueur.

Manoa Valley

Paesano Ristorante Italiano
2752 Woodlawn Drive
Honolulu, HI 96822
808-988-5923

Web: None
Hours: L 11:00 AM-2:00 PM Mo-Sa
D 5:00 PM-9:30 PM Su-Th
D 5:00 PM-10:00 PM FrSa
Cards: AE MC V
Dress: Resort Casual/Evening Aloha
Style: Ital $$

Menu Sampler:

Breakfast:
N/A

Lunch:
Antipasti: Eggplant Rollatini $7.90, Zuppa Di Clam $9.90, Carpaccio $8.90
Zuppe: Minestrone $3.90, Pasta Fagioli $3.90, Vichyssoise $3.90
Insalate: Paesano Salad $6.90, Caesar Salad (min 2 orders) $6.90
Entrées: Chicken Alla Cacciatore $11.90, Fettuccini Alfredo with Chicken and Broccoli $12.90, New York Steak with mushrooms & onions, choice of pasta, potato or vegetables $14.90, Veal Alla Milanese w/pasta, potato, veggies $13.90
Sandwiches: Meatball Sandwich $8.90, Fish Sandwich $10.90

Dinner:
Antipasti: Zuppa Di Clam/Zuppa Di Mussel $9.90, Artichoke Pepperonata 7.90
Vegetables: Mushrooms with Pepper Sauté $7.90, Eggplant Milanese $6.90
Pasta: choice of linguine, fettuccini or rigatoni. Meatball $11.90/$13.90, Carbonara $12.90/$15.90, Pesto Sauce $11.90/$13.90, Sausage $11.90/$14.90
Entrees: Chicken Paesano-sautéed with garlic, peppers, mushrooms, wine sauce $13.90/$16.90, Linguine alla Primavera $12.90/$15.90, New York Steak with onion & mushrooms or Veal alla Rollatini, or Fish Oreganata $16.90/$21.90

Impressions:

There's a classy little Italian ristorante in Manoa Marketplace called Paesano. As you walk up to the door, the first thing you'll notice is the smell of fresh baked bread. This lure draws people in to experience the fine Italian cuisine. Light and full-sized portions are offered for much of their extensive menu. Those looking for romantic dining should find this quite pleasing.

Oahu Dining

Honolulu

Pagoda Hotel's Floating Restaurant
1525 Rycroft St
Honolulu, HI 96814
808-941-6611
www.pagodahotel.com

Hours: Su Bru 10:00 AM-2:00 PM
B Mo-Sa
L 11:00 AM-2:00 PM XSu
D 4:30 PM-9:30 PM
Cards: AE DC DIS JCB MC V
Dress: Resort Casual
Style: Amer/Japan $$
Ent Card

Menu Sampler:

Breakfast:
Sunday Brunch Buffet: Prime Rib Carving Station, seafood, chicken and fish specialties, poached eggs Florentine, scrambled eggs, bacon, sausage, omelet station (10 fillings), sushi, shrimp and vegetable tempura, crepes, local dishes, French Toast and Belgium waffles, desserts- $18.95/adults, $8.95/children(5-10)

Lunch:
Kama'aina Lunch Buffet: Shrimp and Vegetable Tempura, sushi, poke, four entrees, wok fried noodles, potatoes, salad bar, desserts including soft serve ice cream-adults $11.95/children $5.95. On Saturday, this lunch buffet adds Carved Roast Sirloin of Beef and more special entrées- $14.95/adults, $6.95/children

Dinner:
International Buffet-Monday-Thursday-adults $21.95/children $9.95 featuring Roast Prime Rib Au Jus, Snow Crab Legs, Shrimp and Vegetable Tempura
International Buffet-Friday–Sunday- adults $23.95/children $11.95 featuring Roast Prime Rib of Beef Au Jus, Shrimp &Vegetable Tempura, Island Sashimi, Fish of the Day, & three of the chef's special entrées.

Impressions:

We don't usually endorse buffets, but this is one we can get behind. Pagoda's offerings have a higher level of sophistication than you'll find in most places of this type. Better yet, diners are offered a variety of themes on different days, so you can choose your specialty. The setting is interesting, as this restaurant seems to float on an ornamental fishpond in a charming Japanese garden. Leave the tourist haunts behind and go rub elbows with the locals at the Pagoda!

Windward

Pah Ke's Chinese Restaurant

46-018 Kamehameha Hwy
Kaneohe, HI 96744
808-235-4505
Web: None
Hours: LD 10:30 AM-9:00 PM
Cards: AE MC V
Dress: Casual
Style: Chi $

Menu Sampler:

Breakfast:
N/A
Lunch/Dinner:
Appetizer: Crispy Won Ton $3.50, Crispy Gau Gee $4.50, Deep Fried Scallops with Taro $7.50, Pah Ke's Chicken Salad $5.95, Squid with Salt & Pepper $6.25
Roast Meat: Whole Peking Duck with 18 buns $26.00, Half Roast Duck $9.00, Shoyu Chicken $5.75, Char Siu $5.25, Roast meat Combination $10.25
Soup: Watercress with Pork or Beef Soup $5.75, Bird Nest with Shredded Chicken Soup $10.00, Hot & Sour Soup $5.50, Egg Flower Soup $5.00
Entrees: Sautéed Beef with Ginger & Green Onions $5.75, Pork with Bitter Melon $6.25, Mongolian Beef $5.95, Steamed Porkhash with salted fish $6.75, Sautéed Pork with Shrimp Sauce $5.50, Chicken with Cashew Nuts $6.95, Chicken with Oyster Sauce $5.95, Fresh Scallops with Chinese Peas $8.95, Fish Fillet with Sweet & Sour Sauce $7.95, Sautéed Shrimps Szechuan Style $8.50, Abalone with Black Mushrooms $22.00, Lobster Tails with Vegetables $16.00
Sizzling Platters: BBQ Sizzling Beef $8.50, Seafood Satay $8.95
Casseroles: Pot Roast Pork with Taro $6.95, Seafood Combination $9.75
Eggs: Char Siu Egg Fu Yung $4.95, Shrimp Fu Yung $6.25
Noodles: Seafood Combination Fried Noodles $7.50, Hung To Mein $6.95

Impressions:

Aficionados of road tripping and health-centered Chinese cuisine will appreciate Pah Ke's in Kaneohe. Sure, it might take a little bit of effort to get there, but we guarantee you'll enjoy the drive. Then after you arrive your meal will complete the scene. All the usual Hong Kong favorites are offered along with some spicier dishes for accent. Local products are used whenever possible and absolutely no MSG finds its way into the preparations. Although it's located in the corner of a strip mall, Pah Ke's attracts an upscale local crowd. No one should feel out of place. With Pah-Ke's reasonable pricing, neither should their wallets!

Oahu Dining

Honolulu

Palomino Restaurant
66 Queen St
Honolulu, HI 96814
808-528-2400
Web: None
Hours: L 11:15 AM-2:30 PM Mo-Fr
D 5:00 PM-10:00 PM
Cards: AE DC DIS MC V
Dress: Evening Aloha
Style: Amer/Euro/Med $$$

Menu Sampler:

Breakfast:
N/A
Lunch:
Soups and Salads: Local Style Portuguese Bean Soup $5.25, Creamy Bleu Cheese Salad with Toasted Hazelnuts, romaine, bacon, tomato $6.95
Sandwiches: Cheddar Burger with Pepper Bacon on toasted sesame roll $8.95
Pasta: Lobster Ravioli with herb mascarpone $16.95, Carbonara $12.95
Entrées: Spit Roasted Pork Loin with herb crust & wild mushroom sauce $15.50, Grilled Wild Mushroom Salad w/toasted walnuts, Gorgonzola $12.95
Dinner:
Starters: Dungeness Crab Dip with artichoke hearts, sweet onions, Parmesan, cracked pizza crisps $12.50, Smoked Salmon Bruschetta w/goat cheese $9.50
Entrées: Asiago-Almond Crusted Sea Scallops, caramelized sweet onions, roasted red peppers and asparagus, Gloria Ferrer Cuvee beurre blanc $22.95, Huli Huli Chicken, Lemon & Sage or Garlic & Rosemary $16.95, Kabocha Pumpkin Ravioli w/sage pasta, Chinese kale, toasted hazelnuts, sage brown butter $15.95, Spit Roasted Chicken Cannelloni w/roasted garlic cream $15.95

Impressions:

Palomino is the glamour queen of downtown Honolulu restaurants. This upscale dining spot and watering hole overlooks the Honolulu Harbor and busy Nimitz Highway. The menu has a Mediterranean foundation with a Continental twist. Rotisserie-roasted meats and innovative pupus complement the great seafood choices offered on the ever-changing menu. Great signature drinks and a solid wine list make this happening place a popular choice for the downtown business crowd. Palomino is a very cool choice for lunch or dinner. The parking deck in the building is a big plus. Enter off Bethel Street.

Honolulu

Panda Cuisine
641 Keeaumoku St.
Honolulu, HI 96814
808-947-1688
www.pandacuisinehawaii.com
Hours: L 10:30 AM-2:30 PM
D 5:00 PM-10:00 PM
D 10:00 PM-2:00 AM Mo-Sa
Cards: MC V
Dress: Resort Casual
Style: Chi $$

Menu Sampler:

Breakfast:
N/A
Lunch/Dinner:
Dim Sum: Sixty Items prepared by five Dim Sum chefs from Hong Kong.
Appetizers: Fried Stuffed Crab Claws (2) $9.95, Minced Seafood with Lettuce (4) $13.95, Spiced Pig's Fore Shank $9.95, Double Cut with Jelly Fish $14.95
Shark's Fin & Abalone: per person-Braised Superior Shark's Fin (Whole) $75.00, Braised Whole Abalone $36.00, Shark's Fin with Crab Meat $12.95
Soup: Spinach with Tofu Soup $9.95, Abalone and Scallop Soup $26.95, Minced Beef Soup 9.95, Hot and Sour Soup 9.95, Egg Flower Soup 9.50
Entrées: Live Dungeness Crab Baked with Garlic & Butter Sauce $Mkt, Live Maine Lobster baked with ginger & green onion $Mkt, Baked Fresh Prawns with Salted Pepper $12.95, Sizzling Oyster with Black Bean Sauce 13.95, Kung Pao Chicken 10.95, Cantonese Roast Duck (Half) 15.95, Lamb Hunan Style $13.95, Sizzling Tenderloin Steak, Chinese Style $16.95, Mu Shu Pork (4) 11.95, Sizzling Beef with Satay Sauce 12.95, Kung Pao Beef 11.95
Other Items: Spicy Eggplant in garlic sauce with meat $9.95, Fried Rice, Foo Kin Style $11.95, Shrimp Pan Fried Noodle $11.95, Beef w/Chow Fun $9.95

Impressions:

There is an interesting cluster of upscale local dining establishments mauka of the Ala Moana Shopping Center. In the middle of all this you'll find Panda Cuisine. This traditional fine Chinese restaurant starts the day early with dim sum and ends in the wee hours with a light dinner. Meanwhile those visiting during peak meal times will find an extensive menu covering many regions. Sam's Club is across the street, so parking can be an issue at times. Take a cab.

Oahu Dining

Honolulu

Pineapple Room
Macy's
Ala Moana Shopping Center
Honolulu, HI 96814
808-945-8881
www.alanwongs.com
Hours: B 9:00 AM-10:45 AM SaSu
L 11:00 AM-3:00 PM
D 4:00 PM-8:30 PM XSu
Cards: AE DC DIS JCB MC V
Dress: Resort Casual
Style: Haw-Reg/Pac-Rim $$$

Menu Sampler:

Breakfast:
House Made Corned Beef Hash and two eggs with Pineapple Room ketchup $7.50, Spicy Chorizo Scrambled Eggs on vegetable & cheese quesadilla $10.50, Big G's Taco Omelet with avocado salsa and chili sour cream $10.50, Hawaiian Style Eggs Benedict-poached eggs on Kalua pig taro hash cake with lomi tomatoes and luau leaf hollandaise $9.00, Loco-Moke-O w/veal jus $12.50
Lunch:
Thai Style Chicken Cobb Salad w/lemongrass basil dressing $12.50, Korean BBQ'ed Chicken Sandwich, kim chee, bean sprouts, marinated watercress $12.50, Sweet Chili Glazed Mahimahi, w/miso togarashi butter sauce $15.00
Dinner:
Entrées: Guava and Pecan Glazed Lamb, baby vegetables, taro mashed potato, natural jus $32.00, Miso Glazed Salmon w/stir fried vegetables, kim chee vinaigrette $21.00, Pineapple BBQ'ed Baby Back Ribs w/garlic mashed potatoes, sautéed beans, sweet corn $24.50, Seared Peppered Ahi w/roasted garlic potato, haricot vert, bacon, whole grain mustard vinaigrette $25.00, Kiawe Grilled NY Striploin, garlic mashed potatoes, green peppercorn sauce $28.00

Impressions:

Pineapple Room is one of Alan Wong's ventures with Chef de Cuisine Steven Ariel presiding. The menu contains a wonderfully eclectic group of fresh island dishes prepared with classic touches. There are very few department store dining rooms that approach this level of sophistication. Wong's genius and Ariel's expertise combine to make any meal served here an event. Drive up to the third floor parking level of the Ala Moana deck and you can walk in and be seated.

Waikiki

Prince Court Restaurant

Westin Hawaii Prince Hotel
100 Holomoana St
Honolulu, HI 96815/808-944-4494
www.westinhawaiiprincehotel.com

Hours: B 6:00 AM-10:30 AM
SaSuBru 11:15 AM-1:00 PM
L Mo-Fr 11:30 AM-2:00 PM
D 6:00 PM-9:30 PM
Cards: AE DIS JCB MC V
Dress: Evening Aloha
Style: Amer/Japan $$$ Ent Card

Menu Sampler:

Breakfast:

Daily Buffet: 6-10:30 AM-- $19.50 with miso soup with toppings, salads, fruit, cereal, granola, eggs, meats, waffles, traditional and Japanese breakfast entrees
Sa & Su Brunch Buffet: 11:15AM-1PM-- $27.50 with special weekly entrees, saimin, sushi, sashimi, omelet station, antipasti, pasta, crab legs, prime rib

Lunch:

Weekday Buffet: $23.50-'East Meets West" tempura, sushi, shabu shabu. A la Carte-Soba Noodles w/Seared Ahi $10.50, Traditional Curries $12.50

Dinner:

Seafood Dinner Buffet: FrSaSu--$42.00 with crab, sashimi, assorted poke, grilled salmon, prime rib, roasted pig, ahi cakes, stir-fry's, and dessert specials
A la CarteOfferings: Appetizers: Portobello Mushroom and Crab Hash Napoleon with wilted spinach and roasted garlic butter, Cabernet reduction $13.50. **Entrees:** Fresh Pacific Snapper with wild mushroom and lobster ragout $29.00, Grilled Rib Eye Steak w/oven dried tomato & shiitake mushroom relish with redskin mashed potato $29.00, Lobster Tail, Shrimp & Sea Scallops w/grilled vegetables & snap peas, coconut saffron cream $30.00

Impressions:

This is a lovely room with a great view. Outside, the Ala Wai Boat Harbor forms a beautiful backdrop. Inside, you'll find high quality meats, seafood, and produce served in upscale preparations. Although an ala carte menu is always available, many choose to partake in the wonderful buffets and weekend brunches. Chef Goran Streng maintains high standards in all regards. Reservations are suggested, especially for the popular weekend brunch.

Oahu Dining

Windward

Punalu'u Restaurant & Tundaleo's Bar
53-146 Kamehameha Hwy
Punalu'u, HI 96717
808-237-8474
Web: None
Hours: LD 11:00 AM-8:00 PM
Cards: MC V
Dress: Casual
Style: Isl/Sea $$

Menu Sampler:

Breakfast:
N/A

Lunch/Dinner:

30 Shrimp prepared a variety of ways-Shrimp Scampi, Coconut Shrimp, Coconut & Basil (coconut milk & basil), Tempura, Hot & Spicy, Pineapple Shrimp (sautéed in garlic & olive oil), Li Hing Mui Shrimp (sautéed with pineapple & li hing mui) $14.95, for another $2.00 choice the meal and add vegetables, bread, and rice, fries or mashed potatoes
Seafood Entrees $12.95-Mahi or Ono with white sauce $12.95, Seafood Platter $12.95, New York Steak $12.95, Hamburger with fries $5.50, Mushroom Cheeseburger with fries $5.95

Impressions:

Punalu'u Restaurant has roots that go back to when it was known as Ahi's in Kahuku. After that venerable establishment burned, owner Logan Ahi moved his operation to this site. Other endeavors beckoned and the original owner sold the business that we now know as Punalu'u Restaurant. Today this rambling old roadhouse makes a great stop for those driving this misty windward highway. If you're looking for Old Hawaii, here is one place you can find it.

Punalu'u's specialty is locally raised shrimp served in various fashions. They're all great in their own way, but don't get caught up trying to determine which sounds best and miss a couple of very important points. First, if you order a shrimp dish by itself, all you will get is lots of shrimp on a plate of chopped cabbage. This might be great for sharing as a pupu, but if you plan on eating the entire serving yourself, be sure to ask for the meal version to round things out. Then, if making a selection proves difficult, go with a combination, which allows you to request two or even four preparations on a single plate.

Windward

Rainbow Diner & BBQ

54-126 Kamehameha hwy
Hauula, HI 96717
808-293-1693
Web: None
Hours: BLD 9:00 AM-7:00 PM XWe
BL 9:00 AM-3:00 PM We
Cards: MC V
Dress: Casual
Style: Amer/Kor $$

Menu Sampler:

Breakfast:
Served from 9:00 AM-2:00 PM. Two Eggs, Bacon, choice of rice, hash browns, garlic bread and toast $3.50/$5.75, Loco Moco $7.25, Pancakes $4.50, Breakfast Sandwich of eggs, cheese, and choice of meat $3.25, add vegetables $3.95, Steak and Eggs-8 oz NY Steak, rice, hash browns, toast for garlic bread $9.25
Lunch/Dinner:
Plate Lunches: With rice and your choice of three different sides-macaroni salad, bean sprouts, cabbage, seaweed, corn, kimchee. Kalbi $8.25/$4.95, Fish Jun with mahi, or Chicken Katsu Curry $7.95/$4.75, Chopped Steak Stir Fry $7.50/$4.50, BBQ Beef or Chicken $6.95/$3.95, Bi Bim Bap $6.95/$3.95
Shrimp & Seafood: ✯Butter & Garlic Shrimp $10.95, Hot & Spicy Shrimp $10.95, Coconut Shrimp $12.95, Macadamia Nut Shrimp $12.95, Salmon Steak $8.95, Deep Fried Mahi Mahi $10.95, Fried Shrimp Tempura $10.95
Salads: Tossed Salad $5.25Chicken Salad-grilled, fried or spicy $6.95
Sandwiches: Hamburger $2.50, Cheeseburger $3.50/$5.00, Bacon Cheeseburger $4.00, Mushroom Burger $4.00, Deluxe-add lettuce, tomato, and onion $1.00, Fried Shrimp Burger $4.75, Grilled Chicken Burger $4.50, Teri Beef Burger $4.50/$6.00, Mahi Burger $4.75/$6.75

Impressions:

We were on a quest for shrimp trucks when we chanced upon this new place in Hauula. The sign said “Shrimp”, so in we went. We had decided to make butter garlic shrimp our comparison dish at each establishment we visited. The version we were served displayed depth and complexity unmatched at the other places on our list. It was truly “finger-lickin’ good”. Lots of Korean items appear on the menu giving us a hint as to our shrimp prep’s origins.

Kapahulu

Rainbow Drive-In

3308 Kanaina Ave.
Honolulu, HI 96815
808-737-0177
Web: None
Hours: B 7:30 AM-10:30 AM
LD 10:30 AM-9:00 PM
Cards: None
Dress: Casual
Style: Amer $

Menu Sampler:

Breakfast:
Breakfast Special of Two Eggs, choice of fries, rice or white/wheat toast, choice of ham, Spam, Portuguese sausage, wiener, BBQ steak, beef or pork cutlet, boneless chicken, hamburger patty, mahimahi, or chili $4.25, Corned Beef hash and one egg with gravy $3.50, Sweet Bread French Toast $3.50
Lunch/Dinner:
Plate lunch includes rice and macaroni salad. Mix Plate of BBQ boneless chicken and mahimahi $5.90, Hamburger Steak $5.25, Boneless Chicken with Brown Gravy $5.25, Beef or Pork Cutlet $5.45, Ham Steak $5.90, Shoyu Chicken $5.25, Beef Curry $5.25
Sandwiches: On Wheat or White. Ham $2.15, Tuna $2.25, Deviled Egg $2.25, Hamburger $1.35, Mahimahi $2.75, BBQ Beef or Pork $2.75, Hot Dog $1.50

Impressions:

At one time Rainbow Drive-In may have been out in the country, but today the city of Honolulu buzzes around it. Meanwhile, the same families line up at the windows to enjoy their version of comfort food. In keeping with tradition, the offerings are simple but filling. Check out the prices. This is affordable dining regardless of your standards. For a taste of the past, drive out Kapahulu toward the H1 and stop at the Rainbow Drive-In.

Waikiki

Restaurant Suntory Authors' Favorite

Royal Hawaiian Shopping Center
2233 Kalakaua Ave
Honolulu, HI 96815
808-922-5511
www.suntory.co.jp/restaurants/index.html
Hours: L 11:30 AM-1:30 PM Mo-Fr, 12:00 PM-2:00 PM SaSu
D 5:30 PM-9:30 PM
Cards: AE DC DIS JCB MC V
Dress: Resort Casual
Style: Japan $$$$

Menu Sampler:

Breakfast:
N/A
Lunch:
Teppan-yaki Service: All Teppan entrées include salad, miso soup, vegetables, and white rice. Shrimp & Scallops $15.50, New York Steak or Sirloin $19.00, Filet $19.00, Chateaubriand $22.00, Gourmet Sampler Lunch $24.00
Washoku Teishoku: Entrées include salad. Sashimi Teishoku $18.50, Sukiyaki Teishoku $15.00, Tempura Zarusoba $12.50, Ebi Tempura Teishoku $12.50
Dinner:
Appetizers: Chawan-mushi, the chef's creation of shrimp, chicken, and vegetables steamed in creamy egg custard $4.50, Ebi tempura $12.50
Teppan-yaki Courses: $62.00-$120.00 includes appetizer, salad, One or more entrées such as lobster or filet, rice, tsukemono, miso soup, ice cream
Shabu-Shabu or Sukiyaki: $39.00 includes assorted appetizers, rice, tsukemono, Shabu-Shabu/Sukiyaki and ice cream.
Sushi Bar Service

Impressions:

Like everywhere else in the world, modern Japanese dining habits have evolved through contact with other cultures. Restaurant Suntory goes against this trend by offering traditional Japanese dishes free from outside influences. The pursuit of authenticity continues as the chef at the teppanyaki table prepares your meal in true Japanese style rather than putting on a display of fancy knife work and pyrotechnics. Dinner can get pricey, but lunch is quite affordable. Parking is available in the Royal Hawaiian Shopping Center deck behind the complex. Make sure to get your parking ticket validated!

Honolulu

Royal Garden

Ala Moana Hotel
410 Atkinson Drive
Honolulu, HI 96814
808-942-7788
www.royalgardens.com
Hours: L 11:00 AM-2:00 PM
L 10:00 AM-2:00 PM SaSu
D 5:30 PM-10:00 PM
Cards: AE DC DIS JCB MC V
Dress: Evening Aloha
Style: Chi $$$

Menu Sampler:

Breakfast:
N/A
Lunch:
Dim Sum- Extensive selections of steamed items and regular menu service.
Lunch/Dinner:
Appetizers: Deep Fried Taro Ball with crab meat filling $14.95, Char Siu-barbeque fillet pork $9.50, Deep Fried Spring Roll $8.50, Cold Jelly Fish $9.50
Soup: Crab Meat, Pork and Diced Melon Soup $8.95, Hot & Sour Soup $9.50, Chicken Cream Corn Soup $8.95, Seafood with Vegetable Soup $10.95
Entrées: Fried Stuffed Scallop with minced shrimp paste (house specialty) $14.95, Minced Pork and Chinese Sausage & spinach $9.95, Sauteed Shrimp with Szechuan Sauce $15.95, Whole Peking Duck $40.00, Almond Chicken $10.50, Beef with green onion and ginger $10.95, Shredded Pork with bell pepper & chili $9.95, Fried Milk with King Crab Meat (house specialty) $12.95
Casseroles: Abalone & Duck's Webs $29.50, Hawaiian Prawns w/long rice $17.95, Roast Pork & Tofu in Shrimp Sauce $10.95, Braised Chicken $10.95
Dessert: Lychee Sorbet $3.50, Red Bean Soup $2.95, Almond Float w/Fruit Cocktail $2.95

Impressions:

The Royal Garden offers excellent Chinese cuisine, but the dim sum service is a special treat. Just sit back and watch the parade of carts move around the tables and point to your selections. Though you might find a bit of a communication barrier, sign language works. Just be careful when they start passing out the chicken feet! Park on the second floor of Ala Moana.

Hawaii Kai

Roy's Hawaii Kai

Authors' Favorite

6600 Kalanianole Hwy
Hawaii Kai Corporate Plaza
Honolulu, HI 96825
808-396-7697
www.roysrestaurant.com
Hours: D 5:30 PM-9:30 PM
Cards: AE DC DIS JCB MC V
Dress: Resort Casual
Style: Asian/Euro $$$$

Menu Sampler:

Breakfast/Lunch:
N/A
Dinner:
Appetizer: Hawaii Kai Style Crispy Crab Cakes, spicy sesame beurre blanc $12.50, Wood Grilled Mongolian Spiced Baby Back Ribs $10.50, Seared Shrimp On A Stick, cucumber namasu, kim chee, spicy wasabi cocktail sauce $10.50, Pan Seared Hudson Valley Duck Breast w/Thai Mac Nut vin. $11.50
Salads and Vegetables: Mongolian Grilled Chicken Salad with Maui butter lettuce, candied pecans & sesame soy emulsion $9.50, Crispy Calamari & Asian Glass Noodle Salad w/Thai style vinaigrette $9.50, Mixed Greens $7.50
Entrées: Hibachi Grilled Salmon, spun vegetable salad, ponzu sauce $10.50/$25.50, Roy's original Blackened Island Ahi, spicy hot soy mustard butter sauce $13.50/$28.50, Japanese Style Misoyaki Butterfish, sweet ginger wasabi butter sauce $13.50/$28.50, Char Broiled Honey Mustard Short Rib of Beef, Scalloped Potatoes, Poi, Lomi-lomi Tomatoes $26.50, Shiso & Garlic Seared Large Shrimp, Maine lobster white truffle essence $23.50, Roy's Meatloaf, crispy onion rings, natural mushroom gravy $8.50/$17.50

Impressions:

East of Diamond Head in the Hawaii Kai Town Center you'll find the original home of the now global Roy's restaurant chain. Roy Yamaguchi was one of the founders of the Hawaii Regional Cuisine movement. His magic comes through combining flavors and ingredients in intriguing ways. The ever-changing menu couples with an interesting and affordable wine list. Look for Roy's along the highway on the Honolulu side of the lagoon. There's plenty of parking in the lot.

Oahu Dining

Leeward

Roy's Ko Olina
Ko Olina Golf Course
92-1220 Alii Nui Drive
Kapolei, HI 96707
808-676-7697
www.roysrestaurant.com

Hours: L 11:00 AM-2:00 PM
D 5:30 PM-9:30 PM
Cards: AE DC DIS JCB MC V
Dress: Resort Casual
Style: Haw Reg/Pac Rim $$$

Menu Sampler:

Breakfast:
N/A

Lunch:
Starters: Roy's Blackened Island Ahi with spicy soy mustard butter 13.50, Chicken & Rock Shrimp Spring Rolls w/Chinese black bean dragon sauce 8.50
Entrées: Thai Chicken Satay Salad, chopped peanuts, garlic chips 10.50, Roy's Classic Macadamia Nut Fresh Fish w/Maine lobster sauce 13.50, Kiawe Grilled Kobe Beef Hamburger 13.50, Kona Lobster Wrap w/lettuce, tomatoes 13.50
Appetizers on the Bridge Bar: Hot Iron Shrimp on a Stick with hot wasabi cocktail sauce 9.50, Crispy Asian Seafood Mandoo with sunomono, siracha aioli 8.50, Hawaii Kai Style Crab Cakes with spicy sesame butter sauce 12.50

Dinner:
Appetizers: Hibachi Grilled Wild Salmon, sprout salad, Japanese citrus ponzu 11.50, Dim Sum Canoe for two- ribs, ahi, spring roll, shrimp, crab cake 26.50
Entrees: Jade Pesto Steamed Fresh Fish with Chinese style sizzling soy sauce 27.50, Kiawe Grilled Filet Mignon with white bean & smoked bacon demi glace 30.50, Pepper Basil Crusted Opah, Roy's ale buffalo sauce, polenta fries $28.50

Impressions:

Half an hour west of Honolulu developers have created a new resort area called Ko Olina. Recently, well-known local restaurateur Roy Yamaguchi opened his second Oahu location in the Ko Olina Golf Course clubhouse. Roy's signature style includes a display kitchen and plenty of hustle and bustle. Neither his food nor the ambiance is quiet. Diners can expect a flavor punch. Lunch is served making this a good stop for those out driving around the island.

Honolulu

Ruth's Chris
Restaurant Row
500 Ala Moana Blvd
Honolulu, HI 96813
808-599-3860
www.ruthschris.com
Hours: D 5:00 PM-10:00 PM
Cards: AE DC JCB MC V
Dress: Evening Aloha
Style: Stk $$$$

Menu Sampler:

Breakfast/Lunch
N/A
Dinner:
Appetizers: Barbecued Shrimp with white wine, butter, garlic and spices $10.95, Onion Soup Au Gratin $6.95, Mushrooms Stuffed With Crabmeat $10.95, French Fried Maui Onion Rings $5.95, Seared Ahi Tuna $ Market Price
Salads: Caesar $6.95, Fresh Asparagus & Hearts of Palm $6.95, Sliced Tomato & Maui Onion, crumbled blue cheese & vinaigrette $6.95, Spinach Salad $5.95
Entrées: Filet $29.95, Petite Filet $27.95, Rib Eye $32.95, New York Strip $34.95, T Bone $38.95, Veal Chop with hot and sweet peppers $29.95, Broiled Marinated Chicken $19.95, Center Cut Pork Chops $23.95, Lamb Chops (3) with mint jelly $30.95, Steak & Lobster $Market Price, Fresh Catch of the Day-ask your server about selections, $Market Price, Lobster Tails $Market Price
Side Orders: Au Gratin Potatoes $6.95, Shoestring Potatoes $5.95, Lyonnaise $5.95, Cottage Fries $5.95, Baked-1#-$5.95, Sautéed Mushrooms $6.50, Creamed Fresh Spinach $5.95, Fresh Spinach or Broccoli Au Gratin $6.95, Fresh Asparagus with Hollandaise $7.95, Broiled Tomatoes $5.95
Desserts: Bread Pudding w/ Whiskey Sauce $6.95, Crème Brulee $7.25

Impressions:

Ruth's Chris operates a chain of upscale steak houses offering high quality food and service. The Honolulu location can be found in Restaurant Row overlooking Ala Moana Boulevard. Their forte is serving custom-aged beef broiled at 1800 degrees and delivered sizzling at your table. When the waiter informs you that they only use salt and pepper, we suggest ordering your steak well seasoned. The rich side dishes are ample enough to share. Don't miss the great wine list! Park in the deck at the rear of the building and get your ticket validated.

Honolulu

Ryan's Grill

Ward Centre
1200 Ala Moana Blvd.
Honolulu, HI 96813
808-591-9023
Web: None
Hours: Bru 10:00 AM-3:00 PM Su
L 11:00 AM-5:00 PM Mo-Sa
D 5:00 PM-1:00 AM Mo-Sa 3:00 PM-1:00 AM Su
Cards: AE DC MC V
Dress: Resort Casual
Style: Amer/Ec $$

Menu Sampler:

Brunch:
Punaluu Sweet Bread French Toast $14.95, Huevos Rancheros Wrap with chicken and black bean salsa $14.95, Ryan's Loco Moco with two eggs $11.95, Eggs Benedict $15.95, Smithfield Ham and Tillamook Cheddar Omelet $16.95

Lunch/Dinner:
Pupus: Jamaican Jerk Fries with a sweet-hot Thai chili and coconut aioli $5.50, Oyster Shooters each $1.95, Chicken Egg Rolls with spicy peanut dipping sauce $7.95, Hot Dungeness Crab & Artichoke Dip with focaccia bread $11.95
Soups & Salads: Classic Caesar w/garlic croutons $5.95, French Onion Soup with Emmenthaler $5.95, House Salad w/Mandarin oranges and sweet-hot vinaigrette $6.50, Chicken Salad w/sesame dressing & won ton strips $6.50
Entrées: Hot Dungeness Crab Sandwich $11.95, Bay Shrimp Fettucine w/mushrooms & marsala $12.50, Guava-Glazed Baby Back BBQ Ribs $12.95, Kiawe Grilled Salmon & Chili-Rubbed Prawns w/BBQ hollandaise $25.95, Top Sirloin w/Crispy Fried Maui Onions $18.95, Vegetable Pizza $10.95
Desserts: Key Lime Pie $4.95, Haupia Crème Brulee $5.95, Fruit Sorbet $4.95

Impressions:

At Ryan's Grill the entire menu is served all day long until 1:00 AM. This can be great news for travelers who arrive in Hawaii many time zones away from home. The menu is an interesting mix of traditional mainland fare with eclectic spins. Complete bar service and creative pupus complete the scene. This is a popular spot for happy hour. Parking is available in the Ward Centre lot.

Honolulu

Sam Choy's Breakfast, Lunch & Crab

580 Nimitz Hwy
Honolulu, HI 96817
808-545-7979
www.samchoy.com

Hours: B 6:30 AM-10:30 AM Mo-Fr
B SuBuf 9:00 AM-12:00 PM
L 11:30 AM-4:00 PM
D 5:00 PM-10:00 PM
Cards: AE DC DIS JCB MC V
Dress: Casual
Style: Isl $$$

Menu Sampler:

Breakfast:
Homemade Corned Beef Hash & Eggs $6.25, Omelets $6.25-$11.95, Belgian Waffle $4.95, Fried Rice topped w/two eggs $5.75, French Toast Platter $7.25
Sunday Buffet: $13.95/adults, $5.95/children-omelet station, mixed green salad with Sam's Creamy Oriental Dressing, fresh fruit tray, muffins, several hot entrees and rice, Home Fries, bacon, sausage, two special hot entrees
Lunch:
"BLC" bacon, lettuce & crab sandwich $10.50, Sam's Favorite Burger $7.50, Kona Flaming Wok with chicken, beef, or vegetarian $8.95, Paniolo Steak with grilled onion $10.95, Moi-Moi Saimin $11.50, Fried Poke Lunch $9.50
Dinner:
Pupus: Fried Calamari with kim chee furikake $7.95, Korean Spicy Chicken Wings $6.95, Sam's Original Fried Poke $7.95, Wok of Manila Clams $8.95
Entrées: Wok Fried Ginger-Onion Maine Lobster on buttered garlic pasta $27.95, Garlic Roasted Island Chicken with garlic mashed potatoes $16.95, Our Own Ehu Ale Beer Batter Fish with fries and cole slaw $14.95, Chowder $3.95

Impressions:

Sam Choy made his mark by taking local favorites up market. What better place to showcase this approach than in an old factory along the Nimitz Hwy. Inside, a huge display kitchen serves three "local kine" meals a day. The concepts might be simple, but the presentations aren't. Basics are fused together creating layers of flavor that never would have been dreamed of on the old plantations. Due to its location this Sam Choy restaurant has a heavily local trade. Visitors will find it convenient on their way to and from the airport.

Kapahulu

Sam Choy's Diamond Head Restaurant
449 Kapahulu
Honolulu, HI 96815
808-732-8645
www.samchoy.com

Hours:	D 5:30 PM-9:00 PM Mo-Th
	D 5:00 PM-9:30 PM Fr-Su
	SuBruBuf 9:30 AM-2:00 PM
Cards:	AE DC DIS JCB MC V
Dress:	Resort Casual
Style:	Haw-Reg $$$

Menu Sampler:

Breakfast:

Big Aloha Sunday Brunch Buffet: $22.95/adults, age 5-12 $1/year. Many vegetable, pasta and fruit salads, pokes, hot entrees, curries, prime rib, five spice roast duck, fresh island fish, omelet station, desserts

Lunch:

N/A

Dinner:

Pupus: Brie Cheese Wontons with homemade pineapple papaya marmalade $7.50, Seared Ahi Sashimi $10.95, Fried Poke-traditional poke seared on a hot grill $8.95, Honey Hoisin Glazed Lamb Ribs with tropical island slaw $8.95
Entrées: Seafood Laulau with mahi, shrimp, scallops and vegetables wrapped in ti leaves and steamed $26.95, Macadamia Nut Crusted Chicken Breast with a shiitake mushroom cream sauce and papaya pineapple marmalade $21.95, Hawaiian Style Seafood Bouillabaisse of half Maine lobster, Alaskan king crab leg, scallops, shrimp, & fresh fish simmered in an aromatic tomato broth $31.95, Da Choy's Cut Filet-9 oz filet with roasted garlic, baked potato, sautéed onions and green beans $29.95, Fresh Vegetable Luau Pasta with cream sauce $17.95
Desserts: Chocolate Marquise $7.00, Pineapple Cheesecake $7.00

Impressions:

Sam Choy always manages to include local comfort food in his creative menu. What would dinner at Sam's be without some kind of laulau on the table? To get a better picture of his creative style you can check out his web site, catch one of his guest appearances with Emeril, or watch "Sam Choy's Kitchen" on the local stations. Expect to experience that around-the-kitchen-table feel. Sam's personal warmth, generosity, and love of creative food are always extended to the public. Hawaiians call that Aloha! Parking is provided under the building.

Waikiki

Sansei Seafood Restaurant & Sushi Bar
Waikiki Beach Marriott Resort & Spa
2552 Kalakaua
Honolulu, HI 96815
808-931-6286
www.sanseihawaii.com
Hours: D 5:30 PM –10:00 PM
Cards: AE DC DIS JCB MC V
Dress: Resort Casual/Evening Aloha
Style: Asian Fusion/Sea $$$

Menu Sampler:

Breakfast/Lunch:
N/A

Dinner:
Sushi Rolls: California Roll with crab, avocado & cucumber $6.25, Sansei Special Roll of spicy crab, fresh cilantro and veggies inside out with sweet Thai Chili sauce $8.95, Fresh Ahi Sashimi $11.95, Yaki Maki Sushi $14.95
Appetizers: Ahi Tataki $9.95, Sansei's Rock Shrimp Dynamite-crispy tempura rock shrimp tossed w/creamy garlic masago aioli $8.95, Sashimi Combo $11.00, other items 3.95-13.95-Kapalua "Butterfry" of fresh snapper, smoked salmon, crab and veggies in a crispy panko batter roll, served with a tangy ponzu sauce
Entrees: All priced from 16.95-29.95. Shichimi Seared Fresh Atlantic Salmon topped with fresh shiitake mushrooms & asparagus in a mild Japanese pepper sauce, Spicy Crab Stuffed Whole Lobster Tail served over homemade garlic mashed potatoes with our ginger lime chili butter & shiitake mushroom cabernet sauces, Roasted Peking Duck Breast over sautéed spinach with a rich foie-gras demi-glaze, Grilled Filet of Beef Tenderloin crusted with mild chili-porcini mushrooms served over roasted garlic mashed potatoes with a shiitake mushroom unagi demi-glaze, Roasted Japanese Jerk Chicken, served over homemade garlic mashed potatoes with a fresh herb beurre blanc sauce.

Impressions:

Until recently this popular place was located in Restaurant Row near downtown Honolulu. Now visitors will be able to enjoy the Sansei experience a short stroll from their hotels. The owner got his start in a small sushi bar on Maui. Instead of relying strictly on tradition, he branched out and pushed the envelope of contemporary sushi. Unique appetizers and entrées followed as the creativity continued. The resulting menu will satisfy grazers and serious diners alike.

Waikiki

Sarento's Top of The "I" Authors' Favorite

Renaissance Ilikai Hotel
1777 Ala Moana Boulevard
Honolulu, HI 96814
808-955-5559
www.tri-star-restaurants.com
Hours: D 5:30 PM-9:00 PM Su-Th, 5:30-9:00 PM SaSu
Cards: AE DC DIS JCB MC V
Dress: Evening Aloha
Style: Ital $$$$

Menu Sampler:

Breakfast/Lunch:
N/A
Dinner:
Appetizers: Escargot w/creamy polenta, spinach, local mushrooms & garlic parmesan gratin $11.95, Smoked Salmon "Sandwich", crème fraiche $11.95
Soup & Salad: Minestrone $5.50, Caesar Alla Sarento's $8.95, Salad Gabriella with grilled marinated baby artichokes, tomatoes, Shrimp $10.95
Entrées: Filet Marc Anthony brushed with Italian country mustard, buffalo mozzarella & crispy Maui onions, served in a porcini demi $33.95, Rack of Lamb, eggplant Caponata, roasted fingerlings, pomegranate syrup $36.95, Pan Roasted Opakapaka with roasted Cremini mushrooms and watercress salad, topped with jumbo lump crab, simmered in lemon butter $Mkt, Kiawe Smoked Pork Chop, Maui onion jam "Agrodolce" Yukon mashed potatoes, mustard balsamic $26.95, Linguine Con Vongole $22.95, Penne Calabrese with fresh basil, diced eggplant, tomatoes, Italian sausage & goat cheese $21.95

Impressions:

Food enthusiasts are naturally skeptical of dining rooms located on top of tall buildings. Why? History has shown us that the view often comes first, leaving the food and service to bring up the rear. We're happy to report that this is not the case at Sarento's. The first thing one notices after getting past the power of the room and location is the polite, attentive service. Then comes dinner. You'll find an impressive menu to choose from, leaving the only problem being what to order. This also applies to the wine list where the selections seem endless. Plan to arrive before sunset and get the best of the daytime and evening vistas.

Waikiki

Seafood Village
Hyatt Regency Waikiki
2424 Kalakaua Avenue
Honolulu, HI 96815
808-971-1818
www.seafoodvillage.com
Hours: L 11:00 AM-2:00 PM
D 5:30 PM-10:00 PM
Cards: AE CB DC JCB MC V
Dress: Resort Casual
Style: Chi $$
Ent Card

Menu Sampler:

Breakfast:
N/A
Lunch:
Cantonese Dinner menu plus the Hong Kong style dim sum service. Char Siu Bao, Spring Rolls, Shrimp Dumplings, Manapua, Shrimp Shu Mai, Pork Hash, Half Moon, Taro Puff, Won Ton, Seafood and custard tarts at reasonable prices.
Dinner:
Appetizers: Crispy Spring Rolls (3) $4.95, Fried Stuffed Crab Claws (2) $8.95
Salads: Oriental Chicken Salad $4.50, Fresh Roast Duck Salad $4.95
Soup: Lobster & Spinach Soup $8.95, Seafood Hot & Sour Soup $3.75, Chicken & Shiitake Mushroom $4.50, Braised Top Grade Shark's Fin $88.00
Entrées: Sizzling Tenderloin Black Pepper Sauce $18.95, Honey Garlic Tangerine Beef $13.95, Twin Vegetables with Bamboo Fungus $12.50, Fresh Kahuku Shrimp Peppery Salt $17.95, Boneless Chicken Kung Pao Style $10.95
Rice & Noodles: Shrimp and Vegetable Fried Noodles $18.95, Char Siu Fried Rice $12.95, Seafood Combination Noodles $18.95, Garlic & Duck Meat Fried Rice $14.95, Lobster Meat & Vegetables Noodles $28.95, Broccoli with Tofu in wine sauce $10.95, Shanghai Cabbage with Virginia Ham $10.95

Impressions:

On the Ewa side of the Hyatt Regency entrance there's a staircase leading downstairs to a special Chinese dining experience. At lunch their Hong Kong style dim sum service is fun and affordable. The dinner menu is truly massive and features the live seafood for which the restaurant is named. This is fine Cantonese dining within walking distance of all the central Waikiki hotels.

Waikiki

Shanghai Bistro
Discovery Bay
1778 Ala Moana Blvd.
Honolulu, HI 96815
808-955-8668
Web: None
Hours: LD 11:30 AM-10:00 PM Su-Th
LD 11:30 AM-12:00 AM FrSa
Cards: AE DC DIS JCB MC V
Dress: Resort Casual
Style: Asian $$

Menu Sampler:

Breakfast:
N/A
Lunch:
Ala Carte menu available. Chef Chang's Peking Duck Burger on wheat bun, cucumber, green onions, carrots, wasabi cream, French fries $9, Five Course Gourmet Lunch for $8.95 of salad, soup, appetizer, entrée, dessert.
Dinner:
Appetizers: Baked Cream Cheese Scallop with cheese & avocado $4, Crispy Bacon Tofu Rolls $5, Crab Meat in Taro Basket with mayonnaise $4, Golden Seafood Treasure Bag with cream cheese, shrimp, scallops $5, Stuffed Quail $8
Salads: Vietnamese Salad with bean sprouts, basil, cucumbers, carrots, rice noodles, Vietnamese ham, peanuts $7, Thai Papaya Salad $7
Soups: Ground Spinach Tofu Soup $6, Shanghai Bamboo Cup of chicken, pork, daikon, ginger in a clear broth $6, Spicy Thai Seafood Soup $11
Entrees: Bistro Pork Chops w/mushrooms, onions, black pepper, soy sauce $14, Signature Kung Pau Chicken $15, Black Pepper Shrimp Steak-Garlic Rice $18

Impressions:

Chinese dining experiences have historically been broadened by reaching out to new geographic regions. When Cantonese dining became routine, enterprising proprietors introduced the exciting flavors of Hunan and Szechuan. Then came dim sum satisfying our urge to graze. The chef at Shanghai Bistro has combined all of this into a cornucopia of playful contemporary cuisine. Disparate elements and techniques are fused into dishes that defy labels. It's all presented in an expansive setting defined by fine wood and custom table appointments.

Waikiki

Shogun

Pacific Beach Hotel
2490 Kalakaua Ave
Honolulu, HI 96815
808-921-6113
www.pacificbeachhotel.com
Hours: B 6:00 AM-10:00 AM
L 11:00 AM-2:00 PM
D 5:30 PM-10:00 PM
Cards: AE DC DIS JCB MC V
Dress: Evening Aloha
Style: Japan $$$

Menu Sampler:

Breakfast:
Daily Buffet: $17.50/adults, $9.25children -American and Japanese traditional menu items-fruits, scrambled eggs, meats, fish, nori, tofu, croissants, Danish
Lunch:
Weekday Lunch Buffet: $10.95/adults, $6.95/ children, featuring three hot entrees, sushi, poke, sashimi, tako poki, shrimp tempura, yaki soba, rice, oshinko, lomi lomi salmon, salad bar, dessert table and soft serve ice cream
Weekend Lunch Buffet: $15.95/adults, $9.00/children, all of the above plus snow crab legs, beef or seafood teppan, and three "chef special" hot entrees
Dinner:
Sushi Bar Dinner Special-5:30-10 PM**-** All you can eat Nigiri Sushi with a one and a half hour limit. Seating available only at the sushi counter $39.95
Tea House Style Dinners-5:30-10 PM-only with 48 hour advance ordering-private rooms-minimum party of ten-three entrees, adult $19.95/children$11.95, four entrees, plus Kobachi, tsukemono, rice & tea $21.95/adult, $13.95/children
Dinner Specials-all include miso soup, tsukemono, kobachi, rice and tea. $12.95-$22.95 offering dishes such as salmon misoyaki, tonkatsu, spicy garlic chicken, butterfish misoyaki, cold beef shabu shabu, sukiyaki

Impressions:

Shogun serves authentic Japanese cuisine either buffet style or as a complete dinner. Along one wall you'll find the top of a three-story aquarium, and on the other there's a sushi bar. Sounds sensible enough! After dinner karaoke becomes part of the fun. Lunch at Shogun is a culinary adventure at reasonable prices.

Honolulu

Side Street Inn Authors' Favorite
1225 Hopaka Street
Honolulu, HI 96814
808-591-0253
Web: None
Hours: L 10:30 AM-1:30 PM Mo-Fr
D 4:00 PM-12:30 AM
Cards: None
Dress: Casual
Style: Isl/Pac Rim $$

Menu Sampler:

Breakfast:
N/A
Lunch:
Pan Fried Island Pork Chops 9.00, Teriyaki Rib Eye 7.25, Broiled Mahi 6.50, Chicken or Tofu Vegetable Stir-Fry 6.25, Yakisoba 5.75, Saimin 4.00
Sandwiches: Cheeseburger 4.50, Teriyaki Chicken 4.25, Grilled Mahimahi Deluxe 4.75, Smoked Turkey Deluxe 4.75, Chicken Cutlet 4.25
Salads: Cold Somen Salad 5.00, Shrimp Caesar Salad 6.50, Cobb Salad 7.00
Daily Specials-all plates come with rice and choice of tossed or mac salad- Furikake Catch Mkt $, Chicken Hekka 4.50/5.50/6.00, Mochiko Chicken 4.75/5.75/6.00, Spicy Pork Eggplant 4.50/5,50/6.00, Chinese Style Steamed Catch Mkt $, Hawaiian Plate 7.25, Misoyaki Chicken 4.75/5.75/6.00
Dinner:
Asian Grilled Lamb Chops $21.00, Hoisin or Lilikoi Baby Back Ribs $13.50, Chinese Style Crispy Chicken $8.50, Kal Bi with Kim Chee $15.50, 12 oz New York Steak $18.00, Pan Fried Ahi Belly Mkt $, Deep Fried Calamari $9.75

Impressions:

This unassuming establishment came by its name honestly. It truly is a rambling little inn and is definitely located on a side street. We first heard about this place from an airline crew who spend their layover eating and relaxing in its friendly confines. One visit convinced us that they had found something special.

Side Street Inn is a pupu lovers delight. Every day at 4 PM the kitchen starts turning out an amazing variety of ala carte specialties. Any one of these could be a meal in itself, so sharing makes tremendous sense. Quality and originality are hallmarks witnessed by the local chefs who appear here after their own closings.

Waikiki

Singha Thai Authors' Favorite

1910 Ala Moana Blvd.
Honolulu, HI 96815
808-941-2898
www.singhathai.com
Hours: D 4:00 PM-11:00 PM
Cards: AE CB DC DIS JCB MC V
Dress: Evening Aloha
Style: Thai $$$

Menu Sampler:

Breakfast/Lunch:
N/A
Dinner:
Appetizers: Shrimp Spring Rolls with shrimp, minced pork, vermicelli noodles, mushrooms, onions and carrots in crispy rice paper $7.95, Grilled Beef Salad with lemongrass garlic dressing-mild, medium, or hot $8.95, Crispy Duck Lumpia with spicy hoisin sauce $8.95, Curry Puffs with dressing $7.95
Soups: Tom Yum Kung (for two)-spicy lemongrass soup with shrimp, mushrooms, chili paste, cilantro and lime juice- mild, medium or hot $9.95, Ginseng Chicken Soup with Chinese herbs and Ginseng (for two) $9.95
Curries: Baked Boneless Breast of Duck with panang curry sauce $18.95
Noodles: Pad Thai with chicken breast, tamarind sauce & peanuts $12.95
Rice: Vegetarian Fried Rice with mixed vegetables and egg $10.95
Entrées: Siamese Fighting Fish-crispy whole fish served with spicy Thai chili lime sauce $29.95, Asian Style Osso Buco with pearl onions, diced pumpkin and chestnuts $25.95, Singha Steak & Prawns w/sweet potato cake $30.95. Sample Chef Chai's Award-Winning Thai Chili Ginger Sauce or Thai Light Black Bean Sauce over chicken, sea scallops, lobster tail or fresh local fish $15.95-$30.95

Impressions:

Walk across Ala Moana Boulevard from the Hilton Hawaiian Village and you'll find an elegant dining spot serving traditional Thai and contemporary Pacific Rim cuisines. Singha Thai earned its reputation for excellence by offering light, healthy dishes that literally explode with flavor. For a real sampling of exotic tastes, try the recommended food and wine pairings served family style. As an added treat, the Royal Thai Dancers perform nightly from 7 to 9 PM.

Kaimuki

Sis Kitchen
1137 11th Avenue
Honolulu, HI 96816
808-732-0902
www.siskitchen.com
Hours: LD 11:00 AM-9:00 PM XTuSu
D 4:00 PM-9:00 PM Su
Cards: MC V
Dress: Casual
Style: Korean $$

Menu Sampler:

Breakfast:
N/A
Lunch/Dinner:
Lunch Specials: Served 11:00 AM-2:00 PM Mo-Fr. The following are served with side vegetables and rice; Bulgogi (sliced rib-eye steak) 5.95, Dak Gui (BBQ Chicken) mild or spicy 5.95, Bento (Miso Butterfish) 6.95
Appetizers: Mandoo-dumplings, steamed or fried 5.95, House Salad with grilled chicken breast with our homemade dressing 7.95
Soups and Noodles: Dduk Mandoo Kook-dumplings & sliced rice cake served in mild homemade broth 7.95, Hot Kooksoo-noodles in homemade broth 7.95
Rice: Bibimbop-seasoned shredded vegetables, beef and fried egg over rice 7.95, Kim Chee Fried Rice with chopped kim chee, onion and Spam 7.95
Entrees: Served with rice and side dishes. Kim chee Jigae-hot and spicy kim chee pot stew 8.95, Soft Tofu Jigae- soft tofu stone pot stew 8.95, Grilled Miso Butterfish 12.95, Garlic Shrimp sautéed to golden brown in garlic butter sauce 12.95, Croaker grilled or deep-fried 10.95, Spicy Squid and assorted vegetables stir fried in hot chili pepper sauce 9.95, Meat Jun (fritter) 9.95, Bulgogi & Dak Gui 11.95, Kalbi-marinated beef short ribs 12.95, Combination of Bulgogi, Dak Gui, Kalbi 14.95, Spicy Marinated BBQ Sliced Pork 10.95

Impressions:

The Kaimuki area of Honolulu is gathering a fine collection of quality ethnic eateries of which Sis kitchen is a valued new addition. This is dining Korean style with a healthy, fresh approach. Portions are quite large, so be careful not to over order. Sis Kitchen is located in the same block as the Waialae Avenue restaurant row spots and shares the city parking lot behind the buildings.

Honolulu

Sorabol
805 Keeaumoku St
Honolulu, HI 96814
808-947-3113
Web: None
Hours: 24/7
Cards: AE JCB MC V
Dress: Casual
Style: Kor $$

Menu Sampler:

Breakfast:
$6.95-Kim Chee Pot Stew, Soft Tofu Pot Stew, Char Broiled Mackerel Pike, Bean Sprout Soup, Beef and Vegetable Soup (spicy), Bean Paste Stew
Lunch:
Plate style with steamed rice, kim chee, and vegetables. Barbecued Marinated Pork/Chicken $7.50, Barbecued Marinated Prime Ribeye $8.00, Fish Fritter or Beef Fritter Plate $7.50, Combination lunch plates are available $9.50
Special Lunch: BBQ Pork Baby Back Ribs $12.50, Sushi Regular $20.00
Dinner:
All are served with pickled vegetables, kim chee, steamed rice and soup.
Bul Go Ki (barbecued marinated ribeyes) $15.95, Marinated and Seasoned Sirloin $17.95, Char-Broiled Hairtail Fish $13.95, Steamed Halibut $13.95, Dumplings in beef soup $8.50, Seaweed Soup $8.00, Chicken Soup with Ginseng and Sweet Rice $15.95, Noodles mixed with beef and vegetables $8.50, Sliced Pork and Kim Chee with spicy sauce $12.95, Char-Broiled Mackerel Fish $10.95, Marinated and Seasoned Tripe $16.95, side orders of sushi available.

Impressions:

If you would like to have an authentic Korean dining experience, pay a visit to Sorabol. Menus of this type can be a bit intimidating with listings of variety meats and unfamiliar fish, but if you stay with the marinated and barbecued dinners you just might find yourself singing its praises. Most dishes are accompanied by an assortment of pickled vegetables including kim chee, which is a zesty salsa made from coarsely chopped cabbage and chili peppers. Spicy! Steamed rice is a complementary neutral flavor that offsets the excitement in the rest of your meal. The restaurant is roomy, casual, and bustles with activity 24 hours a day. There's plenty of free parking in the lot beside the building.

Diamond Head

South Shore Grill
3114 Monsarrat Ave
Honolulu, HI 96815
808-734-0229
Web: None
Hours: LD 11:00 AM-8:00 PM
Cards: None
Dress: Casual
Style: Isl $

Menu Sampler:

Breakfast:
N/A

Lunch/Dinner:
Plates: All plates come with rice, tuna mac salad and South Shore Slaw OR Fries and Slaw. Fish Tacos-2 fish tacos lightly floured or grilled $6.75, Kal-Bi-1 lb. of delicious marinated short ribs $6.95, BBQ Chicken-Korean style marinated chicken $5.75, Fresh Island Fish-mahi grilled w/pesto, garlic butter, Cajun or house $6.95, Mix Plate-1 Fish Taco, 1 Kal-Bi, 1 BBQ Chicken $7.95
Sandwiches: All sandwiches are served on toasted Ciabatta bread and topped with chipotle aioli, south shore slaw, lettuce and tomato. Chicken Breast-Cajun, mac nut pesto, or house soy sesame $5.95, Grilled Mahi-Cajun, mac nut pesto, garlic butter, or house soy sesame $5.75, South Shore Grill Burger-1/2 lb of hand pattied ground chuck served on a bed of crispy shoestring onions, topped with chipotle aioli, south shore slaw, lettuce and tomato $5.75, Caprese-fresh buffalo mozzarella, tomatoes, mac nut pesto, sweet basil leaves & EEOO $4.25
Salads: organic greens with a house vinaigrette-House Salad $3.50, Grilled Chicken Breast Salad $5.25, Grilled Mahi Salad $5.95
Desserts: Baked in House Desserts Daily.

Impressions:

South Shore Grill Is located in the former Teddy's Bigger Burger location on Monsarrat. This makes perfect sense, as the new chef is the spouse of the burger palace's owner! The husband and wife team recognized that there was a market in this area for upscale fast food. They took a deceptively simple menu and added depth across the board. Everything is tweaked to add new dimensions of taste and flavor. Carry-out and inside seating are both available.

Honolulu

Sunset Grill

Restaurant Row
500 Ala Moana Blvd
Honolulu, HI 96813
808-521-4409

Web: None
Hours: L 11:00 AM-4:00 PM XSaSu
D 5:00 PM-10:00 PM
Cards: AE DC DIS JCB MC V
Dress: Evening Aloha
Style: Ec/Pac-Rim $$$ Ent Card

Menu Sampler:

Breakfast:

N/A

Lunch:

Pupus: Caesar Salad $8.95, Fried Lobster Ravioli w/roasted garlic & Gorgonzola sauce $9.95, Grilled Marinated Duck Breast Salad $14.95
Pastas: Scampi over Linguine $18.95, Blue Crab Amontillado w/asparagus flamed over penne pasta and a garlic cream sauce $18.95, primavera $16.95
Sandwiches: Reuben with Swiss cheese & sauerkraut on Molasses Bread $9.95
Entrées: includes vegetables. Hoisin Barbecue Pacific Salmon with jasmine rice $18.95, St. Louis Ribs with garlic mashed potatoes $18.95, Petite Filet $17.95

Dinner:

Pupus: House Made Cured Salmon Carpaccio with crostini $12.95, Ahi Poke local style with Maui onions and macadamia nuts $Market, Calamari $7.95
Salads: Chicken & Gorgonzola with greens, candied walnuts, Granny Smith apples with a red wine vinaigrette $13.95, Blackened Salmon Spinach $13.95
Pastas: Scampi $18.95, Kiawe Grilled Chicken Primavera over linguine with roasted tomato sauce $18.95, Spicy Sausage & Tiger Shrimp over penne $21.95
Entrées: Kiawe Grilled Filet Mignon with garlic mashed potatoes and Zinfandel reduction demi glace $25.95, Seafood Mixed Grill of Shrimp, Salmon, and Scallops w/a champagne mustard sauce on basil pesto linguine $18.95

Impressions:

Sunset Grill draws its ideas and ingredients from around the world. Your dining partners are just as likely to have lamb from Colorado as clams from Manila. Throw in a little Tex-Mex seasoning and hoisin sauce and the kitchen becomes a pretty wild place. Wine enthusiasts will love this place.

Oahu Dining

Waikiki

Surf Room
The Royal Hawaiian
2259 Kalakaua Ave
Honolulu, HI 96815
808-923-7311
www.royal-hawaiian.com
Hours: SuBru 11:00 AM-2:30 PM
B Buf 6:30 AM-11:30 AM
L 11:30 AM-2:30 PM XSu
D 6:00 PM-10:00 PM
Cards: AE DC DIS JCB MC V
Dress: Evening Aloha
Style: Pac-Rim $$$$

Menu Sampler:

Breakfast:
Sunday Champagne Brunch: carved meats, hot entrees, traditional breakfast items, seafood, salads, fruits, desserts $33.95/adults, $23.95/children
Breakfast Buffet: Traditional breakfast items buffet style $22.25 or a la carte: Pecan Waffle $10.75, Three Egg Gourmet Omelet with hash browns $16.25
Lunch:
Salads & Soups: Roast Five-Spice Chicken Salad with Mac Nuts and Crispy Noodles $12.95, Chilled Light Creamy Maui Onion Soup w/onion rings $6.25
Entrées: Sauteed Mahi Mahi with baby spinach, mango-jicama salsa and jasmine rice $16.25, Royal Hawaiian Seafood Melt Sandwich $13.95
Dinner:
Appetizers: Pepper Spiced Gravlox Summer Roll $10.50, Pan Seared Sea Scallops $13.50, The Royal Sampler $18.00, Shrimp Cocktail $13.00
Salads: Baby Romaine Salad $8.00, Spinach Salad with Fresh Tuna Confit $12.00, Lobster Nicoise Salad & Kahuku Corn Pancake $14.00
Entrées: Teriyaki Glazed Grilled Ahi Fillet $28.00, Sautéed Garlic Jumbo Prawns $32.00, Broiled Beef Tenderloin $36.00, Fresh Maine Lobster $46.00, Royal Hukilau Seafood Bounty – as an entrée $44.50, w/any entrée $16.50

Impressions:

The Surf Room flows from a lovely indoor dining room to a beachfront terrace. Likewise offerings run from the daily resort mega breakfast buffet to romantic Pacific Rim dining. Such is the life of the signature restaurant at the Pink Palace. Stop by and experience the lifestyle at this Waikiki Beach landmark.

Honolulu

Sushi Sasabune
1417 S King St
Honolulu, HI 96814
808-947-3800
Web: None
Hours: L 12:00 PM-2:00 PM Tu-Fr
D 5:30 PM-10:00 PM Mo-Sa
Cards: AE DC MC V
Dress: Casual/Evening Aloha
Style: Japan $$$

Menu Sampler:

Breakfast:
N/A
Lunch/Dinner:
Sashimi/Appetizer: Abalone $15.00, Tuna/Albacore $8.00, Baby Squid $7.00, Y-Tail Collar $3.50, Monk Fish Liver $7.00
Sushi: $$ are per person 4 orders minimum. Toro $10.00, Tuna $4.40, Red Snapper $4.20, Halibut $6.00, Yellow Tail $4.50, Salmon $4.00, Scallop $6.50, Shrimp/Prawn $6.50, Albacore $4.20, Skip jack $5.50, Spanish Mackerel $6.00, Travelly Jack $6.00, Mackerel $4.20, King Mackerel $5.00, Oyster $4.50, Jumbo Clam $8.00, Surf Clam $6.50, Sea Urchin $8.00, Salmon Egg $6.00, Octopus $5.00, Eel $7.00, Egg $4.00, Negitoro Sushi $8.00, Crab Roll $5.00, Salmon Belly R. $5.00, Eel Roll $6.00, Umeshiso Roll $4.50

Impressions:

The American public is accustomed to being in control particularly when they're picking up the check. This works fine on our home turf, but it doesn't always play well when venturing into uncharted waters. Since most of us didn't grow up eating traditional Japanese sushi, perhaps a little education is called for.

Sushi Sasabune operates on the principle that the chef knows best. He knows what's available, how to present it, and the method for maximum enjoyment. Those seeking more than a California Roll would do well to sit down at this sushi bar, and let the master present his culinary performance.

Please note that this experience doesn't come cheaply. The fish and seafood are sourced globally at considerable cost. Those interested in the full presentation can expect per person costs in the $60-$80 range.

Niu Valley

Swiss Haus
Niu Valley Shopping Center
5730 Kalanianole Hwy
Honolulu, HI 96821
808-377-5447
swisshausllc@juno.com

Hours: SuBru 10:30 AM-1:00 PM
D 5:30 PM-9:00 PM XMo
Cards: AE DC DIS JCB MC V
Dress: Resort Casual
Style: Euro $$

Menu Sampler:

Breakfast:
Sunday Brunch: $16-salads, cold cuts, hot dishes, assorted desserts
Lunch:
N/A
Dinner:
Appetizers: Croute Emmental-creamed mushrooms on toast with sliced ham, glazed with Swiss cheese $5.00, Fresh Steamed Clams $8.50, Escargot $6.75
Soups: Swiss Onion Soup glazed w/Swiss cheese $4.25, Soup of the day $2.00
Salads: Spinach Salad with lemon and olive oil dressing, bacon bits and chopped egg whites $4.25, Salat Teller-assorted salad plate $6.75, Swiss Haus Salad of mixed greens, mushrooms, tomatoes tossed with house dressing $3.25
Complete Dinners: include soup of the day, salad, vegetable and coffee or tea. Veal Medallions Florentine-sautéed veal on a bed of spinach topped with bacon and glazed with Swiss cheese with rosti potatoes $19.50, Entrecote Café de Paris-New York Steak sautéed with special herb-butter sauce with baked potato or French fries $24.50, Trout Caprice-fillets of sautéed fresh rainbow trout on a bed of creamed mushrooms, topped with banana, parsley potatoes $18.50
Light Dinners: Bratwurst $7.50, Vegetarian Pasta with garlic cream sauce $9.75, Weinerli-a European style frankfurter with Swiss potato salad or French fries $6.25, Croute Emmental-creamed mushrooms on toast with ham $8.75

Impressions:

For a change of pace, try this affordable dining spot east of Diamond Head. Swiss Haus features authentic European cuisine that you just don't see offered around Honolulu. It's located in the Niu Valley Shopping Center past Kahala on the main highway and is really quite easy to find. Wait until rush hour is over.

Waikiki

Tanaka of Tokyo

Renaissance Ilikai Waikiki Hotel
1777 Ala Moana Blvd
Honolulu, HI 96815
808-945-3443
www.tanakaoftokyo.com

Hours: L 11:30 AM-2:00 PM Mo-Fr
D 5:30 PM-Closing
Cards: AE DC DIS JCB MC V
Dress: Resort Casual
Style: Japan $$$
Ent Card

Menu Sampler:

Breakfast:
N/A
Lunch:
Appetizers: Calamari Appetizer with butter and lemon $5.50, Teppan Fried Rice with egg $1.50, Miso Soup $1.50, Sautéed Scallop Appetizer $3.75
Entrées: Tanaka Sirloin Special $13.75, Seafood Combination (shrimp and scallops) with sauce $11.25, Salmon Steak $12.75, Chicken Teriyaki $9.00, Sukiyaki Steak $10.25, Shrimps $10.75, Scallops $11.75, Filet $14.25
Dinner:
Appetizers: Alaskan King Crab steamed in a ti leaf wrap on your teppan grill $12.00, Shrimp grilled and flambéed at your table $5.50, Blackened Ahi $9.75
Entrées: All come with pickled vegetables, tossed salad, miso soup, steamed rice, grilled shrimp appetizer, teppan vegetables, Japanese green tea and dessert. Shogun-combination of prime filet, whole lobster tail and scallops $58.00, Tanaka Sirloin $24.50, Teppanyaki Salmon $19.25, Shrimp $19.25, Chicken Teriyaki $15.50, Lobster-large tail served in shell $36.50, Scallops $20.75
Dessert: Vanilla, Green Tea, or Watermelon Sherbet or Kona Coffee $1.50

Impressions:

Teppanyaki dining has long been a special occasion favorite with eastern and western diners. At Tanaka Of Tokyo chefs prepare dinner with flashing knives and showman-style flair while verbally interacting with the diners. Of course talking story with others around your table is part of the fun. If you don't know, ask and someone is sure to help you. This is a great place for bargain hunters. Lunch is an unbeatable value, and coupons abound for dinnertime specials.

Diamond Head

Tavola Tavola

3106 Monsarrat Avenue
Honolulu, HI 96815
808-737-6600
Web: None
Hours: D 5:30 PM-9:30 PM
D 5:30 PM-10:00 PM FrSa
Cards: AE DC JCB MC V
Dress: Evening Aloha
Style: Ital $$$

Menu Sampler:

Breakfast/Lunch:

N/A

Dinner:

Antipasti: Fried Calamari and Zucchini with Tartar Sauce $12, Marinated Seafood Salad $12, Salmon Balloon filled with fresh diced vegetables $13, Crepes topped with Salmon and Creamy Sauce $13, Sautéed Squid in tomato sauce $14, Raw Albacore Tuna with arugula, balsamic & olive oil $11
Pasta: Spaghetti with small sausage meatballs and tomato sauce $13, Soft Polenta with a zucchini and calamari sauce and truffle essence $16, Spinach Lasagna with meat sauce $12, Homemade Spinach Pasta with shrimp and cherry tomatoes $15, Homemade Pasta with fresh clams in white wine sauce $16, Homemade Wide Pasta with medley of mushrooms & Bolognaise sauce $15, Shrimp Risotto with asparagus $17, Asparagus Soup $9
Secondi: Today's Fresh Fish with sautéed vegetables and aromatic olive oil $25, Butterfly Shrimp grilled with fresh herb olive oil $19, Grilled Baby Lamb Chops with spinach and roasted potatoes $27, Grilled Ribeye Steak with spinach and roasted potatoes $25, Lamb Stew with green beans $21, Grilled Sausage Patties with soft polenta $19, Four Course Degustation Meal $50

Impressions:

Tavola Tavola is located in a classy little building up near the base of Diamond Head. There behind Kapiolani Park, an Italian-trained Japanese chef prepares an interesting array of southern Italian dishes. Don't expect to see pasta with heavy sauces coming out of his kitchen. In this fine dining establishment the flavors of the ingredients are allowed to come through naturally. Everything from the table service to the house made pastries is strictly upscale, but the atmosphere remains comfortable and welcoming. The parking area is small, so look across the street.

Hawaii Kai

Teddy's Bigger Burgers

Koko Head Marina
7192 Kalanianole Hwy
Honolulu, HI 96825
808-394-9100
Web: None
Hours: LD 10:30 AM-9:00 PM
Cards: None
Dress: Casual
Style: Amer $

Menu Sampler:

Breakfast:
N/A
Lunch/Dinner:
Teddy's Burgers-Big 5 oz-Bigger 7 oz-Biggest 9 oz. and are served with Special Sauce, Lettuce, Tomato, Onions, Pickles. Additional Toppings are Cheese $.40, Bacon $.80, Avocado $.80, Pineapple $.80, Mushrooms $1.00, Chili $1.00 Teddy's Original Burger 4.15/4.95/5.75, Teddy's Teri Burger 4.70/5.45/6.25, Teddy's Spud Burger (Hashbrown patty added) 4.70/5.45/6.25, Teddy's Monster Double 5.95/7.30/8.35
Other Items: Grilled Chicken Breast Sandwich-plain, teri, garlic, Ranch or Cajun, Veggie Burger, Fish Sandwich 5.25, Salad 3.00, Grilled Chicken Salad 5.50, Fries 1.50/2.00, Spicy, Garlic, Ranch or Cheese Fries 2.00/2.55, Onion Rings 2.55, Fish & Chips $7.30
Fountain: Sodas 1.30/1.80, Floats 2.75, Extra Thick Shakes 3.75, Malts + .35

Impressions:

The formula for Teddy's Bigger Burgers was worked out here on Oahu by a couple of guys who really didn't want to live anywhere else. Things started out on a backyard grill and moved up to a small sandwich shop near Diamond Head. Recently Teddy's went mainstream and opened the new Koko Marina location.

The heart of the menu is Teddy's burger served medium with a "special" sauce. These juicy sandwiches come in three sizes suitable for just about any appetite. Backing the headliner comes some great fries and shakes. Additional specialties are offered to suit the tastes of the non-burger crowd. They were recently given the award of "Hawaii's Best" by local media. Teddy's is conveniently located near Hanauma Bay and welcomes returning water sports enthusiasts.

Oahu Dining

Waikiki

The Banyan Veranda
Sheraton Moana Surfrider
2365 Kalakaua Ave
Honolulu, HI 96815
808-922-3111
www.moana-surfrider.com
Hours: SuBru 9:00 AM-1:00 PM
B 7:00 AM-11:00 AM Mo-Sa
D 5:30 PM-9:00 PM
Cards: AE DC DIS JCB MC V
Dress: Evening Aloha
Style: Asian/Cont $$$

Menu Sampler:

Breakfast:
Sunday Brunch: $42.50/adults, $21.50/children. Soups, salads, fish, sushi, carved meats, seafood, hot entrees, omelet/waffle stations, pastries & desserts
Fixed Price Breakfast: $24.50-Juice, platter of fruits, muffins & breads served tableside. Choice of three entrees, Mac Nut or Banana Pancakes, Omelet, Eggs
Lunch:
N/A
Afternoon Tea: Mo-Sa 1 PM-4:30 PM, Su 3-4:30 PM, Earl Grey, Jasmine, Darjeeling and English Breakfast, or Our House Blends made with local flowers, plants and berries, large selection of teas, scones with Devonshire Cream and preserves, finger sandwiches, salmon roll and sweet pastries $28. Tea & Champagne (Two glasses) $34.
Dinner:
Entrees: Baked Lobster Tail with Shrimps, Scallops and Clams on creamy mushroom risotto $33, New York Steak with herb butter & cognac flamed demi glace $33, Pan Roasted Chicken Breast on spinach & artichoke hearts $26

Impressions:

This hotel is referred to as the "First Lady of Waikiki" as it was built when very little else was out here. Sitting in a rocking chair on the front veranda watching Kalakaua Avenue go by gives one an "anachronistic rush" of looking both backward and forward in time. The Banyan Veranda is located in a lovely courtyard facing the beach. The brunch and buffet items reflect the culinary traditions of the many cultures whose paths have crossed in the islands. Of course, afternoon tea is served. This is a wonderful place to dine.

Honolulu

The Bistro at Century Center

1750 Kalakaua Ave.-Third Floor
Honolulu, HI 96826
808-943-6500

Web: None
Hours: L 11:00 AM-2:00 PM Mo-Fr
D 5:30 PM-10:00 PM Su, Tu-Th
D 5:30 PM-12:00 AM FrSa
Cards: AE DIS JCB MC V
Dress: Evening Aloha
Style: Cont $$$$

Menu Sampler:

Breakfast:

N/A

Lunch:

Appetizers: Slices of Scottish Salmon served over crème fraiche with ikura, caper berries, dill, onions, and assorted dark breads $9.00, Eggplant and Goat Cheese Soufflé over an oven roasted tomato fondue $9.00
Salads: Bistro Salad w/Maui onions, Kamuela tomatoes & choice of vinaigrette-roasted shallot, raspberry, or balsamic $7.00, Caesar Salad $9.00
Entrees: Ahi Nicoise prepared with seared sashimi grade (#1) yellow fin tuna $15.00, Portobello Mushroom Wellington baked in puff pastry, over fresh spinach $15.00, Gnocchi of spinach & potato over roasted tomato coulis $14.00

Dinner:

Appetizers: Escargot A La Bistro-chanterelles & morels done Duxelle with asparagus coulis and Maryland Crab $11.95, Foie Gras-seared $19.95
Entrees: Steak Diane-brandy flambé presentation with potato gnocchi $29.95, Australian Rack of Lamb carved tableside with dauphine potatoes, fresh artichoke, and pomegranate au jus $38.95, Duck A L'Orange $28.95
Desserts: Bananas Flambé $10.95, Crème Brulee $7.50, Tiramisu $7.95

Impressions:

If you're looking for a taste of yesteryear with a foot firmly in the present, The Bistro is it. You'll find a menu with definite Continental roots dusted with island ingredients served in a luxurious atmosphere of thick carpets, tuxedoed waiters, candlelight, and tableside preparations. This is an experience to savor; one to share with that special someone. Located on the third floor of a high-rise across from the Hard Rock Café, The Bistro at Century Center is a separate world from the bustle outside its doors. Use the validated deck parking or valet service.

Waikiki

The Cheesecake Factory
2301 Kalakaua Ave.
Honolulu, HI 96815
808-924-5001
www.thecheesecakefactory.com
Hours: 11:00 AM-11:00 PM Mo-Th, till 12 AM FrSa
10:00 AM-11:00 PM Su
Cards: AE DC DIS JCB MC V
Dress: Casual
Style: Ecl $$

Menu Sampler:

Breakfast:
Sunday Brunch: served until 2:00 PM, Eggs Benedict with Canadian bacon 10.95, with fresh spinach, bacon and tomato 11.95, French Toast Napoleon of grilled brioche bread with strawberries, pecans, chantilly cream 9.95
Lunch/Dinner:
Appetizers: Fire Roasted Fresh Artichoke with spicy vinaigrette and garlic dip 8.95, Thai Lettuce Wraps with satay chicken strips, carrots, bean sprouts, and coconut curry noodles wrapped in lettuce leaves with three sauces 10.95
Appetizer Salads: Endive, Pecan and Blue Cheese in light vinaigrette 8.95
Pizza: Pesto Chicken Pizza with oven-dried tomatoes and pine nuts 9.95
Specialties: Grilled Portabella on a Bun with grilled red onion, cheese, spicy mayo, fries 9.95, Spicy Cashew Chicken over rice 14.95, Bistro Shrimp Pasta with basil-garlic-lemon cream sauce 16.50, Herb Crusted Filet of Salmon with lemon sauce, asparagus and mashed potatoes 17.95, Shepherd's Pie with mashed potato topping and parmesan cheese 13.95, Chino-Latino Steak with a Thai Tamarind Sauce, grilled red onion, tomato and steamed white rice 18.50
Salads: Barbeque Ranch Chicken Salad w/crispy fried onion strings 12.95
Sandwiches: Grilled Japanese Eggplant Sandwich, garlic aioli, fries 9.95
Desserts: Black-Out Cake-fudgy chocolate cake, chocolate chips, almonds 6.50
Cheesecakes: 36 kinds-slice 6.25-7.50, or whole cheese cakes at the counter

Impressions:

Though we tend to shy away from Mainland "chain gangs", this is one we endorse. The Cheesecake Factory's sharing-size portions of tasty menu items offer diners a higher than expected level of culinary depth. The restaurant's artfully designed layout maintains a feeling of intimacy in this otherwise oversized facility. Valet parking is available, but if you park in the deck make sure to have your ticket validated because this one can be really expensive!

Hawaii Kai

The Chef's Table Authors' Favorite

Hawaii Kai Towne Center
333 Keahole
Honolulu, HI 96825
808-394-2433
Web: None
Hours: L 11:30 AM-2:00 PM XMo
D 5:30 PM-9:00 PM XMo
Cards: MC V
Dress: Resort Casual
Style: Austrian $$$

Menu Sampler:

Breakfast:
N/A
Lunch:
Dinner:
Small Beginnings: Roasted Mushrooms in Cheeses and Walnut Sauce $6.00, Garlic Steamed Clams in sweet butter wine and herb sauce $9.00, Wine Country Escargots baked in herb and garlic butter $8.50, Jumbo Shrimp Cocktail $6.00
Soups: Special $2.75, Roasted Onion Beet Soup glazed with smoked cheese $4.75, Gulyas Soup "Gypsy Style"-paprika beef and potato soup $5.00
Salads: Spinach and Mushroom Salad with hot bacon vinaigrette $5.50, Chef's Table Mixed Salad of greens, mushrooms and shrimp in House dressing $4.00
Austrian Specialties: Wienerschnitzel-pan fried veal cutlet and onion potatoes $17.50, Jaegerschnitzel- sautéed pork steak in mushroom sauce and spetzli $17.00, Sauerbraten, red cabbage, and spetzli $20.00, Beef Goulash $16.50
Fish and Shellfish: Salmon Steak, grilled, pan-fried, or poached, with lemon caper butter $17.00, Trout Fillet baked with mushroom in green peppercorn sauce $18.00, Pan Seared Scallops, mushroom butter sauce, pasta, veg $19.00

Impressions:

We refer to The Chef's Table as a strip mall surprise. Located in the very same shopping center as Hawaii Kai's Costco you'll find a gourmet restaurant with an Austrian chef serving upscale Bavarian cuisine. Inside this lovely room an open display kitchen turns out rich, flavorful dishes using only prime ingredients. The daily specials are particularly interesting, so be sure to ask what's available. This restaurant provides a wonderful contrast to the fusion cuisine offered in so many of Hawaii's better dining spots. Free parking is plentiful in the lot out front.

Honolulu

The Contemporary Museum Café
2411 Makiki Heights Drive
Honolulu, HI 96822
808-523-3362
www.tcmhi.org
Hours: L 11:30 AM-2:30 PM XMo
L 12:00 PM-2:30 PM Su
Cards: AE DC DIS JCB MC V
Dress: Resort Casual
Style: Ec $$

Menu Sampler:

Breakfast:
N/A
Lunch:
Appetizers: Hummus & Warm Pita $5.50, Crostini of the Day-baguette toasts with a ramekin of various toppings $3.95, Kay's Deviled Eggs topped with pesto, sundried tomato pesto & tapenade $4.25, Garlic Shrimp 7.75
Soups & Salads: Ancho Chicken Taco Salad $9.50, Soup du Jour $2.95/$4.95, Bread $1.00, Asian Noodle Salad-cilantro-ginger pesto pasta with baked tofu, vegetables and greens $8.95, Contemporary Garden Salad with herb vinaigrette or creamy gorgonzola dressing $3.95, Southwestern Chop Chicken Salad with grilled chicken, jicama, corn, black beans and greens with creamy cumin-lime vinaigrette and tortilla chips $9.25
Sandwiches: Served with tortilla chips and hummus. Falafel Burger with feta and yogurt sauce 8.95, Curried Chicken Salad Wrap of chicken, celery & apple with curried mayo wrapped in a tortilla with tomato, lettuce & pineapple chutney 9.25, Mozzarella & Prosciutto Sandwich with roasted peppers, tapenade and arugula on focaccia $9.50, Turkey & Provolone Sandwich $9.25
Desserts: Changing Menu Daily of homemade delicacies.
Dinner:
N/A

Impressions:

If you like cuisine with your culture or vice versa you'll enjoy a visit to The Contemporary Museum Café. The culinary style here is eclectic with fresh flavorful ingredients made into soups, salads, sandwiches, and desserts. The museum is a former family estate with 3 ½ acres of gardens set on a ridge overlooking the city. For current exhibitions you can check the web site at www.tcmhi.org. Don't forget to stop at the unique gift shop before you leave.

Waikiki

The Hanohano Room

Sheraton Waikiki Hotel
2255 Kalakaua Ave
Honolulu, HI 96815
808-922-4422
www.sheraton-hawaii.com
Hours: D 5:30 PM-9:30 PM
Cards: AE DC DIS JCB MC V
Dress: Evening Aloha
Style: Cont/Pac-Rim $$$$

Menu Sampler:

Breakfast/Lunch:

N/A

Dinner:

Starters: Kataiffi Wrapped Kauai Shrimp with shredded filo, fried crisp, with ginger remoulade on seaweed salad 11, Escargot with macadamia nuts and Parmesan cheese 11, Miyagi Oysters with salsa, pickled Maui onion, ogo, and Japanese cucumber ponzu 13, Pan Seared Scallops with champagne sauce 12
Soups and Salads: Maui Onion Soup with Gruyere cheese 8, New England Style Clam Chowder with sweet Kahuku corn and sourdough croutons 8, Waimanalo Valley Salad with champagne vinaigrette 8, Fresh Spinach Salad topped with apple-smoked bacon, Hamakua mushrooms (for two) 24
Entrées: Garlic and Rosemary Roasted Chicken with morel sauce 29, Lemongrass Crusted Onaga baked with taro in a ginger cream, Waimanalo Swiss chard, ruby port gastrique 33, Steamed Moi with Waimanalo Herbs and yuzu sesame soy sauce 33, Garlic Marinated Rack of Lamb with a Dijon mustard crust and pineapple sage jus 39, Fire Roasted Veal Chop marinated in rosemary and served with morel sauce 35, Sautéed Onaga in beurre blanc 35
Desserts: White Chocolate Fondue 8, Tahitian Vanilla Bean Brulee Melon Compote 8, Kula Strawberries Sabayon 8, and Kona Coffee Tiramisu 8

Impressions:

Dining on top of tall buildings has always been an attraction. The view might bring people in, but it takes good food to keep them. This 30th floor restaurant gets things done both ways. The chef blends Continental techniques with what the Sheraton calls the "Flavors of Hawaii" to create a memorable dining experience. Although we find the menu a little hard to define we can't help but like it. Just take the glass express elevator to the top of the Sheraton Waikiki.

Honolulu

The Original OnOn

1110 McCully Street
Honolulu, HI 96826
808-946-8833
Web: None
Hours: LD 10:00 AM-9:00 PM
Cards: MC V
Dress: Casual
Style: Chi $$

Menu Sampler:

Breakfast:
N/A
Lunch:
Specials: 11 AM-2 PM, Soft Duck & Won Ton Noodle in Soup $8.25, Special Seafood Fried Rice $8.25, Seabass Fillet w/ginger & onion on rice $7.75
Lunch/Dinner:
Appetizer Pupu: Pepper Salt Chicken Wings (8) $8.25, Egg Roll $7.25
Northern Chinese Cuisine: Spicy Pork Eggplant $7.25, Kung Pao Chicken $7.95, Mu Shu Pork $8.75, Spicy Shredded Pork $7.25, Mixed Vegetables $7.25
Casserole: Oyster & Pot Roast Pork Casserole $12.50, Lup Cheong, Chicken with Black Mushroom Casserole $10.75, Beef Stew w/Lettuce Casserole $9.50
Soup: Scallop with Egg $9.25, Seaweed with Fishcake $7.95, Hot and Sour Soup $7.50, Chicken Cream Corn $7.25, Green Pea with Egg Blossom $7.25
Entrées: Pork Hash with black bean $7.95, Island Pork Chop Peking Style $8.75, Sweet and Sour Pork $7.25, Stuffed Bittermelon $7.95, Roast Duck $7.95, Chicken with Pea Pod $7.95, Lobster with Cashew Nuts $16.50, Cuttlefish with shrimp sauce $8.95, Fresh Scallop with Chinese Pea Pod $9.95, Fish Cake with Sour Cabbage $7.95, Fried Shrimp with green onion $9.75
Egg: Egg Fu Yung $7.25, Salted Duck $1.65, Sweet Pork Fu Yung $7.25
Chop Suey: Choy Sum w/Oyster Sauce $6.50, House Special Chop Suey $7.25

Impressions:

Those who want to experience a little Honolulu neighborhood culture should enjoy a visit to The Original OnOn. This casual eatery bustles throughout the day as local families and businessmen stop by to partake and talk story. The menu is decidedly Chinese with regional orientation designed to satisfy Oahu appetites. Lunch specials and affordable combination plates are offered for the budget minded. Look for OnOn at the corner of Young and McCully.

Diamond Head

The Patisserie

Kahala Mall Shopping Center
4211 Waialae Avenue
Honolulu, HI 96816
808-735-4402
www.ThePatisserie.com

Hours: B 7:00 AM-10:00 AM
L 10:00 AM-5:00 PM
D 5:00 PM-8:30 PM XSu
Cards: AE MC V
Dress: Casual
Style: Amer/Ger $$

Menu Sampler:

Breakfast:
Popover $.85,Two Egg Ham & Cheese Omelette with toast & jelly $3.95, Eierpfannkuchen-thin German pancake with orange maple syrup- 1 pancake $2.45, 2 pancakes $3.75, Buttermilk Shortstack (3) $2.45
Lunch:
House Specialties: Meatloaf Sandwich $4.95, Assorted Quiche $3.95, Sausage with potato salad & sauerkraut $6.50, Lasagna & tossed greens $3.95
Sandwiches: Bavarian Loaf $4.25, Danish Ham $3.95, Roast Beef $4.50, Pastrami $4.95, Avocado BLT $4.95, Smoked Turkey $4.75, Chicken $4.25
Beverages: Coffee $.87, Cappucino $1.85, Café Latte $1.85, Espresso $1.35
Dinner:
All entrées include tossed salad with creamy ginger dressing, tangy red cabbage & steamed vegetables, rolls & butter. Sauerbraten with bread dumplings $14.00, Oven Braised Lamb Shank with Cabernet Sauce with roasted potatoes $15.00, Pork Tenderloin with Peppercorn and roast potatoes $15.00, Rahm Schnitzel with veal, spaetzle and a chardonnay cream sauce $15.00
Desserts: Tiramisu $1.75, Apple Tart $2.75, Napoleon $1.85, Éclair $1.85

Impressions:

The Patisserie is an anomaly in a land of anomalies. Where else would you find an exceptional bakery serving great German food in a shopping mall? Maybe in Munich but definitely not in Hawaii! Breakfast and lunch are served deli style, but dinner is a sit-down affair complete with tablecloths and wait staff. This is a popular evening spot with the Kahala crowd making reservations a must. The Kahala Mall sits on the east end of the H1 making this an easy place to find.

Honolulu

The Pavilion Café
The Honolulu Academy of Arts
900 S. Beretania Avenue
Honolulu, Hawaii 96826
808-532-8734
www.honoluluacademy.org
Hours: L 11:30 AM-2:00 PM Tu-Sa
Cards: AE JCB MC V
Dress: Resort Casual
Style: Amer/Ec $

Menu Sampler:

Breakfast:
N/A
Lunch:
Soup of the Day $3.50, White Bean Salad on Arugula and Wilted Radicchio with shiitake mushrooms, balsamic vinaigrette and Reggiano $8.95, Beef Tenderloin Sandwich with red onion Dijon & caper relish $10.95, Warm Big Island Goat Cheese & Nalo Green Salad with seasonal fruit and honey-thyme vinaigrette $9.95, Roast Turkey Breast Sandwich with Emmenthaler Swiss cheese & house made chutney on whole wheat bread $8.50, Feta, Tapenade & Hau'ula Tomato Sandwich on house made focaccia $8.95, Piadina of flatbread, arugula, chopped tomatoes, basil, fresh mozzarella & prosciutto $8.95
Wine Carte: Whites-glass $4.50/$5.50, bottles $18.50-$39.50, Reds-glass $5.50, bottles $19.50-$32.50, Café Wines-glass $4.50/$5.50, bottles $17.50-$34.50, Signature Wine Selections-bottles up to $25.00, corkage $10/bottle
Desserts: Sorbets, gelatos, ice creams $3.00, Dessert Specials such as Chocolate Pot de Crème, Fresh Fruit Crisp or Tart, Chocolate Walnut Torte $5.95
Dinner:
N/A

Impressions:

The Honolulu Academy of Arts has many treasures inside, and one of them is The Pavilion Café. This open-air dining spot with its contemporary decor is located in the interior courtyard of the museum. Seating about 120, The Pavilion Café offers a short menu that is long on interesting flavor combinations. The chef prides himself on using only the freshest of ingredients and it shows. Because of the popularity of the café, reservations are recommended and accepted at 15-minute intervals. Validated parking is available.

Kapahulu

The Pyramids

758-B Kapahulu Ave.
Honolulu, HI 96816
808-737-2900
Web: None
Hours: L Buf 11:00 AM-2:00 PM Mo-Sa
D 5:30 PM-10:00 PM Mo-Sa
D 5:00 PM-9:00 PM Su
Cards: AE DC DIS JCB MC V
Dress: Casual
Style: Med $$

Menu Sampler:

Breakfast:
N/A
Lunch:
All You Can Eat Buffet $8.95-Chicken, Lamb & Beef Shawerma, Rice, Fries, Greek Salad, Pita, Potato Salad, Tomato Salad, Rice Pudding, Falafel
Dinner:
Appetizers: Baba Ghanouj-baked onions and eggplant with tahini, lemon, cumin, and fresh garlic $6.95, Spanakopita (Spinach Pie) with Egyptian Salad $3.95, Stuffed Grape Leaves served with yogurt sauce (10) $11.95, (5) $6.95, Feta Salad $4.95, Pyramids Special of hommos, tabbouleh, falafel, baba ghanouj and grape leaves (4 persons) $19.95, Feta Salad with tomato & cucumber $4.95
Entrées: All are served with salad and pita bread. Kosa-layers of zucchini, onion rings, mushrooms & tomato slices topped with a creamy béchamel $12.95, Mousaka with fried eggplant, ground beef and béchamel $14.95, Kebbeh-marinated ground lamb & beef, cracked wheat, onions, raisins and pine nuts $14.95, Reiash-lamb ribs marinated for two days then charbroiled over low heat $18.95, Chef's Complete Dinner/person (minimum of two) $26.95

Impressions:

Before anyone makes any comments about curb appeal, let's just say we passed The Pyramids by a few times before venturing inside. That first visit was an eye opener. After stepping through the door, a tastefully decorated room greeted us with some of the best Egyptian and Mediterranean cuisine we've had anywhere. Lunchtime is a particularly good value. For a small price, patrons can sample a variety of dishes from a buffet. Then at dinner authentic belly dancers complete the mood. Parking is a problem. Do yourself a favor and take a cab.

Honolulu

The Willows Authors' Favorite

901 Hausten Street
Honolulu, HI 96826
808-952-9200
www.willowshawaii.com

Hours: Bru Buf 10:00 AM-2:30 PM Su
L Buf 11:00 AM-2:00 PM Mo-Fr
L Buf 10:00 AM-2:30 PM Sa
D Buf 5:30 PM-9:00 PM
Cards: AE DC DIS JCB MC V
Dress: Resort Casual
Style: Amer/Haw $$$

Menu Sampler:

Breakfast:
Sunday Brunch Buffet-Belgian Waffle Station, Salads, Prime Rib, Baked Whole Snapper, The Willows Famous Curry, Seafood Bar, Entrees, Dessert Station $27.95, Keiki 4-10 $13.95, Seniors 65+ 10% off

Lunch:
Buffet Mo-Fr $16.95, Keiki 4-10 $8.50, Seniors 65+ 10% off. Soup Station, Salads, Carving Station with Roast Turkey & Prime Rib, The Willows Famous Curry, Saimin Station, Entrees, Dessert Station; Saturday Lunch Buffet $19.95, Keiki 4-10 $9.95, Seniors 65+ 10% off, adds a Seafood Station (Snow Crab Legs) to the weekly menu.

Dinner:
Dinner Buffet Mo-Fr 5:30 PM-9:00 PM, SaSu 5:00 PM-9:00 PM $27.95, Keiki 4-10 $13.95, Seniors 65+ 10% off. Soup Station, Salads, Carving Station of Roast Turkey with brown gravy & cranberry sauce or Prime Rib with horseradish sauce & au jus, The Willows Roasted Portobello Mushrooms with Balsamic Beurre Blanc, Saimin Station, Suckling Pig, Entrées such as Teriyaki Chicken, Baby Back Ribs, Steamed Mussels, Fresh Catch, Dessert Station with a sundae station, fresh fruits, pies and cakes.

Pupu Bar for $10, Monday through Friday, call for hours

Impressions:

For a glimpse into the lives of local people as they celebrate milestones in life come to The Willows. Weddings and private parties are given special attention here. Here you'll have your choice of crowd-pleasing buffets served in a lovely garden setting or tapas style dining in the Rainbow Room.

Oahu Dining

Waikiki

Tiki's Grill & Bar

Aston Waikiki Beach Hotel
2570 Kalakaua Ave.
Honolulu, HI 96815
808-923-8454
www.tikisgrill.com
Hours: LD 10:30 AM-Midnight
Cards: AE DC DIS JCB MC V
Dress: Casual
Style: Amer/Asian/Isl $$

Menu Sampler:

Breakfast:
N/A
Lunch:
Appetizers: Coconut Shrimp $8.95, Steamed Manila Clams & saffron coconut cream sauce $8.95, Kauai Shrimp Summer Rolls w/peanut dipping sauce $5.95
Soups & Salads: Island Fish & Clam Chowder $4.95, Warm Spinach Salad w/mac nut crusted goat cheese $6.95, Curried Pea/Water Chestnut Salad $5.95
Entrées & Sandwiches: Kalua Pig Sandwich w/caramelized Maui Onions & guava BBQ sauce $8.95, Grilled Monchong w/pineapple chutney & rice $14.95
Dinner:
Appetizers: Calamari Katsu-panko crusted w/lemon grass beurre blanc sauce $7.95, Kalua Pig Quesadilla w/ jack cheese, corn relish & guacamole $6.95
Soups & Salads: Oriental Chicken Chop Salad w/sweet-sour sesame dressing $7.95, Island Nicoise Salad with medium rare seared ahi $10.95
Entrées: Chef's Signature King Salmon glazed and served with a lemon grass beurre blanc sauce, mashed sweet potatoes & Asian slaw $15.95, Filet Mignon with grilled onions, mushrooms & roasted garlic butter, mashed potatoes $22.95, Pan Seared Ahi with Cajun spices over Kalua pig mashed potatoes $16.95, Tiki's Cheeseburger-1/2# chuck on house-made Kaiser roll $7.95

Impressions:

There's a new "in" place to go on Waikiki Beach known as Tiki's Grill & Bar. The proprietors positioned Tiki's to appeal to locals and visitors alike. First, they started off with a great chef and an imaginative menu. Then, they added a large bar serving all kinds of drinks and pupus. Finally, they located the place on the third floor of a hotel overlooking the ocean. The mix seems to be working as the crowds have been coming since the day Tiki's opened. Both lunch and dinner can be casual affairs, or you can step up in the evening to more complex entrées.

Chinatown

To Chau Restaurant Authors' Favorite

1007 River Street
Honolulu, HI 96814
808-533-4549
Web: None
Hours: 8:00 AM- 2:30 PM
Cards: None
Dress: Casual
Style: Viet $

Menu Sampler:

Breakfast/Lunch:
Pho: Vietnamese Beef Soup consisting of a clear, rich beef broth garnished with slices of rare steak and well cooked brisket, flank, tendon, tripe, fresh herbs and vegetables over rice noodles in three sizes: X-Large Bowl $5.50, Medium Bowl $4.50, Regular Bowl $4.00. Different combinations of meat for the pho are from the above list plus beef balls. Fresh basil, bean sprouts, jalapenos included.
Appetizers: Shrimp Rolls (2) of shrimp, pork, fresh herbs, and vermicelli rolled in rice paper with special sauce $3.50, Spring Rolls (6) of minced pork, crab, shrimp, and mushrooms wrapped in rice paper and deep fried $6.00
Plates: BBQ Chicken Rice Plate $6.00, Pork Chop Rice Plate $6.00
Beverages: French Filtered Coffee Hot or Iced $1.50, Hot Jasmine Tea $.50, French Filtered Coffee w/Condensed Milk $2.00, Fresh Lemonade Juice $1.50, Lemonade w/soda water $1.55, Salty Lemonade $1.50, Soy Bean Milk $1.00
Dinner:
N/A

Impressions:

At first glance, the plain unadorned storefront of To Chau might easily be passed by as a bit too "provincial". That is until you get to the head of the line and the door opens. Then the aroma of rich broth and fresh herbs surrounds you and pulls you in. Pho (fuh) shops are a staple in Vietnam. People from all walks of life slurp the rich soup for breakfast and lunch. First, you select the type of meat you want in your pho, and then a generous bowl of beef broth loaded with rice noodles arrives. Alongside the bowl you'll receive a plate of fresh herbs and bean sprouts. These are added gradually as the soup is eaten. To add them all at once would cool the soup and dull the bright flavor of the herbs. Garnish your pho with lime and chilies, add your favorite sauce, and join the party!

Waikiki

Todai

1910 Ala Moana Blvd
Honolulu, HI 96815
808-947-1000
www.todai.com
Hours: L 11:30 AM-2:30 PM
D 5:30 PM-9:30 PM
Cards: AE MC V
Dress: Resort Casual
Style: Japan/Sea $$$

Menu Sampler:

Breakfast:
N/A
Lunch/Dinner:
Buffet Style serving over 40 kinds of sushi, 15 hot meat & seafood entrees, tempura, salads, and 20+ bite-sized desserts and a crepe station.
Lunch: $14.95 Monday-Friday, $16.95 Saturday and Sunday
Dinner: $25.95 Monday-Friday, $26.95 Saturday and Sunday
Dinner service adds mussels, clams, jumbo shrimp, snow crab legs to the buffet.
Children less than 5 feet tall are 50% off; Seniors 65+ are 20% off

Impressions:

Todai is Waikiki's ultimate Japanese buffet. People wait at the door before they open to get in line for the abundance waiting inside. The assortment of dishes is nearly overwhelming. They offer over forty different kinds of sushi alone! The main buffet is 160-feet long and has an amazing variety of choices. You can't do it all so don't try. All of the dishes are labeled to help the uninitiated better enjoy this dining experience. To finish things up they have a dessert buffet and a crepe station. Lunch is a great value. Although the price goes up, seafood lovers can go crazy at dinner when a variety of shellfish dishes are added to the display.

Kapahulu

Tokkuri-Tei

Authors' Favorite

611 Kapahulu Ave #102
Honolulu, HI 96815
808-739-2800
Web: None
Hours: L 11:00 AM-2:00 PM Mo-Fr
D 5:30 PM-12:00 AM Mo-Sa
Cards: AE DC DIS JCB MC V
Dress: Casual
Style: Japan $$$

Menu Sampler:

Breakfast:
N/A
Lunch/Dinner:
Beverages: imported and domestic beers, wines, many sakes
Sashimi: Maguro 11.00, Hamachi 11.00, King Crab with Tosa Vinaigrette 9.95
Bata Itame: Fresh Asparagus sautéed with butter, seasoned w/soy sauce 4.95
A La Carte: Tofu Steak 4.50, Spinach in Soup w/whirlpool egg 4.50, Uni & Geso cooked in an abalone shell 12.75, Salmon Skin Salad over silky tofu 7.50
Kushi Yaki: Skewers-2/order. Yaki Tori 2.50, Gyu Yaki 8.50, Ume Yaki 3.50
Yaki Mono: Grilled Eggplant 3.00, Teri Yaki Squid 6.50, Tomorokoshi 3.00
Age Mono: Ebi Tempura 7.50, Mandoo 3.50, Flounder 9.95, Mini Katsu 3.50
Rice & Noodles: Unagi Donburi 9.50/17.50, Cold Buckwheat Noodles 5.50
Nabe Mono: Yose Nabe (Bouillabaisse) 23.95, Shabu Shabu 25.95
Shiru Mono: Manila Clam Soup 3.00, Nameko Mushroom Soup 3.00
Teishoku: Complete Dinner-rice, miso soup, salad, pickles, & Imo Yokan. Tokkuri Teishoku-sashimi, ebi tempura and 4 oz Prime Beef Steak 17.95
Sushi Rolls: Spicy Scallop Roll 6.50, Baked Alaska Roll 9.50, Opae Roll 9.50

Impressions:

This place doesn't look like much from the street. It's located in the corner of a modest shopping plaza up Kapahulu from the Honolulu zoo. But when you go through the door, magic happens. This is a Japanese tavern, and like taverns the world over, the draw is food, drink, and socialization. An international crowd gathers here to enjoy all of the above. Over the years the owners have developed an extensive menu of "tasty tidbits" guaranteed to feed the party. The food at lunch is great, but go in the evening for the full experience.

Diamond Head

Tokyo Tokyo

Kahala Mandarin Oriental Hawaii Hotel
5000 Kahala Avenue
Honolulu, HI 96816
808-739-1500

Web:	None
Hours:	L 11:00 AM-2:00 PM XSa D 5:30 PM-10:00 PM
Cards:	AE DC DIS JCB MC V
Dress:	Resort Casual
Style:	Japan $$$

Menu Sampler:

Breakfast:
N/A
Lunch:
Japanese Sushi Lunch: Featuring sushi, tempura, sashimi miso soup $20.00, Selection of entrees: Two selections $15, Three Selections $20
Dinner:
A la Carte: Gomadofu-homemade sesame tofu with shrimp & pumpkin $17.00, Fresh Oysters on the half shell with spicy ponzu, orange ponzu and sea salt $9.00, Paper Thin Sliced Live Flounder Sashimi with marinated pimento $17.00
Salads: Seasonal Tomato Salad with basil lemon dressing $12.50, Avocado and King Crab Salad, mayonnaise sauce, topped with flying fish caviar $17.00
Entrées: Prix Fixe 8 course $95/person, 6 course $60/person; Finest Tenderloin Steak cooked on your own with heated stone served with garlic ponzu sauce on the side-Kobe Beef $59.00, Black Angus Beef $25.00, Broiled Free Range Chicken basted with teriyaki sauce $15.00, Blue Fin Tuna cooked over a wire grill with Bincho charcoal at your table, wasabi and soy sauce $29.00

Impressions:

As you enter the Kahala Mandarin you'll see a casual yet upscale dining venue featuring both traditional and contemporary Japanese cuisine. The owner of this fine dining restaurant is known for teasing patrons with contrasting tastes that work. The purveyor of these delicacies also owns the famous Wasabi Bistro on Kapahulu. We are big fans of both establishments and recommend them highly. Visitor parking is available in the deck, but it is quite expensive so make sure to get your ticket validated.

Waikiki

Trattoria
2168 Kalia Road
Honolulu, HI 96815
808-923-8415
Web: None
Hours: D 5:30 PM-10:00 PM
Cards: AE DC DIS JCB MC V
Dress: Evening Aloha
Style: Ital $$$
Ent Card

Menu Sampler:

Breakfast/Lunch:
N/A
Dinner:
Alla Carta/Antipasti: Caesar Salad (tableside prep) $9.50, Chef's Special Green Salad $7.25, Stracciatella of chicken broth, Parmesan cheese, egg and fresh parsley $3.50/$4.50, Fresh Clams steamed in white wine, garlic, shallots and herbs with red or white sauce $10.75, Broiled Scampi Prawns $13.95
Pasta: Canneloni alla Milanese-crepes wrapped around a combination of veal, chicken and beef baked and topped with layers of marinara, Bolognese, and cream sauce $15.95, Lasagna al Forno Fatta in Casa $13.95, Sauce choices—Pesto Genovese –a creamy sauce of olive oil, garlic, fresh basil and roasted nuts $13.95, Salsiccie alla Calabrese-medium hot Italian sausages with anise seeds, cooked in marinara sauce $16.95, Puttanesca-sauteed anchovies in melted butter, cooked in hot sauce with tomatoes, black olives and pimientoes $15.25
Entrées: Served with vegetables and the chef's pasta of the day. Veal Marsala with mushrooms $24.95, Chicken Parmesan $23.95, New York Steak seared & topped with butter, garlic and shallots sauce $26.95, Scampi alla Trattoria $26.75, Pescatora-fresh clams in the shell, garlic, herbs, your choice of pasta with white or red sauce $21.95, Aragosta alla Fra Diavolo-Lobster sauteed in olive oil with shallots, tomato, white wine and spices served in the shell $27.95

Impressions:

Trattoria is a long-time Waikiki favorite. Although the entrance suggests informality, inside you'll find starched white tablecloths and hand-painted frescoes. The kitchen's approach is more fine dining than pasta with marinara. We view veal to be a benchmark in Italian restaurants and theirs is of good quality and well prepared. It can get busy in this area so make reservations.

North Shore

Turtle Bay Resort Restaurants

57-091 Kamehameha Highway
Kahuku, HI 96731
808-293-8811
www.turtlebayresort.com
Hours: See Below
Cards: AE DC DIS JCB MC V
Dress: See Below
Style: Diverse

Menu Sampler:

Palm Terrace Restaurant: Casual Dress
B: 7 AM-11 AM, Menu: Sweet Bread French Toast with Coconut Syrup and Macadamia Nut Butter $7.95, Eggs Benedict $11.25, Poached Eggs on Shrimp and Crab Hash with Papaya Salsa $12.50, Hawaiian Silk Smoothie $4.50
L: Lunch Buffet 11 AM-2 PM (if available), menu 11 AM-5 PM, Pan Seared Caramelized Salmon w/baby spinach, arugula roasted sweet peppers, asparagus, balsamic dressing $12, Shredded Kahlua Pork BBQ Sandwich, fries $12
D: Dinner 5 PM-10 PM, Lobster Pesto Salad with lilikoi vinaigrette $13.50, Double Cut Passion Fruit Pork Chop, garlic mashed potatoes, fruit salsa $24

Sunset Room: Resort Casual
Sunday Brunch: 10 AM-2 PM $29.95/adults, $25.45/62+, $15.00/age 4-11. Lavish selection of fruits, omelets, waffles, traditional breakfast items, vegetables, carved meats and seafood with a beautiful panoramic view of Kahuku Point and Turtle Bay. Reservations not required but recommended.

21° North: Evening Aloha
D: Tu-Sa 6 PM-9:30 PM. Reservations required. Appetizer of Pan Seared Scallops, creamy Kahuku corn polenta, Osetra caviar, truffle mushrooms vinaigrette $13, Five Spice Lacquered Peking Duck, jasmine rice, kiwi and cilantro salad, vanilla plum glaze $32, Grilled Beef Tenderloin, Yukon gold garlic mashed potato, Madeira demi-glace $32, Chef's Tasting Menu-five courses $76, $95 with wine selections.

Impressions:

The Turtle Bay Resort has recently undergone an extensive renovation, and the results were worth the wait. All three restaurants offer patrons stunning ocean views and progressive levels of dining sophistication. These rooms attract an interesting mix of customers from around the north shore as well as around the globe. This diversity is evident in the menus as well as through the clientele.

Oahu Dining

Kaimuki

Verbano Italiano Ristorante

3571 Waialae Avenue, #101
Honolulu, HI 96816
808-735-1777
www.verbanohawaii.com

Hours:	L 11:00 AM-2:30 PM Mo-Fr
	D 5:00 PM-10:00 PM
Cards:	AE DIS MC V
Dress:	Casual
Style:	Ital $$ Ent Card

Menu Sampler:

Breakfast:
N/A
Lunch:
Appetizers: Bruschetta-grilled homemade bread, eggplant, ricotta cheese, fresh tomato, basil, olive oil & balsamic $5.90, Calamari Fritti $7.90
Salads: Spicy Spinach Seafood Salad with shrimp, scallops, & calamari $9.90
Pasta: Fettuccini Carbonara $8.90, Linguini Chicken Anchovies Olio $9.90, Pollo & Melanzane Di Casino of sautéed chicken with bacon, ham, spinach, baked eggplant & mushrooms, garlic, pasta & cheese $10.90
Dinner:
All of the above items plus the following:
Appetizers: Escargot sautéed with fresh garlic, lemon, butter & wine $6.90, Clams Florentina of baked clams, fresh garlic, spinach, bacon, butter & wine $8.90, Roast Peppers with Anchovies $6.90, Carpaccio $7.90
Salads: Caesar Salad $4.90, Italian Salad of romaine, pickled carrot & celery, tomato, pepperoncini, salami, black olives, anchovies, cheese $3.90
Entrees: Steak Tuscana of grilled steak topped with mushrooms, anchovies, capers, chili pepper sauce in olive oil $15.90, Fettuccini Carbonara with sautéed onion, bacon, ham, tossed with egg & butter or marinara $11.90, Vongole Di Tuscan of chopped clams sautéed with garlic, onions; served with spicy tomato sauce $11.90, Veal Marsala with mushrooms, butter & marsala wine $14.90, Seafood Ravioli of homemade pasta with mixed seafood items; your choice of tomato, cream or pesto sauce $13.90

Impressions:

Verbano is one of those special finds that combines a solid menu, pleasant atmosphere, and reasonable prices. The mood here is a step above the casual neighborhood Italian eatery, so dress accordingly. A local favorite!

Honolulu

Vino Authors' Favorite

Restaurant Row
500 Ala Moana Blvd
Honolulu, HI 96813
808-524-8466
www.sanseihawaii.com

Hours: D 4:30 PM-9:30 PM WeTh
D 4:30 PM-11:00 PM Fr
D 7:00 PM-11:00 PM Sa
Cards: AE DC DIS JCB MC V
Dress: Resort Casual
Style: Asian/Euro $$$

Menu Sampler:

Breakfast/Lunch:
N/A
Dinner:
Salad: Vino's Nalo Green Salad-Waimanalo greens, Wailua asparagus, salami, olives, tomatoes, onions and shaved cheese $7.50, Little Vino Caprese of heirloom tomatoes, crisp bufala mozzarella with fresh herbs, balsamic $7.50
Pasta Perfect: Contemporary-house made spinach pasta filled with butternut squash and a mushroom ravioli topped with a sage brown butter sauce $6.95, Traditional-house made ravioli-sweet fennel sausage, baby spinach, ricotta cheese and a slow cooked marinara sauce $6.50
Heartier Fare: Mini Veal Osso Buco in a rich veal and red wine reduction $11.95, Grilled Ligurian Monster Shrimp with roasted garlic butter and tomato concasse $11.50, Asparagus Milanese, farm fresh quail egg and garnished with truffle oil $6.95, Eggplant Napoleon-chilled roasted vegetable terrine with an oven dried tomato and smoked pepper vinaigrette $7.50, Seared Foie Gras with a port wine and fig reduction, fleur de sel $16.95, UN-Caesar Salad $6.95

Impressions:

Those looking to gather with friends and linger over tapas and fine wines need go no further than Vino in Restaurant Row. This place has the feel of a private club. Its cozy and intimate ambiance is a good match for the sophisticated crowd at the tables. Italian inspired tastes dominate the brief but enticing menu. Wines are available in two or five ounce portions allowing patrons to sample both food and drink. The wait staff brings it all together with personal unhurried service.

Waikiki

Wailana Coffee House Authors' Favorite

1860 Ala Moana Blvd
Honolulu, HI 96815
808-955-1764
Web: None
Hours: 24/7
Cards: AE DIS JCB MC V
Dress: Casual
Style: Amer/Isl $

Menu Sampler:

Breakfast:
Corned Beef Hash, two eggs, butter grilled banana & toast $5.95, Three Egg Omelets $6.25-$7.25, Eggs Benedict with smoked ham and turkey, hashed browns $7.75, Belgian Waffle $4.95, Blueberry Pancakes $4.95, Papaya $3.50

Lunch:
Burgers-served on a toasted bun with lettuce and pickle. Mushroom Burger $5.50, Paniolo Burger with chili beans and chopped onions $5.95, Patty Melt on European Rye w/chopped onions and French fries $6.50, BBQ Pork on a toasted bun w/French fries $6.25, Any sandwich w/ Salad Bar $3.25, Mahi Mahi Sandwich w/French fries $6.50, Fisherman's Wharf Salad w/asparagus $8.50

Dinner:
Choice of soup, salad bar or minted fruit cocktail, French fries, whipped potatoes or steamed rice (baked potato 5-10 PM) & roll. Teriyaki Steak w/soup, salad bar, or minted fruit cocktail, choice of starch & roll $10.50, Broasted Chicken (4 pcs) w/fries & cole slaw $8.75, Deep Fried Scallops $9.95, Fish & Chips w/tartar sauce $7.75, Fried Saimin $5.25, Spicy Battered Butterfly Shrimp $10.75, Breaded Tenderloin Cutlet w/mushroom sauce $9.25

Happy Hour: 12-9-Mai Tai $2.50, Karaoke 9-1

Desserts: Hot Fudge Ice Cream Cake $3.75, High Rise Ice Cream Pie $4.50

Impressions:

This bustling restaurant should be franchised and sent to the neighbor islands. They offer good food at reasonable prices in pleasant surroundings and have 24/7 service for the entire menu. What more can you ask for? The choices are extensive and there's something to please just about everyone in your group. An attractive lounge with TVs for viewing sporting events is located right across from the entrance. This dining spot is especially kind to travelers whose body clocks are totally out of whack and want something to eat at 4 AM!

Manoa Valley

Wai'Oli Tea Room

2950 Manoa Road
Honolulu, HI 96822
808-988-5800

Web:	None
Hours:	B 8:00 AM-12:00 PM SaSu
	L 10:30 AM-2:00 PM Mo-Fr
	L 12:00 PM-2:00 PM SaSu
	Tea 2:00 PM-4:00 PM with res.
Cards:	MC V
Dress:	Resort Casual
Style:	Amer $

Menu Sampler:

Breakfast:
Wai'Oli Waffles-cinnamon apple, blueberry, strawberry, banana, or mac nut 8.25, Guava & Berry French Toast, whipped cream, caramelized pecans 10.25, Continental Breakfast-1/2 papaya, pastry & coffee or tea 6.00, Quiche w/rice or potato & toast 8.50, Frittata w/rice or potato & toast 8.75, Eggs Benedict 10.50
Tea: Selection of Fresh Baked Goods and Finger Sandwiches 18.75
Lunch:
Wai'Oli Chicken Curry Salad served in pita bread, cole slaw $9.75, Fresh Catch of the Day Sandwich $12.50, Chicken & Cheese Quesadilla with pineapple chutney, Mexican salad, sour cream, guacamole $10.25, Gourmet Shrimp Salad with avocado $12.75, Homemade Soup with Fresh Bread $3.50/$5.75

Impressions:

In the mountains behind Waikiki there's a private place called the Manoa Valley. This is home to the University of Hawaii and the Wai'Oli Tea Room. Those interested in period architecture and lovely gardens will appreciate this gracious dining spot. The menu isn't extensive but adequate, particularly at breakfast. We like the fresh baked goods. Expect a leisurely pace.

Kapahulu

Wasabi Bistro
1006 Kapahulu Ave.
Honolulu, HI 96816
808-735-2800
Web: None
Hours: L 11:00 AM-2:00 PM Mo-Sa
D 5:30 PM-10:00 PM
Cards: AE JCB MC V
Dress: Casual
Style: Japan $$

Menu Sampler:

Breakfast:
N/A
Lunch:
Starters: Tofu Salad $6.75, Maui Onion Tempura $5.50, Fried Gyoza $3.75,
Entrées: Includes miso soup, green salad, Japanese pickles & rice-Chicken Teriyaki $8.25, Braised Fish of the Day $11.25, Pork Tenderloin Cutlets $11.00, Baked Scallops Special $10.00, Soft Shell Crab $6.95, Beef Katsu $10.00
Lunch Combinations: include miso soup, salad, pickles & rice-choice of two items-Chicken Teriyaki, California Roll, Shrimp & Veg. Tempura, etc. $10.95
Dinner:
Cold Starters: Seafood Sunomono $5.50, Maguro Tataki-seared tuna $8.95
Hot Starters: Calamari Salad $7.25, Soft Shell Crab with ponzu sauce $7.75
Dinner Entrées: include soup, salad, pickles & rice-Rib Eye Beef Teriyaki $20.75, Butterfish Yakizakana $20.75, Una-Juu broiled eel over steamed rice $18.50, Shrimp & Vegetable Tempura $15.75, Salmon Katsu $14.75
Sushi: Rainbow Roll (8 pcs) $11.50, Shrimp Tempura Roll $9.25
Signature Dishes: Wasabi #1 Special of crab meat and avocado wrapped with white fish, baked with wasabi secret sauce $7.95, Baked Scallops Special-scallops and mushrooms over our "Dynamite Rice" $10.00

Impressions:

Kapahulu has its own little restaurant row and right in the middle of it sits the Wasabi Bistro. This Tokyo style Japanese takes things up a notch. Not only do they serve some of the best starters and sushi you'll find in Waikiki, but they also offer a full gamut of traditional entrees and combinations. Those who'd like to experience fine Japanese cuisine without a high price tag would do well to try lunch here. You won't be giving that much up since the mid-day menu is nearly as extensive as that at dinner. Parking is available on premises or by valet.

Chinatown

Won Kee Seafood

Chinatown Cultural Plaza
100 N. Beretania St
Honolulu, HI 96817
808-524-6877

Web: None
Hours: L 11:00 AM-2:30 PM
D 5:00 PM-10:00 PM
Cards: AE DIS JCB MC V
Dress: Casual
Style: Chi $$
Ent Card

Menu Sampler:

Breakfast:
N/A
Lunch/Dinner:
Appetizers: Crispy Egg Rolls (3) $4.50, Roast Pork Char Siu $4.50, Steamed Clams $12.00, Wine Chicken and Jelly Fish $9.50, Fresh Oyster $2.00
Soup: Hot & Sour Soup $3.00, Chicken Corn Soup $2.50, Abalone Soup $5.50, Beef Egg Drop Soup $2.50, Steamed Abalone and Shark Fin Soup $20.00
Entrées: Sautéed Scallop with Vegetable $12.95, Jumbo Shrimp braised with curry sauce $16.00, Roast Duck w/plum sauce $9.50, Fresh Clam w/ginger and scallion $12.00, Spicy Deep Fried Pork Ribs $9.50, Cold Ginger Chicken $9.500
Seafood: Sweet and Sour Crispy Shrimp $12.95, Island Prawns Braised with Curry Sauce $18.00, Oyster with Scallion and Ginger Sauce $12.00, Deep Fried Spicy Squid $10.50, Mixed Seafood in Taro Basket $12.95
Meats, Poultry: Sizzling Beef with Maui Onions $10.50, Spicy Garlic Chicken $9.50, Spicy Deep Fried Pork Ribs $9.50, Pepper Steak in Taro Basket $9.50
Noodles & Rice: Fried Noodle or Chow Funn with Seafood $9.00, Yong Chow Fried Rice $8.00, Pan Fried Chow Funn with shrimp and chicken $8.00

Impressions:

When you walk into Won Kee, the first thing you'll notice is the fish tanks along the wall. Many Chinese restaurants utilize in-house tanks to ensure absolute freshness for their more particular patrons. This is a fine dining establishment with massive hand carved furniture and a menu to match. Seafood is their mainstay, but they offer a variety of other traditional dishes as well. Parking is available across the street or in the cultural center deck.

Honolulu

Yanagi Sushi Authors' Favorite

762 Kapiolani Blvd.
Honolulu, HI 96813
808-597-1525
www.yanagisushihawaii.com
Hours: L 11:00 AM-2:00 PM
D 5:30 PM-2:00 AM Mo-Sa
D 5:30 PM-10:00 PM Su
Cards: AE DC DIS JCB MC V
Dress: Resort Casual
Style: Japan $$

Menu Sampler:

Breakfast:
N/A
Lunch:
Double Combination Lunch-served with miso soup, rice & pickled vegetables-Tempura, Chicken Teriyaki $7.95, Broiled Salmon, Chicken Teriyaki $7.95
Special Combination Lunch-served with salad, appetizer, miso soup, rice, pickled vegetables & ice cream-choice of two entrées $14.95, three $17.95
Dinner:
Pupus: Toro (ahi belly) Tataki $Mkt, Fried Prawn $3.75, Dynamite $7.50
Soups & Salads: Lobster Miso Soup $6.95, Sashimi Salad $9.95
Nabemono: Shabu Shabu of strip loin, vegetables & noodles $19.95, Shabu Shabu Deluxe adds assorted fresh seafood $26.95, Sukiyaki $19.95
Broiled Fishes: Butterfish $10.25, Ahi Teriyaki $8.25, Khal Bi $14.25
Tempura: Ala Carte-Shrimp $8.50, Vegetable $7.50, Tonkatsu $8.75
Roll Sushi: Honeymoon Roll-unagi, shrimp, avocado, crab eggs, sesame seeds $8.50, Spicy Tuna Roll $4.95, Salmon Skin $4.95, Spider Roll $9.50

Impressions:

Want to join the local movers and shakers for some Japanese cuisine? Get that car out of the garage and head downtown. There at the intersection of Clayton and Kapiolani you'll find the home of Yanagi Sushi. When you arrive, give your keys to the valet and he'll take care of the parking situation. Then, get ready to enjoy a great dining experience. Inside you'll have your choice of seats at the sushi bar or in the dining room maze. There's just about everything Japanese on the menu throughout the day and until very late in the evening. You can't get a Sunday lunch here, but otherwise it's all-day every-day. We really like this one!

Diamond Head

Yen King

Authors' Favorite

Kahala Mall Shopping Center
4211 Waialae Ave.
Honolulu, HI 96816
808-732-5505
Web: None
Hours: LD 10:00 AM-9:30 PM
Cards: AE MC V
Dress: Casual
Style: Chi $$

Menu Sampler:

Breakfast:
N/A
Lunch/Dinner:
Gourmet Buffets: 11 AM-2 PM $9.50/adults, $6.00/children age 3-12; 5 PM-9 PM $13.95/adults, $7.50/children age 3-12
Soup: Hot & Sour Soup $4.50, Won Ton Soup $5.95, Sizzling Rice Soup $5.95
Entrées: Mongolian Beef (hot) $7.50, Peppery Beef Sizzling Platter $8.50, Mu Shu Pork $7.95, Sweet and Sour Pork $7.50, Dry Fried Chicken (hot) $7.95, Crackling Chicken (1/2) $8.95, Peking Duck (1/2) $15.00, Kung Pao Squid (hot) $8.95, Shrimp with Tofu $8.95, Velvet Shrimp $10.50, Happy Family $9.95, Oyster Sautéed in Ginger & Onion Sauce $10.50, Crispy Fried Scallop $11.50, Hot Eggplant with Scallop $11.50, Braised Whole Fish $Mkt
Vegetarian: Egg Fu Yong $5.95, Spinach, Garlic & Wine Sautéed $7.95, Black Mushroom & Chinese Green $5.95, Vegetarian E-Mein Sautéed $6.95
Noodles & Rice: Yen King Chow Mein or Fried Rice $5.95
Dessert: Almond Tofu $1.95, Glazed Banana or Glazed Apple $4.50
Daily Lunch Plates: includes hot & sour soup & rice-2 items $6.25/3- $7.95
Daily Dinner Specials: includes hot sour soup & rice, 2 items $7.25/ 3-$8.95

Impressions:

Yen King does a couple of things very well. First, you'll have to go some to find better Szechuan cooking. If you like a little zip on your plate you'll really enjoy the spicy hot specialties. Then, if grazing is more your style give the buffet a try. This isn't your neighborhood hot bar. Howard calls it his gourmet buffet, and he doesn't miss the mark by much. Kahala Mall shoppers appreciate being able to sit down to an excellent meal without spending much of their time or budget. Daily specials make for a value priced alternative at both lunch and dinner.

Honolulu

Zaffron
69 N. King St
Honolulu, HI 96817
808-533-6635
www.zaffronhawaii.com
Hours: L 11:00 AM-2:00 PM XSaSu
D Buf 5:00 PM-9:00 PM We-Sa
Cards: AE DIS MC V
Dress: Resort Casual
Style: Ind $$

Menu Sampler:

Breakfast:
N/A
Lunch:
Plate Orders: Chicken Curry-chicken, chole, aloo sabzi, biryani rice, naan $7.00, Mixed Plate of chicken curry, keema mixed vegetable, chole, aloo sabzi, chicken biryani rice, naan $7.50, Vegetarian Curry w/vegetables & rice $7.00
A la carte: Tandoori Chicken $4.50, Peanut Butter Naan $2.00, Beef Curry $5.50, Chole (chick pea curry) $3.00, Fish Curry $6.00, Dhal (lentils) $3.00
Dinner:
Buffet: adults $14.40/children $7.20, Buffet consists of **Four Meat Choices**- Beef Curry, Spicy Beef Keema, Chicken Curry, Tandoori Chicken, Egg Curry, Goat Curry, Kofta, Lamb Curry-**Six Vegetable Choices**- Bean, Bell Pepper, Cauliflower, Bhindi, Choley, Dal, Eggplant Curry, Gobi, Mixed Vegetables, Squash Curry, **Extras**- Fresh Naan Bread, Vegetable Samosa, Vegetable Salad, Raeta, Hot Mint Chutney, **Two Desserts-** Halawa and Kheer
Iced Tea $1.00, Indian Hot Tea $1.25, juices $1.00, & Milk Shakes $3.00
Canned drinks & bottled water are $1.00 each, Lassis (sweet, salty, mango) $3

Impressions:

If you haven't tried Indian cuisine, you can do so now in Honolulu. Dishes like Tandoori chicken and beef curry can open new doors for someone who's had all the fusion cuisine that they care to eat for a while. The lunch plates are quite reasonably priced and very popular. Their dinner buffets are particularly good for the newcomer, because you can sample many new and different items. In keeping with Islamic tradition alcohol is not served at this establishment.

OAHU DINING BY REGION

OAHU DINING BY REGION

Honolulu

Chinatown

Waikiki

Manoa Valley

Kapahulu

Diamond Head

Niu Valley

Kaimuki

Hawaii Kai

Windward

North Shore

Leeward

FOOD & CULTURAL TERMS GLOSSARY

FOOD & CULTURAL TERMS GLOSSARY

a'a	rough clinker lava
aina	the land
abalone	large saltwater mollusk
aburage	deep-fried tofu
adobo	marinated Filipino chicken and/or pork stew
agemono	Japanese cooking method of preparing meats and vegetables by deep-frying
ahi	yellowfin tuna, often served raw as sashimi on a bed of Chinese cabbage with a wasabi and shoyu dipping sauce
ahupua'a	a land division used in old Hawaii consisting of all the lands between two adjoining ridges from the top of the mountain to the ocean
akamai	clever or smart
akua	spirit or god
ali'i	chief or noble
aloha	versatile term that can mean hello, good-bye, and love
Aloha Friday	casual dress day or more importantly the first day of the weekend party that actually starts Thursday afternoon
arroz	rice
arugula	peppery flavored greens
aumakua	guardian spirit
auntie	any older lady, a term of respect

'awa	kava, a beverage made from the ground roots of the intoxicating pepper
azuki	red beans
banh hoi	Vietnamese meat and vegetable roll-up
barbecue stick	char grilled teriyaki meat stick
bean curd	tofu
bean threads	fine thin noodles made from mung bean starch, long rice
bento	Japanese box lunch
black beans	fermented beans used in Chinese sauces
bok choy	a tall variety of cabbage with white celery like stems and dark green leaves
bulgoki	Korean teriyaki barbecue beef
bun	thin soft Vietnamese rice noodles
butterfish	black cod, has a smooth silky texture
carne	meat
cascaron	Filipino fried sweet dumpling
char siu	sweet marinated barbecued pork
chili oil	liquid fire made from chili peppers and oil
Chinese cabbage	a compact variety of cabbage with white celery-like stems and pale green leaves, also known as Napa cabbage or won bok
chorizo	hot and spicy sausage
chow	stir-fry
chow fun	cooked noodles combined with green onions and bits of meat or seafood then stir-fried with sesame oil

chun — Korean method of frying using flour followed by an egg wash

cilantro — Chinese parsley

coconut creme — thick creamy layer on top of a can of coconut milk

coconut milk — liquid extracted by squeezing grated coconut meat

crack seed — sweet or sour snack foods made from preserved fruits and seeds

da kine — what-cha-ma-call-it

daikon — large white Asian root vegetable commonly used as a garnish

dashi — broth made from dried seaweed and flakes of dried bonito

Diamond Head — directional term used on Oahu meaning to go east in the direction of Diamond Head or "Go Diamond Head"

dim sum — Chinese style dumplings

doce — sweet

donburi — thinly sliced meat, vegetables, and coddled egg served in a deep bowl over rice

edamame — lightly salted and boiled young soybeans

egg roll — fried pastry roll with various meat and vegetable fillings

Ewa — directional term used on Oahu meaning to go west in the direction of Ewa or "Go Ewa" which is opposite from Diamond Head and toward Pearl Harbor

fish cake — ground white fish, starch, and salt cooked together by steaming or frying

fish sauce — potent seasoning made from salt and fish

five spice powder	mixture of several spices that usually includes fennel, peppercorns, cinnamon, cloves, and star anise.
furikake	a dry condiment used on rice dishes
fusion cuisine	layers of flavor, texture, temperatures, and techniques created by combining elements from the cuisines of different cultures
ginger	spicy pungent root vegetable used as a flavoring in Asian cooking
gobo	burdock root
grinds	food
guava	sweet red tropical fruit
guisates	Filipino pork or chicken dish made with peas and pimento in a tomato based sauce
hale	house or building
halo halo	tropical fruit sundae made with ice, milk and sugar instead of ice cream
ham har	fermented dried shrimp paste, very funky, a little goes a long way
hana	work
hana hou	do it one more time/encore!
haole	Caucasian
hapa	half as in hapa-haole or half-Caucasian
haupia	coconut custard dessert
Hawaii Regional Cuisine	movement started in the late '80's/early '90's by young local chefs combining island cooking styles and classic techniques with fresh local products to create an exciting new fusion cuisine

Hawaiian chili water	liquid heat made with Hawaiian chili peppers, water, and salt
Hawaiian rock salt	coarse white or pink rock salt
Hawaiian time	later rather than sooner
heiau	ancient Hawaiian stone temple
hekka	a stir-fry dish made with meat and vegetables in a shoyu-based sauce
hibachi	small charcoal cooker
hoisin sauce	thick, sweet, but pungent sauce used in Chinese cooking
holoholo	pleasure trip, to go "holoholo"
hono	bay
honu	turtle
hukilau	pulling of a large fish net by a group
hui	club or association
hula	Hawaiian native dance
huli huli	"turn turn" as in grilling chicken
imu	Hawaiian underground oven made by digging a pit and lining it with hot lava rocks covered by banana plants and food and burying it for several hours, used at luaus for making kalua pork, laulau, sweet potatoes, etc.
inari sushi	cone sushi made by filling fried tofu pockets with sweet vinegar flavored rice
ipo	sweetheart
kaffir lime leaves	leaves of the kaffir lime tree used as flavoring in Thai cooking

kahuna	priest or skilled person
kai	the sea
kaiseki	Japanese fine dining in courses
kal bi ribs	Korean teriyaki beef short ribs
kale	Portuguese cabbage
kalo	taro
kalua pork	shredded pork prepared luau style in an imu pit, also known locally as kalua pig
kama'aina	long time resident or someone who was born in Hawaii
kamaboko	Japanese fish cake
kane	man
kapu	forbidden
kapuna	grandparent or wise older person
katsu	breaded cutlet
kau kau	food, a place to eat
keiki	child
kiawe	dry land hardwood used in smoking and grilling meats
ki'i	statue or image
kim chee	spicy Korean condiment made from fermented cabbage and peppers
koa	valuable hardwood tree, warrior
Koko Head	directional term used on Oahu meaning to go in the direction of Koko Head or "Go Koko Head"
kokua	help

kona leeward

kona wind muggy airflow from the equator

kukui candlenut tree, the source of kukui nut oil

Kula a truck gardening district in Upcountry Maui

kulolo sweet pudding made with poi

kumu teacher as in kumu hula

lanai deck or patio

lau hala woven mats

lau lau flavored meat mixed with taro leaves and wrapped in ti leaves then steamed, often in an imu

laver purple seaweed used in making nori

lechon roasted pig

lei garland of flowers

lemon grass woody lemon flavored grass used as flavoring in Southeast Asian cooking

li hing mui sweet and sour seasoning made from dried plums and salt

lilikoi passion fruit

limu edible seaweed

linguica spicy Portuguese pork sausage seasoned with garlic and paprika

loa long

loco moco local dish consisting of rice, a large hamburger patty or slices of Spam, and fried eggs with lots of brown gravy over all

lolo crazy

lomi	to knead or massage
lomi lomi salmon	salted salmon finely diced with tomatoes and green onions
long rice	clear noodles cooked in broth
lua	restroom
luau	Hawaiian feast, also a dish made from taro leaves, coconut crème, and meat
lulu	calm
lumpia	fried spring roll with meat, vegetable, or dessert fillings
lup cheong	Chinese pork sausage
lychee	sweet white fruit
macadamia nuts	small round nut with creamy but crunchy texture
mac salad	macaroni and mayonnaise
mahalo	thank you
mainland	North America
makai	directional term that is helpful on an island meaning to turn or look toward the ocean
maki sushi	sushi rolled in nori
malasada	wonderful sweet brought here by the Portuguese similar to a fresh sugar donut but minus the hole
malihini	newcomer
malo	loincloth
mana	power or energy from the spirit world
manapua	steamed pork bun

mandoo	Korean dumplings with meat and vegetable fillings
mango	golden fleshed tropical fruit
mano	shark
Manoa	a gardening district near Honolulu, the Manoa Valley
mauka	directional term meaning to look or turn toward the mountain or uphill part of an island
mauna	mountain
mein	Chinese noodles
mele	chant or song
menehune	legendary "little people" of Hawaii
mirin	sweet rice cooking wine
miso	fermented soybean paste
miso soup	light Japanese soup made from soybean paste and garnished with tofu, kamaboko, daikon, green onions, and wakame
mixed plate	plate lunch version of a mixed grill
moa	native Polynesian chicken
moana	ocean
mochi	rice cake
mochiko	sweet rice flour
mo'o	lizard or water spirit
musubi	rice ball
muu muu	loose fitting ankle length dress

naan Indian flatbread

nabemono Japanese cooking method of preparing thin slices of meat and vegetables in a hot broth

'Nalo As in Waimanalo, a garden district on the Windward side of Oahu

nam pla Thai fish sauce

nam prik Thai hot sauce

nani beautiful

nene Hawaiian goose

nigiri sushi oblong sushi

niu coconut

noni native shrub bearing medicinal fruit

nori roasted seaweed pressed into sheets

norimaki sushi rolled in nori

nui big or great

nuoc mam Vietnamese fish sauce

off-island in the islands one does not go "out of town" they go "off-island"

ogo type of seaweed favored by the Japanese

ohana extended family

ohelo native shrub bearing edible berries

okazuya a Japanese delicatessen where fast foods and snacks are served buffet style

ono delicious

opae shrimp

opihi — Hawaiian escargot harvested from rocks along the ocean and eaten raw with salt

oyster sauce — thick brown sauce made from oysters and shoyu often used in stir fry dishes

Pacific Rim Cuisine — a fusion of cuisines involving methods and ingredients from the countries around the Pacific Ocean

pad thai — Thai noodles

pahoehoe — smooth ropey lava

pakalolo — crazy smoke, marijuana, buds; something to decline when offered

pali — cliff

pancit — Filipino noodles

paniolo — Hawaiian cowboy

panko — Japanese breadcrumbs

pao — bread

pao doce — Portuguese sweet bread

papaya — smooth skinned orange-fleshed tropical fruit that can also be used green when peeled and shredded in a salad

pasteles — similar to a tamale except made with bananas instead of corn flour

patis — Filipino fish sauce

pau — finished

pau hana — finished working

pho — Vietnamese noodle soup

pidgin — Hawaiian Creole English

pipi kaula — Hawaiian beef jerky

plantain	cooking banana
plate lunch	island style blue plate special with a main entrée such as teriyaki beef or chicken, two scoops of white rice, and a scoop of macaroni salad
poi	glutinous paste made by pounding steamed taro root, the Hawaiian staple starch
poke	ceviche dish made with cubed fish or sliced octopus mixed with onion and seaweed then marinated in shoyu and spices
pono	righteous
ponzu	tart Japanese citrus sauce
Portuguese sausage	spicy garlic and paprika flavored pork sausage, linguica
pua	flower
pua'a	pig
pueo	owl
puka	hole
pupu	appetizer
pu'u	hill
ramen	curly Japanese wheat noodles
rice noodle	noodles made with rice flour
rice paper	round rice flour wrapper that is soaked in hot water to soften before use
saimin	island noodle soup that has many variations and broths--extras may include Spam, teriyaki beef, green onions, vegetables, hard-cooked eggs, and fish cake

sake Japanese rice wine

sashimi raw fish sliced very thin and served with spicy condiments and dipping sauce

satay tender chicken or beef strips marinated in coconut milk and spices then skewered and grilled

sesame oil aromatic oil made from sesame seeds used sparingly to flavor Asian dishes

shabu shabu chafing dish cookery involving thinly sliced meats and vegetables simmered in broth usually with a tabletop preparation

shaka hand signal using the thumb and little finger used as a greeting

shave ice similar to a snow cone except there is no crunch as the ice is shaved instead of crushed, can be topped with wonderful tropical flavored syrups and served with ice cream and azuki beans

shoyu Japanese soy sauce, Aloha Brand is preferred in the islands as it is not as salty as some other types

soba Japanese buckwheat noodles

somen thin Japanese wheat noodles

Spam canned spiced pork lunchmeat

spring roll fried rice paper roll with various fillings

starch rice or potatoes

sukiyaki Japanese beef, tofu, vegetable, and noodle dish with shoyu based sauce commonly cooked at the table

summer roll fresh rice paper roll with various fillings

sushi small slices of vegetables, fruits, fish, or meat combined with tangy rice

sweet bread	rich egg bread commonly called Molokai or Portuguese sweet bread
sweet rice	also known as sticky rice or glutinous rice
tako	octopus
talk story	to have a casual conversation
tapa	cloth made from pounded tree bark
taro	starchy root plant used in making poi
teri	teriyaki
teishoku	a complete Japanese meal including soup, salad, entrée, pickled vegetables, and rice
tempura	meat, seafood, or vegetables fried in a light batter coating
tendon	meat and vegetable tempura served over rice
teppanyaki	Japanese cooking method of grilling vegetables, seafood, meat and rice tableside by a knife-wielding chef, very entertaining
teriyaki	sweet tangy shoyu based marinade
Thai basil	herb used in Thai cooking, has a purple flower and sharper taste than sweet basil
ti	broad-leafed plant whose leaves are used for plates, hula skirts, and for wrapping foods and religious offerings
tobiko	flying fish roe, caviar
tofu	soybean curd available fresh or fermented
tom yum	spicy Thai soup
tonkatsu	fried cutlet
tsukemono	pickled vegetables

tuong ot	Vietnamese hot sauce
tutu	grandmother
two scoop rice	two scoops of cooked white rice
uala	sweet potato
udon	thick Japanese wheat noodles
ulu	breadfruit
vertical food	a physical manifestation of fusion cuisine where the elements of the dish are stacked
wahine	woman
wai	water
wakame	a seaweed condiment
wasabi	spicy Japanese horseradish paste often combined sparingly with shoyu to make a dipping sauce for sushi and sashimi
wiki wiki	hurry up, very fast
wok	round bottomed cooking pot used over very high heat to quick sear or stir-fry chopped meats and vegetables
won bok	Chinese cabbage
won ton	Chinese meat dumplings
wor	vegetables
yakimono	Japanese cooking method of preparing meats and vegetables by broiling or grilling
yakiniku	tabletop grilling
yakisoba	grilled noodles
yakitori	grilled meat and vegetable kebabs

HAWAIIAN FISH & SEAFOOD GLOSSARY

HAWAIIAN FISH & SEAFOOD GLOSSARY

Hawaii IS the island state and what could be a more fitting headliner on a Hawaiian menu than the bounty of the sea? Just like everything else found in this Pacific paradise there are unique spins to the fish and seafood offerings. With this in mind we have created a separate glossary to help you explore and better appreciate the aquatic offerings found in Hawaii's dining spots.

Visitors need to be aware that finfish are nearly always listed by their Hawaiian names on island menus. That's no problem for those who grew up in Hawaii, but the rest of us would do well to brush up on the subject first. How else would you know that an ahi is a prize big eye or yellow fin tuna, and that a tako isn't the same as a taco? The word tako in Hawaii means octopus, and receiving one instead of the other could come as quite a surprise!

Most people don't realize that longliners stay out for several days at a time, but trollers come in every night and that the difference in the quality and freshness of their catch can be noticed. If you are paying for fresh island fish you want to make sure that you get it. You might see the term "day boat" used in some of the finer restaurants to describe the freshest of fresh fish and seafood. Regardless, make sure to ask and always insist on fish that has never been frozen.

As long as we're on the subject of getting what you're paying for, let's take a look at the economics of fish and seafood in Hawaii. There's a misconception that just because people see "water water everywhere", the aquatic resources must be limitless and the prices low. Nothing could be farther from the truth. The high cost of production through aquaculture and harvest in the wild along with huge local and foreign demand drive prices to the upper limit of the menu.

In closing, when you decide to take the plunge and go out for fish or seafood, make it a point to trust the recommendations at the restaurant. The chef knows how to match species and preparations for the best possible results. Just let your waiter know what you have in mind and listen to his suggestions. You'll be far happier in the end if you go with the flow than if you try to have it your way.

ahi — big eye or yellow fin tuna

aku — skipjack tuna, most common spring through early fall, robust flavor, firm texture, often served as poke or in sushi, primarily caught by commercial pole-and-line fishermen and recreational trollers

akule — big-eyed scad, a local favorite, primarily caught by netting or by hook-and-line fishermen

ama ebi	sweet shrimp or langoustines, harvested with traps from deep water, available locally but often imported
a'u	billfish of any type
big eye ahi	big eye tuna, most common from mid-fall through mid-spring, moderate beef-like flavor, medium firm texture, favored for sashimi and poke, primarily caught by long-line boats
ehu	red snapper, moderate flavor, most common during winter, medium firm texture, primarily caught by deepwater hook-and-line fishermen
hapu'upu'u	grouper or sea bass, most common spring and fall, moderate flavor, medium firm texture, primarily caught by deepwater hook-and-line fishermen
hebi	shortbill spearfish, most common mid-spring through early fall, moderate flavor, medium firm texture, primarily caught by commercial long-line boats
kajiki	pacific blue marlin, most common summer through fall, moderate flavor, firm texture, primarily caught by commercial long-line boats and recreational trollers
Keahole lobster	clawed "Maine" lobsters raised on the Big Island through aquaculture, available all year
Kona lobster	spiny or rock lobster, primarily caught by divers working the reef or by trapping, usually imported, available all year
lehi	silver mouth snapper, most common during late fall and winter, moderate flavor, medium texture, primarily caught by deepwater hook-and-line fishermen

mahimahi — dolphinfish, most common spring and fall, moderate almost sweet flavor, medium texture, ask if the fish is fresh "island fish", primarily caught by commercial and recreational trollers

moi — pacific threadfin, the royal fish, now raised locally through aquaculture, mild flavor, delicate texture, available all year

monchong — bigscale or sickle pomfret, available all year, robust flavor, medium firm texture, primarily caught as a by-catch of tuna long-liners and deepwater hook-and-line fishermen.

nairagi — striped marlin, most common winter and spring, moderate flavor, medium firm texture, primarily caught by commercial long-line boats and recreational trollers

onaga — ruby or long-tailed red snapper, most common late fall and winter, mild flavor, medium texture, primarily caught by deepwater hook-and-line fishermen

ono — wahoo, most common late spring through early fall, mild almost citrus-like flavor, medium firm texture, primarily caught by commercial and recreational trollers with part of the catch harvested by commercial long-line fishermen

opae — shrimp, now raised locally through aquaculture, available all year

opah — moonfish, most common spring through summer, robust flavor, medium texture, primarily caught by commercial long-line fishermen fishing over seamounts

opakapaka — crimson snapper, most common fall and winter, mild flavor, delicate texture, primarily caught by deepwater hook-and-line fishermen

opihi	small limpet, found on coastal rock faces in the surf zone, eaten raw with salt as "Hawaiian escargot"
papio	juvenile pompano or crevally, medium flavor, firm texture, caught by shore casters, shallow water trollers, and bottom fishermen
shutome	broadbill swordfish, most common spring and summer, moderate flavor, medium firm texture, caught at night by commercial long-line fishermen
tako	octopus or squid, primarily caught by divers working in shallow water or by jigging
tombo	albacore or "white meat" tuna, most common mid-spring through mid-fall, moderate flavor, medium texture, primarily caught by commercial long-line fishermen and small-boat hand line fishermen
uku	grey snapper, most common mid-spring through mid-fall, moderate flavor, medium firm texture, primarily caught in deep water by hook-and-line fishermen but is also caught near the surface by recreational trollers
ula	spiny or rock lobster, primarily caught by divers working the reef or by trapping
ula papapa	slipper lobster, primarily caught by divers working the reef or by trapping
ulua	adult pompano or crevally, medium flavor, firm texture, caught by shore casters, shallow water trollers, and bottom fishermen
yellow fin ahi	yellow fin tuna, most common mid-spring through mid-fall, moderate beef-like flavor, medium firm texture, favored for sashimi and poke, primarily caught by commercial long-line boats and commercial and recreational trollers

Printed in the United States
51700LVS00003B/316-324